A PLUME BOOK

HOW TO LISTEN TO GREAT MUSIC

Courtesy The Great Courses

ROBERT GREENBERG is a composer, pianist, and a music historian. He has served on the faculties of UC Berkeley, California State University at Hayward, and the San Francisco Conservatory of Music, where he was chairman of the Department of Music History and Literature and director of the Adult Extension Division. He is currently music historian-in-residence with San Francisco Performances and also serves as the resident composer and music historian to NPR's *Weekend All Things Considered*. Since 1993, he has recorded over 550 lectures for The Teaching Company.

Founded in 1990, THE TEACHING COMPANY produces DVD and audio recordings of courses by top university professors in the country, which they sell through direct marketing. It is a nine-figure-a-year business and they distribute forty-eight million catalogs annually. They offer more than four hundred courses on topics including business and economics; fine arts and music, ancient, medieval, and modern history; literature and English language; philosophy and intellectual history; religion; social sciences; and science and mathematics.

How to **LISTEN** *to* **GREAT MUSIC**

A Guide to Its History, Culture, and Heart

ROBERT GREENBERG

A PLUME BOOK

PLUME
Published by Penguin Group
Penguin Group (USA) Inc., 375 Hudson Street, New York, New York 10014,
U.S.A. • Penguin Group (Canada), 90 Eglinton Avenue East, Suite 700, Toronto,
Ontario, Canada M4P 2Y3 (a division of Pearson Penguin Canada Inc.) • Penguin
Books Ltd., 80 Strand, London WC2R 0RL, England • Penguin Ireland, 25
St. Stephen's Green, Dublin 2, Ireland (a division of Penguin Books Ltd.) • Penguin
Group (Australia), 250 Camberwell Road, Camberwell, Victoria 3124, Australia
(a division of Pearson Australia Group Pty. Ltd.) • Penguin Books India Pvt.
Ltd., 11 Community Centre, Panchsheel Park, New Delhi – 110 017, India • Pen-
guin Books (NZ), 67 Apollo Drive, Rosedale, North Shore 0632, New Zealand (a
division of Pearson New Zealand Ltd.) • Penguin Books (South Africa) (Pty.) Ltd.,
24 Sturdee Avenue, Rosebank, Johannesburg 2196, South Africa

Penguin Books Ltd., Registered Offices: 80 Strand, London WC2R 0RL, England

First published by Plume, a member of Penguin Group (USA) Inc.

First Printing, May 2011
10 9 8 7 6 5 4 3 2 1

Ⓟ REGISTERED TRADEMARK—MARCA REGISTRADA

LIBRARY OF CONGRESS CATALOGING-IN-PUBLICATION DATA

Greenberg, Robert, 1954–
How to listen to great music : a guide to its history, culture, and heart / Robert
Greenberg.
p. cm.
Includes bibliographical references and index.
ISBN 978-0-452-29708-1
1. Music appreciation. I. Title.
MT6.G76 2011
781.1'7—dc22
2010050220

Printed in the United States of America
Set in Berling • Designed by Chris Welch

PUBLISHER'S NOTE
While the author had made every effort to provide accurate telephone numbers and
Internet addresses at the time of publication, neither the publisher nor the author
assumes any responsibility for errors, or for changes that occur after publication. Further, the publisher does not have any control over and does not assume any responsibility
for author or third-party Web sites or their content.

To my wife and my mother, who sing to me still:

Diane Elizabeth Clymer-Greenberg (1974–2009)

Natalie Ruth Greenberg (1928–2010)

Contents

How to **LISTEN** *to*

GREAT MUSIC

CHAPTER 1

Understanding and Listening to Music

We are hardwired to hear and make music. Yes, we will sigh with pleasure when we hear a favorite theme played by an orchestra, and who hasn't felt a stab of nostalgia, or even brushed away a tear, when hearing a song reminiscent of youth or a lost love? However, such exquisite moments notwithstanding, the musical experience represents something far deeper.

Broadly defined, music is sound in time. Sound is nothing less than our perception of the vibrations, the movement, of the universe around us. Music is an intensification, a crystallization, a celebration, a glorification, of that movement and those vibrations. Pretty heady stuff. Far beyond spoken language—which, with its sounds in time, might rightly be considered a low-end sort of music—music is a universal language; one need not speak Ashanti in order to groove to West African drumming; or German in order to be emotionally flayed by Beethoven; or English to totally freak when listening to Bruce Springsteen. Say it with flowers? Nah. If you really want to get your expressive point across, say it with music.

No human activity occurs in a vacuum, and this is particularly true for the arts. Music, painting, sculpture, cinema, literature, and all of their brother and sister arts are mirrors of the world in which their creators live. Art crystallizes and intensifies human experience, rendering it universal in the process. But let us not mistake the "universal" end product for the circumstances around its creation. Art does not shape its time; rather, the times shape the artist, who then gives voice to his time in his own special way. To understand an artist's world and something of the artist herself are the first requisite steps to understanding the artist's work, its style, and its meaning.

What we're discussing here is context, and that's a large part of what this book is about. By creating a historical context for the composer and music understudy, we will know something of what that composer's contemporaries knew. When we listen this way, with the ears and understanding of a contemporary audience, centuries of accumulated dust and grime are swept away and we perceive the music we're hearing as new, relevant, and utterly alive. When heard contextually, all music becomes contemporary music!

Thus, the goal of this book is to create a degree of understanding— of *context*—that will allow us to hear, to *listen* to, music with new ears.

Along with this historical context, this book will provide the reader with several mutually reinforcing tools to further understand the music under discussion, including terminological tutorials and guided listening of representative musical compositions. A working vocabulary of selected terms is a key to conscious perception. It is my firm belief that we cannot make fine distinctions without a vocabulary capable of framing those distinctions. Winespeak, for example ("it's a youthful, chewy cabernet redolent with shoe leather and yesterday's newspaper") is, for all its silliness, an absolutely necessary syntactical device for addressing distinctions that, once named, can be perceived. For the same reason, a few well-chosen terms will be good for our musical palates.

This book will examine representative musical compositions in two ways. Certain key works will be discussed in detail in the body of the text. In addition, guided listening will be provided for various other works in musical sidebars that I have called Music Boxes. I would encourage you to acquire recordings of these representative works in the format of your choice (CD, MP3, LP, 78; though I would counsel against 8-track cartridges, a nasty format that) and to listen to them while reading about them, and recreationally as well. Only then can historical context, biographical information, and the music itself merge into a singular expressive and intellectual entity.

We all love a good story. Most stories are linear: their narratives trace a sequence of events as cause leads to effect. Despite the way it is often told, history—and this includes music history—does not consist of a single sequence of events but rather of an uneven sequence of concurrent and interactive events. This makes storytelling something of a challenge, and it explains why this narrative will bounce around a bit, from place to place, from composer to composer, and from genre to genre—and back again. That's okay; bounce is good.

Some readers might chafe at the phrase "Great Music" in this book's title, but it is there to identify that the focus here is clearly on the best of Western music. Its inherent conceit aside, it is a phrase we can live with because we are going to conceptualize it euphemistically, as referring to music that is composed. (Yes, not all great music is composed, and not all composed music is great, but this is where I must beg your indulgence lest an endless syntactical/philosophical discussion ensue along the lines of "breath mint or candy mint?") We would begin our terminological vocabulary with the phrase "composed music." The concepts of the composer and of composed music emerged during the tenth and eleventh centuries CE due to the invention (in the ninth century) of music notation. Composed music is notated music, and notated music is music that can be "considered": revised, edited, evaluated, and reevaluated in a manner far beyond music that exists only orally.

Concert music is composed music intended primarily to be listened to. As blanket terms go, this one is a doozy and would include most of the music composed in the last six hundred years, including operas, oratorios, cantatas, symphonies, concertos, string quartets, and piano sonatas. The list goes on; we will not. The most commonly used designation for this same music is *classical music*, a term sure to raise the hackles of the historically sensitive, which includes your author. In music, the word *classical* refers specifically to the period between approximately 1750 and 1800, during which composed music manifested many of the aesthetic principles of "classical art," meaning ancient Greek art. To call the whole kit and caboodle of Western composed music classical music is awkward, especially when a better term is available, and that term is *concert music*.

This book focuses primarily on the concert music of what is known as the common practice period: music composed between 1600 and 1900, what we can consider as comprising the "standard" repertoire. This is music in which the tonal harmonic system and its various melodic and harmonic structures and expressive rituals constituted a basic, common syntax. This is not to say that vocabulary and expressive content didn't change over those three hundred years; they most certainly did. But for the same common syntactical reasons that an English speaker of today can understand a Shakespeare play written in 1600, so the music of the common practice shared a basic syntactical underpinning that spanned three centuries.

Chapters 2–3 and 30–33 bookend our discussion of the common practice. Chapters 2–3 briefly (but vigorously!) trace something of the history of Western music (and the historical and societal events behind that music) from the ancient world through the Renaissance. Chapters 30–33 trace the dissolution of the common practice during the first years of the twentieth century. That dissolution was, in reality, part of an ongoing process of change that had long been operative in Western music and thus the reason why we wrap up our discussion in 1913, with the premiere of Igor Stravinsky's *The Rite of Spring*. The exponential rate of change that our planet has undergone since the turn of the twentieth century is mirrored in the arts. Even a cursory examination of the music of the twentieth century would double the length of this book. When we tackle it, the music of the twentieth century will make a fascinating addendum to the present study.

This book is based on a multimedia course published by The Great Courses called *How to Listen to and Understand Great Music*. The course, which is available in both audio and video formats, uses

actual musical excerpts extensively to illustrate the re
to focus on particular details under discussion. (Ther
included in this book.) This book—any book, for that m
not have the luxury of actual musical excerpts to illustrate and high-
light points as they are encountered. Consequently, the approach
here is different. Music in the Western world has been a mirror of the
religious, political, economic, and social events around the composers since the High Middle Ages. Our understanding of the complex,
interactive events that have shaped the Western world over the last
millennium will therefore inform our ability to grasp how they are
mirrored in composed music. Thus, this book is structured in such a
way that understanding precedes listening.

In lieu of actual musical excerpts, this book employs notated
musical examples. These are meant neither to intimidate nor render academically legitimate a book that is otherwise intended for
a nonacademic audience. They are merely intended to be used as
visualizations of the musical phenomena under discussion. For our
purposes, music notation is nothing but a graphing system. The basic
graph—the grid—consists of five horizontal lines and the spaces
enclosed by those lines. The higher a note is plotted on the graph, the
higher the sound. The more ink used to plot the note—stems, flags,
beams, etc.—the shorter its duration (i.e., the faster the note goes
by). The basic contour of a melody, its rise and fall, can be divined
by simply connecting the dots (the notes) into a continuous shape.
Even if you can't read the music, you can gain a sense of the musical
substance and expressive content just by looking at the contour of
those notes.

That is about 80 percent of what there is to know about music
notation.

In an ideal world, the reader would be able to plunk out these
notational examples on a keyboard in order to get an idea of what
they sound like. We do not, however, live in an ideal world. Thus,
I would encourage those readers unable to play the examples for

themselves either to delegate the job to someone who can, or not to sweat it and to be content with the fact that the musical examples are merely icing and not the informational cake (a strained but appropriate metaphor).

Let the journey begin with the all-important concept of Western music as a mirror of the world itself.

CHAPTER 2

A Mad Dash Through the Roots of Western Music

Music as a Mirror

We're going to make a rather mad dash through the early history of Western music so we might understand the roots of the cultivated, or composed, music of the last four hundred years—what it grew out of, what it retained and what it shed, what it rebelled against and what it embraced. This race through time will allow us to broach some major themes that will give context, historical and musical, to our understanding of music.

Why do we bother with context? Because music mirrors the culture in which it is created. If we learn something about that culture, we will learn something about its music. In the process, we will come to understand the music not just from our contemporary perspective, but from the perspective of the audiences who heard it when it was first created—not always the same thing. Understanding the historical context of a piece of music will change entirely our appreciation of the music and our ability to truly hear it. Simply put, the more we know, the better we hear.

Let's start this contextual journey by considering a few basic assumptions about Western music.

First of all, Western music, for the last one thousand years, has been marked by almost constant stylistic change. Expressively, constructively, and instrumentally different musical styles mirror the vastly different historical environments in which they were created.

Western music has exhibited this almost constant change because of the intrusion of ego: the ego of the composer. The concept of the composer as someone who creates, assembles, and revises musical materials was born roughly a thousand years ago, during the High Middle Ages. It was about seven hundred years ago that composers actually began to sign their work and thus take personal credit for their music.

Let us consider what that means.

When we attach our names to something, we are saying to the world, "This is mine. It represents who I am, what I feel, what I know, what I think. And I'm proud of it!" (Contrast this with the music of the early Church, which was, in the minds of its creators, inspired by God for God.)

When we attach our names to something, we are acknowledging, to some degree, that it reflects both who we are as individuals and something of our life experiences. Because each of us is different, and because we live in a constantly changing world, the nature of the music with which we express ourselves will inevitably change.

As such, over the last thousand years, the very nature of expressive content has changed.

Today, if we ask someone, "What should be expressed in art?" that person will likely expound—as I would, incidentally—that art should somehow express *feeling*. For the last two hundred years or so, much of (most!) Western art has been characterized by something of a fetish for individual feelings. At another time in history, though, personal feelings were not high on the expressive priority list; God and religion were the focal point of musical expression. At other times, pure intellect and intellectual control were considered of highest expressive merit; at still others, artistic restraint and good taste. What is considered expressively relevant has and will change from era to era.

The rate of stylistic change in Western music has increased as the rate of change in Western society has increased. As we will observe, historical periods become shorter and shorter as we move toward the present (and we will periodize, much as we bemoan the inaccuracy of period dates).

All of this is important for understanding and listening to music for a couple of reasons. First, it helps to explain why there is such a dazzling variety of Western music to begin with. Second, by understanding the historical context reflected by the music, it becomes possible to comprehend the style, that is, the compositional and expressive substance of the music. By understanding the historical context, we can better understand and "hear" the music.

We would do well to avoid the notion that art is linear, and that, somehow, it just keeps getting better as we go along. Certainly, art—and for us, music—gets *different* as it goes along. Just as, certainly, the musical language itself—that is, the actual materials available to composers—has grown as we've moved toward the present day.

However, unlike science, technology, and medicine, this doesn't mean that music has gotten "better." Is Claudio Monteverdi's music better than that of Josquin des Prez; is Bach's better than Monteverdi's; Mozart's better than Bach's; Beethoven's better than Mozart's; Brahms's, Mahler's, Debussy's, Stravinsky's, and Schoenberg's better than that which came before? Obviously not.

There is a reason why we turn to the paintings of Vermeer, the sculptures of Michelangelo, and the music of Bach, Mozart, Beethoven, and Brahms, to name just a few, in search of truth and edification, and it has nothing to do with nostalgia for the past. Great art is timeless, and it speaks to us, directly and relevantly, across time.

From an expressive point of view, music history is best conceived in terms of grand cycles. For example, ideas espoused by the ancient Greeks regarding the expressive power of music—ideas we will discuss in just a moment—cycled back to the forefront of Western musical thought about six hundred years ago. The essentially humanistic Greek ideal of music remains our ideal to the present day. But at some point in the near or distant future another vision of music, perhaps as essentially a form of ritual, will cycle back to the forefront of our cultural consciousness. Only time will tell.

Truth and Beauty, Body and Soul: The Role of Music in Ancient Greece

Greek culture was essentially humanistic in spirit; at the end of the day, Greek art and philosophy put humankind at the center of all things. The Greeks believed that music manifested the order and rightness of the cosmos, and they were fascinated by the impact of music on human beings. They believed that music was capable of healing the sick, purifying the mind and body, working miracles in nature, and changing the hearts of people; hence, they attributed miracles to such mythological musicians as Apollo and Orpheus. Finally, the Greeks thought of music as fundamental to activities that were connected with the pursuit of truth or beauty. Music was omnipresent in the Greek world.

"Stavros, Stavros, he's our man; if he can't play it, no one can!"

So ubiquitous was music in the ancient Greek world that music performance was even an event at the Panhellenic Games, the circuit of athletic festivals capped every four years by the festival at Olympia (the Olympic Games). A carved stone dating from the Greek classical period bearing the prizes for various athletic events has survived. The first prize for cithara singers (harp singers, the ancient Greek version of Bob Dylan) was, according to David C. Young writing in 1984, equivalent to roughly $84,750. Most definitely the good old days!

At the very heart of the Greek view of music was something called the doctrine of ethos, which described the moral quality of music and the effect of music on people and nature. The doctrine of ethos was based on the view of Pythagoras (ca. 570 BCE–ca. 495 BCE) and his followers that music was a microcosm of the cosmos, a system of pitch and rhythm that was ruled by the same mathematical laws that governed the whole of the universe.

The Greeks recognized that, among other things, music had the power to heighten and intensify the expressive meaning of words. Indeed, significant portions of many Greek dramas were sung or chanted when they were originally performed, a fact that was to have a huge impact on the thinkers and composers of the Renaissance some two thousand years later.

In 146 BCE, Greece became a Roman state. Roman civilization absorbed and adopted Greek music and art as its own.

In 313 CE the Emperor Constantine issued the Edict of Milan, granting Christians and Christianity equal rights and protection in the empire. In fact, the edict made Christianity the official state religion of the Roman Empire. Christian or not, the empire's days were numbered. As the prestige and power of the Roman emperor declined, that of the Roman bishop, that is, the Pope increased. Gradually, the Pope became the predominant Roman authority in matters of faith and discipline. As Roman municipal authority disintegrated, the Church stood, increasingly, as the last bastion against barbarism, and the last preserver of culture and learning in an increasingly hostile world.

For this we must be eternally grateful to the early Church. We cannot possibly overstate the importance of the Christian Church for its role in preserving, defending, and, ultimately, re-civilizing Europe.

By 600 CE, with the last vestiges of Roman municipal authority more or less gone, the great age of theocracy had begun. During this period (until roughly 1400), God, the Church, and humankind's relationship to God and Church became the central philosophic, spiritual, educational, and artistic issues for Western Europe. We generally call this the theocratic age, encompassing approximately the years between 600 and 1400, the Middle Ages.

Sing It, Don't Swing It: Music in the Early Church

The early Church sought to differentiate itself from pagan and Jewish ritual. To that end, it developed three essential corollaries regarding the nature and use of music in Christian worship. These corollaries will help us to understand the nature and purpose of the music we're going to examine in the next chapter.

1. Music, as a "beautiful" thing, is useful only if it reminds us of divine and perfect beauty.
2. Music must teach Christian thoughts. Nonvocal music cannot do this. Therefore, strictly instrumental music must be rejected.
3. Large choruses, "bright" melodies, and dancing are associated with pagan festivals. These must all be rejected!

Now, for us, today, these corollaries might create the impression that the early Church was a repressive and anti-artistic institution. It was not. It was an island of civility and culture attempting to survive in a sea of barbarity and ignorance. Without strict rules and regulations, without the suppression of the individual ego for the greater good of the greater number, it's unlikely that the early Church would have survived the onslaughts of the first four hundred years of the Middle Ages—often called the Dark Ages.

CHAPTER 3

The Music of the Medieval Church

Hyperbole and the occasional bright spot aside, the years between roughly 600 and 1000 CE—and in particular, 600 to 800 CE—were a wretched time for most of Western Europe. Generally (but accurately) speaking, public safety and the advanced technologies of the ancient world were lost, leaving most Western Europeans to live in extremely primitive conditions. The feudal system, which tied the bulk of the population to the land, was little short of slavery. For the overwhelming majority of people, life was indeed nasty, brutish, and short. The Christian Church, which promised a glorious afterlife following the trials of mortal existence, provided the ray of light and hope in this otherwise dark landscape.

The great legacy of the medieval Church was the Christian conversion of Europe and, with it, the rebirth of European civilization. During these otherwise dismal years, the Church stood as patron of art and education, of civility and literacy. The libraries and scriptoria of the medieval Church managed to save and preserve a body of knowledge and literature that would otherwise have been lost forever.

The role of music in the early medieval Church was twofold. It was used to create a mood conducive to long hours of prayerful contemplation. And it was used to embellish the formal services, to make them more impressive and more solemn. The medieval Church saw music not as a humanistic pursuit, but rather as a tool of ceremony and ritual.

The music of the early medieval Church is today generically referred to as plainchant. It's called plainchant because it is unadorned and unaccompanied, consisting, as it does, of a single unaccompanied melody line, a musical texture called monophony, meaning one sound.

Try it at home! Sing in the shower. Your unaccompanied voice is singing in a monophonic texture. Having left the shower, grab your wife or husband, partner, children, cat, or gerbil (okay, maybe not the cat), and sing the same thing *together*. Despite the fact that there is more than one voice singing, the voices are singing the same single, unaccompanied melody at the same time. It is still monophony; you are still creating a monophonic texture.

MUSIC BOX

Plainchant

The number of different plainchants created over the centuries is *huge*. Yet the characteristic sound of plainchants remains fairly consistent from type to type and century to century. Enter the word *plainchant* in your search engine of choice and begin listening. Plainchant melodies will be characterized by the following:

- a monophonic texture;
- for ease of singing, a relatively conjunct melodic contour (*conjunct* meaning no large intervals between one note and the next) and a restricted range (no notes too high or too low); and
- rhythms based strictly on the articulation of the words being sung (meaning no steady, dancelike beats; if you can dance to a plainchant, you've been sipping too much sacramental wine). Plainchant is music of the soul and the voice, not the pelvis.

Miraculously, plainchant has the same power to calm and enlighten today as it did a thousand years ago, which is, I think, an ongoing testament to its power, beauty, and artistic truth.

The repertoire of medieval plainchant is often referred to as Gregorian chant, in honor of Pope Gregory I, who reigned as Pope (Bishop of Rome) from 590 to 604 CE. Contrary to the popular image, Gregory I had nothing to do with the creation of plainchant. His name is associated with this body of music because it was during his reign that the Roman Catholic Church sought to assert its authority over the churches of Europe by codifying and standardizing liturgical procedures, including music.

Truly, there is no *I* in *chant*. The musical functionaries who created, memorized, and taught by rote the huge body of plainchant to the church community were not making music to express or glorify themselves. Frankly, that's a concept that would have been utterly foreign to them. They were creating music to glorify God, music that would help to create a meditational state during the countless hours church functionaries spent in prayer; music that would facilitate the memorization of huge amounts of liturgical text; music that could calm the mind and render it susceptible to divine influence. This was the role of music in the medieval Church. And while popular music—romantic songs and simple dance music—existed in the medieval world, it was the church music that was ultimately notated (i.e., written down) and which became the basis for the composed music of centuries to come.

In terms of sheer number and variety, the plainchant repertoire represents the single greatest body of music created by Western culture. It is the only music that has survived in written form from the Dark Ages.

The High Life: The High Middle Ages and the Rebirth of Western European Civilization

The impact on music of the rebirth of Western European civilization was profound, and nowhere was it greater than in the invention of composed polyphony between the years 900 and 1000. Let's unpack this.

As the Western European population was Christianized, a degree

of civility and public safety followed. Trade routes were reestab-
lished, wealth was created, and with it, those extraordinary hubs of
interdependent human activity called cities began to dot the Euro-
landscape. Cities can exist only in an environment of cooperative
specialization: different folks govern, import the food, export the
offal, teach the young, and so forth. The Christian Church, the civic
lynchpin of the age, was the dominant spiritual and educational institution in the new European cities. And the buildings with which
the medieval Church celebrated itself became a metaphor for God's
power and magnificence.

The High Middle Ages saw an explosion in architectural technology, as first Romanesque—that is, Roman arch–based architecture—
and then Gothic architectural styles were born. Construction on
the "new" Canterbury Cathedral was begun in 1070. The corner-
stone of Notre Dame in Paris was laid in 1163; in 1260 the Chartres
Cathedral was consecrated; and construction on the great cathedral
of Cologne began in 1248 (though it was not completed until 1880!).

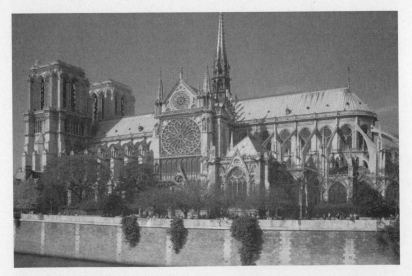

Notre Dame iStockphoto/Thinkstock

That communities could afford to expend their resources on these huge architectural marvels is further evidence of the growing wealth and security of Western Europe in the years after 1000 CE. The complexity and magnificence of design and detail inherent in these Gothic cathedrals are mirrored in the "new music" being composed for worship in these churches, music that features multiple and often very complex simultaneous melodies set in a texture called polyphony.

Polyphony is a musical texture in which two or more principal melodic parts are heard simultaneously. For example, here is a melody we all know as "Row, Row, Row Your Boat" and for which we have varying degrees of affection. In the spirit of pedagogical investigation, I would ask you to sing it:

Now get the gerbil. Sing it together, but in an overlapping fashion, as a round.

While you and the gerbil are each singing the same melody, you are *not* singing it at the same time. Thus, once the second voice enters, two principal melodic parts are simultaneously present, neither of which is more (or less) important than the other. This is an example of polyphony. The word *polyphony* means "many sounds," so what we have here is the simultaneous presence of multiple melodic parts.

From the standpoint of composition, the invention of composed polyphony was the Big Bang. In creating music featuring two or more simultaneous melodic parts, a specialist is going to have to make all sorts of compositional decisions regarding harmony and coordinated rhythm that don't have to be made in the creation of a plainchant. To use a cooking analogy, it's the difference between having cereal for dinner and cooking a five-course meal with paired wines. Preparing such a dinner requires knowledge, planning, taste, technical acumen, and execution.

Composed polyphony also required a universally understood system of music notation. With the development of polyphony and notation came the concept of the composer: the musical creator as a combiner and builder.

MUSIC BOX

Léonin (ca. 1150–ca. 1201), *Organum Duplum* on "Alleluia Pascha Nostrum" ("Hallelujah, Our Passover") (ca. 1180)

Léonin was a musical functionary of the Cathedral of Notre Dame in Paris, and one of the earliest composers whose name we know. The work that follows (in modern notation) is an organum, a two-part composition in which a plainchant ("Alleluia Pascha Nostrum") is joined to a freely composed part. Léonin's is an example of a florid organum, in that the freely composed part is quite ornate and is heard above the long-held tones of the plainchant below it.

This is ornate, carefully *composed* music that needs to be performed by trained specialists working in close cooperation with each other. It is an appropriate metaphor for the twelfth century and the flowering of culture, complex architecture, specialization, and civic cooperation that marked the time.

And the Walls Came Atumblin' Down:
The Fourteenth Century

The neatly closed medieval universe based on the omnipotent power and absolute authority of the Church came to an end during the four-teenth century. It was an end that did not happen quietly. A series of events—the so-called Babylonian Captivity, the Great Schism, and the Black Death—cumulatively brought about the end of the theocratic age.

As the Church was losing its absolute grip, a political and spiritual crisis took place. Increasingly powerful secular rulers began to contest the Church's right to rule and, especially, to tax in their lands. By the mid- to late fourteenth century, the growing power of secular courts resulted in an intellectual and artistic swing toward things nonreligious: secular ideas, secular art, and secular literature. For example, the fourteenth century saw the growth and development of vernacular literature, with much of it—such as Dante's *Divine Comedy*, Boccaccio's *Decameron*, and Chaucer's *Canterbury Tales*—satirizing matters of Church and faith. We are witness to the beginnings of a new humanism and a new classicism, as Roman and Greek art, literature, and philosophy offered pre-Christian models for life, thought, and art in a time of Christian crisis. The impact of all of this on music was profound, as a body of secular composed music intended to intrigue, edify, and entertain its listeners emerged from the pens of composers for the first time since the demise of the ancient world.

Music in the Fourteenth Century

Gnarly Modern Music: The Ars Nova
The musical cutting edge of the fourteenth century was occupied by a group of composers living and working within the institutional confines of Paris's Notre Dame Cathedral. This second Notre Dame School of composers is referred to as the ars nova, the "new art," in order to distinguish them from the first school (which included Léonin and his colleagues), a group referred to as the ars antiqua, the "old art." The music of the fourteenth-century ars nova epitomizes this era of rapid change and diversity. Much of their music is secular, and it is often of daunting complexity, with rhythmic systems carried to incredible extremes.

MUSIC BOX

Guillaume de Machaut, "Quant en Moy" (ca. 1350)

Machaut was born around 1300 and died in 1377. He was the whole package: aside from being the outstanding composer of the ars nova, he is also considered the greatest French poet of his time. Many of his compositions are of extraordinary complexity, including one called "Quant en Moy," which translates as "When, to me."

"Quant en Moy" is a secular polyphonic work that sets to music two different love poems sung by two different singers, a soprano and a tenor, simultaneously. It uses a technique called isorhythm, which assumes that rhythm and pitch can be manipulated separately. In an isorhythmic composition, complex rhythmic patterns are repeated over and over again even as the pitch material develops freely. In "Quant en Moy," the soprano sings a poem in which the isorhythmic pattern is forty beats long, and the tenor simultaneously sings a different poem in which the isorhythmic pattern is twenty beats long. Once every stanza, the patterns merge into something called a hocket, an amazing effect by which the two voices rapidly alternate, like the teeth of a zipper, before sailing off into the next stanza.

It's all eye-crossingly complex. We will not witness such systemic complexity in Western music again until the 1940s and '50s.

Note the following:

- The isorhythmic structure is not a "surface" element of the music but rather a subliminal presence.
- A third melodic part in the instrumental accompaniment consisting of a plainchant holds the whole thing together. God is not absent after all; he may be out of sight, but he's not out of mind. This accompanimental plainchant becomes a metaphor for God's presence in all things, religious and secular.

continued on next page

> • "Quant en Moy" is "spiky" and foreign-sounding to our ears.
> The complementary concepts of harmonic consonance and
> dissonance, as we understand them today, had not yet evolved,
> and the isorhythmic patterns give this music a rhythmic "edge"
> that militates against natural vocal declamation. Nevertheless,
> the music is brilliant, clever, and utterly representative of its time.

It has been suggested that the musical complexity of the ars nova
mirrors the architectural complexity of the Notre Dame Cathedral
itself, with its incredible arches, its flying buttresses, and its riotous
surface detail, and that these Notre Dame–based composers sought
musical analogs for the architectural structures and details they
observed every day.

The secular, intellectually complex music of this period mirrors
a fragmented and anguished age, an age in which composers of such
music sought to create order in an increasingly disordered world. It
was during the fourteenth century that Western music diverged from
the medieval Church's primarily ritual use and ceremonial view of
music, and back toward being a more humanistic art that could be
consumed for personal edification and/or amusement.

Going Gaga for Greek: The Rebirth in Full Swing

The secularism and growing fascination with antiquity that characterized much of the art of the fourteenth century continued unabated
into the fifteenth and sixteenth centuries. It is not an overstatement
to say that the experience of rediscovering ancient Greek and Roman
culture overwhelmed Europe during these centuries, a period now
generally referred to as the Renaissance.

To a great degree, the Renaissance was a response to the break-
down of the absolute authority of the medieval Church. Where the
medieval man said, *Credo ut intelligam*, meaning "Understanding can

come only through belief," the evolving spirit of the fifteenth century said, *Intelligo ut credam*: "Belief can come only through understanding." This intellectual shift can be observed in several major trends:

- **Classicism.** The Renaissance was fascinated by the language, literature, philosophy, art, and architecture of ancient Greece and Rome. But more than just the accomplishments of the Greeks and Romans, the thinkers of the Renaissance were inspired by the ancient view of humankind. Thus inspired, humanism emerged as the dominant intellectual movement of the Renaissance. It focused on human life and accomplishments rather than on religious doctrine and the afterlife.
- **Exploration.** The Renaissance saw the voyages of Christopher Columbus, Vasco da Gama, and Ferdinand Magellan.
- **The Protestant Reformation.** The power of the Roman Church was profoundly shaken by the Protestant Reformation, led by Martin Luther.
- **Education.** The rise of secular power meant the rise of secular education. Aristocrats and the upper middle class hired scholars to educate their children.
- **The printing press.** The dissemination of knowledge took an incalculable leap forward with the invention of movable type around 1450. The first plainchants were published in 1473, and the first polyphony in 1501. Not until the invention of the Internet (thank you, Mr. Gore) will we see an equivalent jump forward in the speed of information transfer.

Sometimes technology is our friend, and sometimes it isn't

Just as e-mail would seem to have done away with the ancient art of handwritten letters, so the advent of printed music brought an end to the exquisite art of hand-copied, illuminated music manuscripts.

We can see these huge hymnals today in the church and cathedral libraries of Europe: massive medieval and early Renaissance collections of plainchant, copied and illuminated by hand on vellum. These volumes are big: stick four legs on 'em and you've got yourself a coffee table. The expense of producing these books was prodigious, so a church would buy one such hymnal for all to share. It would be placed on a stand at one end of the choir loft. Anyone with bad eyes sat close to it, and those with good eyes sat farther away. In such a way, a single book could serve an entire choir.

- **Painting and sculpture.** Inspired by the glories of classical art, Renaissance artists depicted the world around them with a new clarity and perspective. A golden age of art ensued, one that saw the lives and creations of such artists as Donatello, Botticelli, da Vinci, Raphael, Michelangelo, and Titian.
- **And finally, music.** The humanist Greek ideal of music was taken to heart by Renaissance composers, who sought to create more expressive and expressively "meaningful" music based on what ancient Greek writers and philosophers claimed their music was capable of doing. Many important and influential church officials also wanted the Church's sacred music to employ a more emotionally immediate vocabulary than that of earlier times. Those who read ancient literature asked themselves why their contemporary music did not move them the way the ancient Greeks claimed their music moved them. Bishop Bernardino Cirillo, an outspoken critic of the liturgical music of his time, wrote, "Thus the musicians of today should endeavor in their profession to do what the sculptors, painters, and architects of our time have already done, who have recovered the expressive art and power of the ancients" (Grout, Palisca, 4th ed., 199).

Of course, it's one thing to demand that musicians recover "the expressive power and art of the ancients" and another thing actually to be able to do so. The great challenges facing the composers of the fifteenth century were to decide what exactly their music should express and then to figure out how precisely to express it in a way that would move its hearers in a manner analogous to the music of the ancients.

It's the *Words*

At a time when the overwhelming bulk of all composed music was vocal, the composers of the fifteenth century came to realize that the expressive message of the music lay in the words. Therefore, expression in music was indelibly tied to clear vocal articulation: the rise and fall of melody and musical rhythms should be a function of verbal articulation, the better to project the words clearly and unambiguously. For Renaissance composers, clear vocal declamation of the words being sung became the essential element in musical expression: if the words carried the essential expressive message of a piece of music, then the words had to be clearly understood.

Along with this doctrine of articulation was the developing idea that the music itself should reflect and intensify the actual meaning of the words, a process called word painting or tone painting.

The Renaissance expressive notions of clear vocal articulation and word painting found their ultimate manifestations in the Mass and the madrigal, the two most important musical genres of the late sixteenth century.

A musical Mass is the setting of certain parts of the daily Mass to music. Such a Mass was to most Renaissance composers what the symphony was to eighteenth-century composers and opera to a nineteenth-century composer: the ultimate test of compositional prowess. The greatest composers of the Renaissance—Josquin des Prez (ca. 1450–1521) and Giovanni Pierluigi da Palestrina (ca. 1525–1594)—were also the greatest composers of the Mass.

There were a variety of different Masses, all of which were based upon a single, preexisting melody line, usually a plainchant. However, one type, the so-called imitation Mass, employed as its theme a melody drawn from the secular repertoire. The creation and popularity of imitation Masses in the early sixteenth century demonstrate that the composers of these Masses were given an extraordinary degree of creative freedom by a relatively tolerant Church.

Soon enough, Martin Luther's Ninety-five Theses (posted as a protest on a church door in the city of Wittenberg in 1517) put an end to the Church's tolerance and led to the seismic upheaval that was the Protestant Reformation.

The World Turned Upside Down: The Protestant Reformation and the Counter-Reformation

The Reformation shook the Western world to its core. The so-called Counter-Reformation followed, as the Catholic Church, battered but not broken, sought to discover and then address those laxities that it believed had led to the Reformation in the first place. Among the most important acts of the Counter-Reformation was the convening of a task force called the Council of Trent, which met for eighteen years in the northern Italian city of Trento, from 1545 to 1563. Every aspect of the Church fell under the council's scrutiny; and it had something to say about pretty much everything, including music.

Among many other things, the council objected mightily to the increasingly secular and personally expressive nature of late fifteenth- and early sixteenth-century church music. Imitation Masses, overly complex polyphony, and even the *pronunciation* of church-trained singers were censured by the council.

The next generation of church composers, with Giovanni Pierluigi da Palestrina in the lead, managed to create a new sort of sacred music, one in tune with the council's pronouncements. However, for the most part, the council's dictates tended to stifle innovation, which, as a result, was lavished on the secular music of the late sixteenth century, most notably on an emerging genre called the madrigal.

A madrigal is a secular, unaccompanied vocal work for four to six individual voices. What set madrigals apart from other contemporary genres of late Renaissance secular vocal music was that they combined "elevated" poetry with suitably "elevated" music. Another thing that set them apart was their "free" mixing of polyphonic and homophonic sections, something very unusual in music of the late Renaissance. In the artistically repressive environment of the Counter-Reformation, during which experimentation was absolutely verboten in church music, the

Giovanni Pierluigi da Palestrina (1525–1594) The Teaching Company Collection

madrigal, as a secular art form, became the most experimental, the most avant-garde musical genre of its time.

At the heart of the genre lies a compositional technique called word, or tone, painting. Word painting is the creation of a musical gesture that illustrates the meaning of a word or a group of words— for example, by setting the words *running down the hill* with a fast, descending musical scale. Thus, madrigals are "about" their words and about illustrating the meanings of those words, and in this they are the ultimate manifestation of the Renaissance's infatuation with the "word."

In their desire to evoke the word musically, mid-sixteenth-century aestheticians and philosophers wrote lengthy tracts on how best to marry music and words. Whole essays and dissertations were written on what sorts of musical gestures were appropriate to illustrate what sorts of words.

Thus, the madrigal, as a genre, became bound up with finding a musical way to express the literary meaning of a poem. The madrigal became the last expressive step before the invention of opera,

the musical genre that would finally re-create, in modern guise, the
musical/dramatic art of the ancient Greeks.

Thomas Weelkes, "As Vesta Was from Latmos Hill Descending" (1601)

Italian-language madrigals were all the rage in England during the
late sixteenth century. Inspired, English composers took up their
quills and began composing English-language madrigals.

A marvelous collection of English-language madrigals was published in 1601, containing madrigals by twenty-three different
English composers. The collection was assembled by the composer
Thomas Morley, and he called it *The Triumph of Oriana*. All of the
madrigals are dedicated to Queen Elizabeth I, who was then in the
forty-third year of her forty-five-year reign. All of the madrigals
in the collection end with the same epigrammatic last line, "Long
live fair Oriana," Oriana being a mythological name for Queen
Elizabeth.

Despite the fact that it is in English (and not Italian), Weelkes's
"As Vesta Was from Latmos Hill Descending" is, for English speakers, an ideal example of the genre, because we can get the jokes: the
high notes on the word *hill*, falling and rising scales on the words
descending and *ascending*, a sustained note on the word *long*, and so
forth. Despite the silly lengths to which word painting often goes,
the madrigal is verbally illuminating and most entertaining, and this
was precisely what the genre was supposed to be about.

The fourteenth-century crisis of faith that brought about the end
of the absolute authority of the medieval Church triggered a rediscovery and cultivation of ancient (pre-Christian) art, science, and
philosophy in the fifteenth and sixteenth centuries. The thinkers and
artists of the Renaissance transformed this ancient heritage into new
science and art of their own. In the world of Renaissance music, an

all-encompassing effort was made to recapture the expressive oomph the Greeks had ascribed to their music. At the same time, the syntax of music—building on the work of Pythagoras, among many others—grew dramatically, as the tonal harmonic system based on the triad came into being.

We've just concluded a whirlwind tour of some of the major movements in early Western music history. Before we continue on to the more familiar music of the common practice (music composed between approximately 1600 and 1900), we'll take a brief detour in the next chapter to become familiar with some of the terminology that will, when applied in later chapters, help us understand how concert music is put together.

CHAPTER 4

A Necessary and Invigorating Excursion into the Worlds of Music Theory and Terminology

t the time the Renaissance ostensibly began, around 1400 or so, there were profound regional differences in tuning and variations in the kinds of pitches and pitch relationships that could be heard across Western Europe. By the "end" of the Renaissance, around 1600 or so, tuning systems and harmonic practice had gone a long way toward standardization. It is time to grasp the theoretical and terminological bulls by their horns and tackle these issues to the degree that we can understand something of the development of the Western musical language and what took place during the Renaissance in particular.

The rediscovery of Pythagoras and other ancient music theorists stimulated a tremendous degree of experimentation with systems of tuning, scales, and harmony during the Renaissance.

We begin by defining music in the broadest possible terms.

Music is "sound in time" or "time defined by sound." There's nothing subjective about those definitions; we don't say "organized" sounds or "pleasant" sounds, because one person's organization is another's anarchy, and one person's pleasantness is another's ugliness. Our definitions can include everything from a steam engine rolling down the rails to an elegant minuet by Haydn, and that is as it should be.

When we talk about the "time" aspect of music, we're talking about some aspect of rhythm. Rhythm includes everything from the beats in dance music to large-scale musical form, that is, how the large sections in a piece of music are arrayed. For now, we're going to focus our attention on the sound aspect of music: how certain types of sounds, called pitches, are arrayed into melody.

Pitch and Melody

A pitch is a "discrete sound," a sound we can sing. It's a discrete sound with two properties.

First, a pitch has the property of a single fundamental frequency. A fundamental frequency is the rate of vibration along the full length of a sound-producing body (a four-foot-long piano string, for example) and the subsequent sound produced by that rate of vibration. When we sing along with that vibrating piano string, it is its fundamental frequency that we are singing.

The second property of pitch is timbre. *Timbre* means "tone color." So, a pitch has two properties: a single fundamental frequency, which allows us to sing that pitch, and the property of timbre, which allows us to identify what instrument is playing (or singing) that pitch.

Timbre is a product of factors, the most important of which are the overtones (or "partials") given off by a vibrating body. You see, even as the piano string is vibrating at its full length and producing its fundamental, it is also, simultaneously, vibrating in *partial lengths*: in halves, thirds, quarters, and so forth. Each of these partial vibrations also produces a sound, called a harmonic. The degree to which certain of these partials are louder (or softer) than the others, and the way in which they blend with the fundamental, produce an identifiable timbre, a tone color, unique to the sound-producing body, be it a piano string, a clarinet, or a sackbut.

One more term before we move on, and that term is *note*. A note is a "notated" pitch, a pitch with duration. When we notate on paper, part of what we write down is the pitch's duration, meaning for how long that pitch should be sustained. A note is a pitch with duration, and thus notes are where the sound and time aspects of music intersect.

Notes are the building blocks of melody. I would suggest that we think of notes the same way we think of atoms: as that smallest complete musical object with which we can build larger musical structures.

Melody, most simply defined, is any succession of notes.

Living in Harmony: The Tonal System

Harmony in music refers to the simultaneous sounding of two or more different pitches. A chord is a type of harmony, one consisting of the simultaneous sounding of three or more different pitches. The tonal system is that system of chords, of harmonies, that lies at the sonar plexus of the music of the common practice. While the tonal system was perfected during the Baroque era (ca. 1600–1750), it was "invented" during the Renaissance, as composers and theorists reexamined and extended the work of Pythagoras (ca. 570–495 BCE) and his school.

Pythagoras and his followers discovered that the simpler the mathematical ratio between two vibrating bodies, the more blended—the more consonant—the relationship between the sounds they produce.

As an example, let's go back to the four-foot-long piano string: Say the pitch produced by that vibrating string is middle C (which means that the string is vibrating back and forth at its full length some 260 times a second). Half the string would vibrate twice as fast, that is, 520 times a second. The sound produced by half the string is the C an octave above middle C.

These two sounds are so closely related that we perceive them as being the same pitch, one higher (or lower) than the other: pitches an octave (eight white keys on a keyboard) apart.

Thus, an octave is a sonic manifestation of a one-to-two ratio, which, after one-to-one, is the simplest ratio in our universe. Our conclusion: the simpler the ratio between two pitches, the more "blended," the more "consonant" with each other are the sounds they produce. In discovering this, Pythagoras was convinced that what he had discovered was nothing less than a sonic manifestation of the order, the rightness, of the cosmos.

Renaissance theoreticians took Pythagoras's work to the next level. They played the first six "partials" of the harmonic series simultaneously, those fractions (the "parts" of the fundamental), and came up with a harmonic unit that we today call a major triad. This construct consists of three different pitches (thus the designation *tri*-ad) that nevertheless blend together in a very mellow, very homogeneous way.

The theoreticians and composers of the Renaissance jumped for joy over this creation, and eventually created a harmonic system based on the triad. The impact of the development of the triad-based tonal harmonic system on Western music cannot be overstated.

Texture

Texture refers to the number of melodies and the relationship between those melodies in a given segment of music. The three textures we will encounter over the course of this book are monophony, polyphony, and homophony.

Monophony

Monophony, or a monophonic texture, is a melody consisting of a single unaccompanied melody line, such as plainchant.

Polyphony

A polyphonic texture is one in which there are two or more principal melodic parts, each (or all) of equal importance.

There are two words that are synonymous with *polyphony* and *polyphonic*; they are, respectively, *counterpoint* and *contrapuntal*.

The noun *counterpoint* is an Anglicization of the Latin *contrapunctus*, which means "against point," as in "note against note."

The adjective *contrapuntal* comes from the Latin *contrapuncta*, which means "against point." Implicit in the word is "note against note," meaning simultaneous melodic parts of equal importance.

There are two different types of polyphony (or counterpoint): imitative polyphony and nonimitative polyphony.

Imitative Polyphony

An imitative polyphonic texture is one in which the constituent melodic parts all sing and/or play more or less the same melody, but at various time intervals, so that the melody overlaps itself. There are two types of imitative polyphony: strict and nonstrict. A strict imitative polyphonic texture is one in which each constituent part imitates the other parts exactly: strictly. For example, a performance of "Row, Row, Row Your Boat" will feature three voices, or parts, each singing exactly the same thing, but at an interval of time, so that the parts overlap. A piece or passage of music written in strict imitative polyphony is called a *kanon* in German and a round in English. Round is a most useful designation, because it describes the cyclical nature of such a piece; like a dog chasing its tail, a round will keep following itself.

Most imitative polyphony is of the nonstrict variety. In nonstrict imitative polyphony, the voices (or parts) do indeed imitate one another, but not exactly—not strictly—with the advantage being that the music doesn't get caught in a cyclical groove and is free to go wherever the composer wants it to go.

Nonimitative Polyphony

The other main type of polyphony is nonimitative polyphony, which is a different kettle of notes entirely. A nonimitative polyphonic texture is one in which there are two or more simultaneous and different melodies, neither of them more important than the other(s). Once again, you can try this at home! Grab the gerbil and sing "Happy Birthday to You" simultaneously with "In-a-Gadda-Da-Vida." The result might not sound very good, but you will have performed a bit of nonimitative polyphony!

Homophony

A homophonic texture is one in which one melody is predominant and all other melodic or harmonic material is perceived as accompanimental.

The emergence of the tonal harmonic system provided an organizational framework by which the various melodies in a polyphonic texture could be coordinated to be consonant with one another. Equally important, the evolution of the tonal harmonic system provided the means for a single melody to be underlain by a changing harmonic accompaniment. Such a musical texture—in which we perceive one principal melody and all else as being "accompanimental"—is called homophony. Thanks to the advent of the tonal system, composed homophony—that is, harmonized melody—appeared for the first time during the Renaissance.

A homophonic texture is one in which there is a foreground (the thematic melody), a middle ground (the bass line), and a background (the inner voices). We're talking here about musical perspective, which was invented at virtually the same time as artistic perspective. The first great example of the new art of perspective—Tommaso Masaccio's *The Holy Trinity*, on the wall of the Church of Santa Maria Novella in Florence, was painted in 1428, at exactly the time homophony began to evolve! Thinking of artistic perspective may help you remember what we mean by musical perspective and, in turn, homophonic texture.

By the late sixteenth century, the tonal harmonic system based on the triad had, for all intents and purposes, been adopted universally by European composers.

CHAPTER 5

Emotional Exuberance and Intellectual Control

The Paradox of Baroque Art

The secular, ancient Greece–inspired search for humanistic expressive relevance and power that characterized the music of the fifteen and sixteenth centuries continued unabated into the seventeenth century. However, the music of the seventeenth century represents an expressive and technical sea change from that which came before. Opera, a stage drama set to music, was invented in Florence around the year 1600. Although initially an outgrowth of the Renaissance impulse to re-create the musical-dramatic art of the ancients, opera was to transform forever the expressive nature and syntactical content of Western music. Opera recognized and celebrated the emotion felt by an individual person to a degree entirely new in post-ancient European music. The spinoffs from opera—such as the technological innovations spun off from the American space program—constitute a "what's what" of Baroque era musical innovation. The large instrumental ensemble called the orchestra; the genres of concerto and symphony, oratorio and church cantata; the perfection of the tonal system; the ensemble-within-an-ensemble known as the basso continuo; and, most important, the cultivation of emotional expression, of feeling, in vocal and instrumental music all can trace their origins back to the invention of opera.

Thus, we mark the Baroque era as beginning in 1600 and running to 1750.

Is there really any such thing as the Baroque era (or, for that matter, the Middle Ages, the Renaissance, and the Classical and Romantic eras)?

To periodize or not to periodize? That is the question. Whether 'tis nobler in the mind to suffer the slings and arrows of outraged academes by periodizing (and thus to blaspheme through generalization) or to address large-scale stylistic trends without prevarication; 'tis a fardel to bear, and bear it we shall. For such utile aids are not to be scorned, but embraced lest even greater misunderstanding be our lot. O Baroque! O Classical! O Romantic! Though the thorns of despised love be your reward, we will invoke you even as we curse you, for, like our knees, thou art poorly made, but we cannot walk without you.

As period dates go, 1600 is a good one, because it was in 1600 that the first surviving work that we, today, consider an "opera" was performed in Florence, Italy.

During the summer of 1750, nearly 150 years to the day after that opera performance in Florence, Johann Sebastian Bach died in Leipzig. Admittedly, in 1750, few people knew that Bach had died, and even fewer people cared. But in hindsight we now recognize that 1750 marked the end of an era.

The word *baroque* comes from the Portuguese word *barocco*, meaning "a pearl of irregular shape and/or irregular color." During the early eighteenth century, *baroque* became slang for things that were considered gross or bizarre or in bad taste: a derogatory reference to art, architecture, and music that was considered overly extravagant and fussy in its design. By the 1920s, the term had lost its unfavorable connotations, and had come to refer to the flamboyant, extravagant, and detailed art and music of the period dating from roughly 1600 to 1750.

What we call the Baroque era has also been called the age of science and the age of reason, because of the increasing secularization, scientific investigation, and intellectual rationality that characterized the period.

This was the era of Hume, of Locke, of Descartes, of Malthus, of Bacon, of Leibniz. It was the era that saw Galileo Galilei observe the heavens and develop his heretical theory of heliocentricity, by which he claimed the sun, not Earth, was the center of the solar system.

The Baroque was the era of René Descartes, who constructed a system of knowledge that was based entirely on deduction and dismissed sensory input as "unreliable."

The Baroque was the era of Johannes Kepler, who developed a complex mathematical formula by which one could predict the elliptical orbits of the planets. Something that appeared random and magical in earlier times could now be explained rationally based on Kepler's formulas.

Most important, it was the era of Isaac Newton. Newtonian physics is a fascinating blend of religious faith and hard science. Newton claimed that underneath the complexity and visible chaos of the universe there existed systemic order. According to Newton, once man had divined the formulas by which this universal system operates, he would be able to understand the past, deal with the present, and anticipate the future. God was seen as a great watchmaker, and the cosmos as God's own watch.

Newton's worldview, which was a combination of faith and rationality, of religious belief and logic, demonstrates perfectly the dichotomy, the paradox, of Baroque science, philosophy, art, and music.

We read in our modern history books that it was during the Baroque era that rational thought defeated supernatural explanation. This is true, but only up to a point. The impression this statement makes is that Baroque Europe was populated by a bunch of secular humanists for whom spirituality and religion played no role. This impression is inaccurate. Indulge me in a parable. It's the year 1300. You're a student and you ask your teacher, "Master, why is grass green?" Your teacher replies, "My child, grass is green because God in his wisdom has made it so." And you say, "Ah, I should've known! Thank you!" And you go away happy, satisfied with a supernatural explanation for a physical phenomenon.

Fast-forward to 1700, smack-dab in the middle of this "age of science," and you ask the same question: "Master, why is grass green?" Your teacher responds, "My child, grass is green because it contains a chemical called chlorophyll that reflects certain light wavelengths that our brain interprets as the color green, which God in his wisdom has given us." And you say, "Neat-o."

There's the Baroque trip in a nutshell: God and faith are not out of the picture, not by a long shot. Consequently, the Baroque belief that logical systems—the invisible hand of God—rationally governed the complexity of the world manifested itself in art that celebrated detail controlled by symmetry. When we look at a Baroque palace, or garden, or furniture, or a ceiling painting, or an organ, we are immediately struck by two things: First, all the stuff, all the detail. Baroque design typically confronts us with a veritable riot of information. But in spite of its surface complexity, it is never chaotic, disorganized, or confused. Why? That's the second thing that strikes us: its symmetry and balance. Baroque design is about symmetry—rationality and logic—controlling all that exuberant detail.

Baroque design is a metaphor for the same issues that Newton and his scientific colleagues were grappling with: how to reconcile the apparent complexity of the world and cosmos with the spiritual belief that, behind it all, there *must* be order, logic, and control, for God would not have it any other way.

Nowhere is this Baroque duality of detail held in check by logic, of exuberance tempered by control, more apparent than in the music of the age. At its core, Baroque music is about expressive exuberance and surface extravagance carefully tempered and controlled by rhythm; a systemic approach to harmony; and symmetrical (or what we call "cyclical") musical forms.

Opera, the Affections, and Absolutism: How Musical Theater, Emotional States, and Euro-Royalty Revolutionized Musical Expression

From the Baroque era on, so much happens in music that we will have to look at each era from multiple angles, which, taken together, will give us a holistic and detailed view of the music and how to understand it.

One of the distinguishing features of the Baroque era was its fascination with idealized emotional states—spiritual movements of the mind—which were referred to as the "affections." One manifestation of this fascination was the Baroque infatuation with theater, where such idealized emotions could be exposed, magnified, and witnessed vicariously. Another manifestation was the invention of opera, around the year 1600, in which stage plays were set to music, thus intensifying, through music, the affections being felt and expressed by the characters. (For our reference, the plays of Shakespeare were written at exactly the time opera was being invented, between 1590 and 1612.)

A comparison of the characteristics of two different kinds of music will help clarify some differences between music of the Renaissance and that of the Baroque era. Let us imagine a Renaissance madrigal and an aria from a Baroque opera, works composed one hundred years apart: the madrigal in 1580 and the opera aria in 1680.

Both madrigal and opera are secular genres. Both were created to entertain and fascinate their audiences, and both genres represent the artistic cutting edge of their times. Madrigals were composed for vocal ensembles typically ranging in size from four to six voices. The operative expressive technique in a madrigal is word painting, by which a composer links appropriate musical gestures with the words, thus heightening and intensifying the literary meaning of the words. A madrigal, then, is about its words, which a composer will "paint" with appropriate musical gestures.

An operatic aria, on the other hand, is the equivalent of a soliloquy in a stage drama. Composed for and performed by a single singer, real time stops during an aria while the singer, in the guise of a character onstage, reflects on the course of the action and his or her feelings. It is the composer's task to interpret the words being sung in such a way as to give emotional substance to the feelings that lie behind the words.

In summary, a madrigal is about its words, which are illustrated using a technique called word painting, while an opera aria is about the feelings behind its words, interpreted and intensified musically by the composer.

Opera is *theater*, and its emotional impact is a galaxy removed from that of a madrigal. At best, a four-, five-, or six-voice madrigal can evoke only generalized emotions. But an operatic aria is about a person, a character, and his or her emotions, a character on whom we focus laser-like as an individual.

The development of opera represents, musically, the rise of the individual in Western musical culture, and nothing in the last four hundred plus years of Western music history has been more important or has had more far-reaching ramifications than the invention of opera. Whether you're an operaphile or an operaphobe, the importance of opera to the development of Western music is singular, and thus we will revisit opera continually over the remainder of this book.

Absolutism and the Music of the Baroque Era

The decreasing political power of the Church gave rise to the "absolute monarch," who claimed to govern through divine right. These monarchs and their aristocratic minions sought to celebrate themselves through opulent and extravagant art, architecture, and music. The magnificence characteristic of so much Baroque era music (and art) is a testament to its usefulness as a propaganda tool.

By far the biggest dog among the absolute monarchs of the

Baroque was Louis XIV of France, who reigned for an incredible seventy-two years, from 1643 to 1715, and the ultimate example of Baroque extravagance is the palace Louis built for himself at Versailles, all thirteen hundred plus rooms of it. Of course, Versailles was more than a royal residence; it was a statement: its scale was meant to dwarf, stupefy, and intimidate Louis's friends and enemies.

However, for all of its incredible size and detail, what makes the palace at Versailles work, as a piece of architectural art, is its symmetry, symmetry that holds everything in place. Everything is architecturally balanced and logically controlled by the hand of the architect. The overall effect of the buildings and grounds, despite their size, is one of control and order. It is so baroque!

The French Overture

In response to the pomp and extravagance of Louis's court, a specific and important genre of music was invented: the so-called French overture. A musical overture is an instrumental introduction that almost always precedes a musical stage work, be it an opera, a ballet, or a musical theater work. A French overture is something more than that. Invented around 1660, a French overture is a royal and magnificent orchestral composition designed to create a festive atmosphere for the stage event to come and, even more important, to formally welcome the king to the theater. The king for whom the French overture was invented was Louis XIV, who liked his pomp in large doses.

A French overture consists of two sections of music. The first part is characterized by sweeping scales; a slow, plodding tempo; and dotted (meaning long/short) rhythms: ta-tummm, ta-tummm, ta-tummm. The first part of a French overture is majestic and royal and, in every sense, pompous. The second part of a French overture is characterized by imitative polyphony (remember, the nonstrict overlapping of like melodies) and a faster tempo.

Louis XIV's court composer, Jean-Baptiste Lully, was as cut-throat, as politic, as power hungry, and as opportunistic as his boss. Lully, an Italian by birth, came to France at the age of twelve. Through equal parts talent, scheming, and possibly even assassination, Lully climbed the musical ladder, ultimately becoming the master of all music at the French court. His most enduring invention was the French overture.

Such was the influence of Louis the XIV's court, and such was the fame of Lully, that the so-called French-style overture became ubiquitous across Europe for the next hundred years and more. For example, George Frideric Handel, a German-born, Italian-trained composer, began his English-language oratorio *Messiah* with a French-style overture. Talk about a cosmopolitan genre!

MUSIC BOX

George Frideric Handel, Overture to *Messiah* (1741)

Handel's is a French-style overture, undoubtedly the most frequently performed French overture in the repertoire. Typical of the genre, the overture is structured in two large parts:

1. The first part is marked *grave*, "solemn." It is dark in tone, slow in tempo, and marked by dotted (short-long) rhythms. The expressive effect of this opening section, as in any French overture, is one of great gravitas and pomp, a metaphor for the majesty of the king himself.

2. The second part is marked *allegro moderato*, "moderately fast." It is characterized by faster rhythms and imitative polyphony. The expressive impact of this faster section, as in any French overture, is one of great excitement: excitement at the arrival of the king and in anticipation of the theatrical event to follow.

The Science of Music and the Music of Science:
The Language of Music Explodes!

Inspired by the art of the ancient world, the artists of the Renaissance observed and depicted nature and the human body as they actually were. This same clear-eyed spirit of rational investigation characterized science in the Baroque era, during which the visible universe was observed, analyzed, and codified. This visible universe included the aural universe of music. Virtually every aspect of music—from tuning systems and the tonal system to instrument design and music notation—was investigated and codified and, in the process, updated and extended. The syntax of Western music—the actual vocabulary of pitch, rhythm, instrumental color, and expressive devices available to composers—grew exponentially during the Baroque era. This syntax provided the underpinning of the Western musical language until the early twentieth century, which is why we speak of the "common practice" as running from 1600 to 1900, from the invention of opera to the beginning of the twentieth century.

CHAPTER 6

Play It, Don't Say It

The Rise of Instrumental Music

The development of a large-scale instrumental musical tradition during the Baroque era illustrates the fact that the syntactical elements of the era's music had became substantial enough that they could, by themselves, create a viable musical exprience without the need for text or voices. This is incredibly important, so I would ask readers to read that sentence again. I'll wait.

Instrumental music was written during the Renaissance as well, particularly "suites"—that is, collections of dances—for lute, guitar, harpsichord, and other chord- or harmony-producing instruments. There was also courtly dance music, and the fanfares and flourishes created to celebrate royalty and such.

However, fanfares and flourishes constitute occasional music: ritual and/or ceremonial jingles that had little (or nothing) to do with the cultivation of an instrumental musical tradition. The same could be said for the collections of dances that constitute the great bulk of instrumental music created before the Baroque. Renaissance instrumental dance music was about dance first and music second, and the suites that appeared for lute and harpsichord, for example, were as often as not arrangements of preexisting social dances.

Very simply, and with no offense intended to Renaissance music, it wasn't until the Baroque era that instrumental music—conceived for its own sake, with a syntax all its own—began to be cultivated as an art form equal to that of vocal music. This was a big deal, as

Western music diverged from being an art based primarily on the concrete meaning of words and became, increasingly, an abstract art in which the intuition and feelings of the audience were brought to bear in a manner quite new and different.

I would suggest that instrumental music is the most abstract art yet conceived by humankind. Some might quibble with me; but in this I know I'm right. In drawing and painting, representational or not, a physical object exists in at least two dimensions. A drawing or painting is an object we can touch and physically feel. A piece of sculpture exists in three dimensions. It's a concrete thing that "exists," physically, in space. While a work of poetry, drama, or literature might not be "physically concrete" beyond the paper on which it's written, poetry, drama, and literature are written in languages that we can know and recognize. When we read a book or a poem, when we watch a play, we understand, at the very least, the language the author is using, and unless it's Pynchon, Joyce, Gödel, or the lyrics to "I Am the Walrus," we usually understand what the writer is trying to say.

But what is instrumental music? It is music that has no words, no literary information beyond its title to explain why it exists and why it sounds the way it does. It's neither physically dimensional nor concrete. We can touch a score, but a score is not the music; it's merely a chart that tells us very approximately what to play. Music has to be played, and when instrumental music is played, it exists only in the ether as concussion waves assaulting our eardrums.

Instrumental music speaks a language, has a syntax, that for all its glories is nonverbal in nature and has virtually no physical substance whatsoever. Color me a literalist, but as far as I'm concerned, that's about as abstract an art as I can imagine.

What this means to us, here and now, is that understanding the rise of a genuine, large-scale instrumental tradition during the Baroque era is going to require us to continue building our vocabulary. We're going to need to expand on the terms we've already encountered so we can perceive and identify the syntactical elements of this abstract thing called instrumental music.

A Vocabulary for Melody

A brief review.

- A pitch is a discrete sound with two properties: a fundamental frequency (that can be sung) and timbre (tone color).
- A note is a pitch with duration.
- A melody is any succession of notes.

In chapter 4, I suggested that we perceive notes as musical atoms: as being the smallest complete musical objects with which we can build larger musical structures.

Motive

In building most melodies, notes clump together to create "motives," which are then manipulated to create complete melodies. A motive is a brief succession of notes from which melody grows, through the processes of repetition, sequence, and transformation. To run a bit further with the atomic metaphor, if notes are atoms, then motives are molecules, which accumulate to create genuine substance: a complete melody.

For example, hear in your head or sing the melody to "Happy Birthday to You," a melody we know and understand with or without its words. The opening phrase, "Hap-py birth-day to you" represents the thematic motive. When manipulated, it will create a complete thematic melody.

In the second phrase, "Hap-py birth-day to you," the final two notes are higher than they were during the first version of the motive. This is called a sequence: the repetition of a motive or some part of a motive at a higher or lower pitch level. The third phrase, "Hap-py birth-day, dear Ludwig," maintains the rhythm of the thematic motive, but changes its pitches. We would call such an event a transformation of the thematic motive. The fourth and final phrase, "Hap-py birthday to you," represents a near-repetition of the original motive. These four phrases taken together create a coherent and motivically consistent thematic melody.

It was just this sort of motive-driven melody that was the solution to a seventeenth-century musical problem. The problem? Early composers of instrumental music needed a way to create melodic coherence and logic—a way to create melodies that made abstract sense to audiences in the absence of words. Motives and motivic repetition, transformation, and sequence did just that, providing coherence, structure, and meaning to melodies otherwise lacking words. The Baroque was the "great age" of the sequence, which is not necessarily a complimentary statement; it's painfully easy to parody the instrumental music of many Baroque composers (especially the Italian ones), with its endless strings of sequences up and down and down and up. But that's how composers gave coherence to early instrumental music, and as time passed and the instrumental syntax grew, such endless sequential episodes became the exception rather than the rule.

Tune

A tune is a special sort of melody, one with a clear beginning, middle, and end, a melody blessed with a property called lyricism. Lyricism is the quality of being songlike; a lyric melody, then, is one that is conceived vocally. Now, this doesn't mean that tunes—that lyric melodies—are written only for the voice. It's simply a matter of conception. Thus, all tunes are melodies, but not all melodies are tunes. "Happy Birthday to You" is most definitely a tune!

Theme

A theme is the principal musical idea in a given section of music. A theme can be a tune, it can be a motive, it can be a harmony, it can even be just the sound, the timbre, of an instrument (something we will discuss when we get to the French composer Claude Debussy in chapter 31).

Conjunct and Disjunct Melodies

Let us add to our vocabulary of melody two descriptors: *conjunct* and *disjunct*. A relatively conjunct melody is one in which its pitches are relatively close together, for example, the *Ode to Joy* theme from the fourth movement of Beethoven's Symphony no. 9 of 1824:

Note that adjacent notes in this melody are never more than a scale step away from one another, creating a melodic contour as smooth (as *conjunct*) as silk boxing shorts.

Now let's look at a relatively disjunct melody. This is the melody of Richard Wagner's über-famous "Ride of the Valkyries" from his music drama *The Valkyries*. The notes in this melody jump around like a tenor with a wasp in his BVDs. Adjacent notes are anywhere from two and a half steps to a full octave from one another, and the effect is a jagged, sharp-peaked melodic contour: a relatively disjunct melody.

With this new bit of musical vocabulary tucked away, we can return to the Baroque era secure in the knowledge that when the need arises, we'll have the vocabulary to address all sorts of melodies and themes.

As we have observed, the spirit of rational inquiry and investigation characteristic of the Baroque era was applied to the science and language of music as well, resulting in a seismic change in the syntax of Western music. Let's flesh this statement out a bit by observing just a few of the syntactical innovations characteristic of Baroque era music.

Instrumental technology and design underwent explosive change and development during the Baroque. Organ technology, design, and construction reached a peak that has never been exceeded since the baroque. Likewise, the harpsichord was perfected and the piano was invented during the Baroque era.

The growing needs of opera orchestras demanded wind and brass instruments that could blend and play in tune with other instruments. And although future builders would continue to tweak their designs, the flute, oboe, English horn, bassoon, clarinet, natural horn, and trombone came into being more or less as we know them today during the Baroque.

Perhaps most important, it was during the Baroque era that the violin family of instruments—perfected in and around the Italian city of Cremona by such legendary baroque luthiers (makers of stringed instruments) as Amati, Stradivari, and Guarneri—replaced the "da gamba" family of stringed instruments and, in the process, became the backbone of the orchestra, which it remains to this day.

The Baroque genius for systemization and codification focused on tuning systems as well. The "well-tempered tuning system" became standard by the very early eighteenth century. It was a system that divided the octave into twelve different pitches, and allowed for a major scale and a minor scale to be built on any one of those twelve different pitches. The resulting matrix of twenty-four different "scales," or "keys"—twelve major and twelve minor—thus established during the Baroque era remained the basic "pitch palette" for Western composers until the twentieth century.

Meter

Meter, which refers to how beats are grouped in a section of music—by twos, threes, fours, whatever—was also standardized during the Baroque era, as was the bar line, a notational device for separating metric units (meaning measures). Time signatures were invented, by which composers could indicate how many beats were in each metric unit (or "measure"). For example, the time signatures that follow would indicate metric units of, from left to right, two beats, three beats, and four beats. (In a key signature, it's the top number that "counts," by telling us how many beats are in each metric unit. The bottom number tells us what kind of note gets one beat: from left to right, a half note, an eighth note, and a quarter note.)

The science of tonal harmony, begun during the Renaissance, was perfected during the Baroque era. The system is called functional tonality or functional harmony, because Baroque composers and music theoreticians determined that any chord or harmony could be understood as having one of three functions in a composition: tonic chords created a sense of rest or resolution; dominant chords created a sense of tension needing resolution; and subdominant chords transited between the tonic chords and the dominant chords. (We will return to, and demonstrate, these basic harmonies in chapter 14, when we examine musical punctuation marks called cadences.)

A specialized group of instruments evolved during the Baroque whose job it was to articulate the bass line and functional harmonic progressions in a composition. Called the basso continuo, or thorough bass, this group of instruments fulfilled a role very much like the rhythm section in a jazz ensemble. The basso continuo—which typically consists of a chord-producing instrument such as a harpsichord and a bass line instrument such as a cello—was used universally during the Baroque as a control element; the bass line and clock-steady harmonic progressions played by the basso continuo become a veritable cage of harmony controlling the otherwise extravagant and note-filled melodic surfaces of Baroque era music.

MUSIC BOX

Johann Sebastian Bach (1685–1750), Brandenburg Concerto No. 2 (ca. 1720), Second Movement

Basso continuo was used universally during the Baroque era: in the opera house, and in chamber and orchestral compositions. As a result, pretty much any performance of a Baroque work—provided it is not a solo work for keyboard, violin, or cello—will feature a basso continuo. I've recommended J. S. Bach's Brandenburg Concerto no. 2 because it is a work none of us can afford to live without. The slow and quiet second movement provides a perfect environment with which to observe the basso continuo.

Note the following:

- The movement is scored for flute (or recorder), oboe, and violin and a basso continuo consisting of a harpsichord and a cello.
- The cello plays the beat-steady bass line while the harpsichord plunks out the changing harmonies above the bass line with equal regularity.
- The basso continuo creates a "cage" of rhythmic and harmonic control that encloses and contains the complex, intertwining melodic lines above, a brilliant example of the Baroque era musical duality of (melodic) exuberance tempered by (harmonic) control.

Instrument technology, tuning systems, meter, and functional harmony: no aspect of music was left untouched by the rational, scientific spirit of the Baroque. The seventeenth century also saw the emergence of the two dominant compositional styles of the Baroque era: the Italian style and the German style. The next chapter will define these styles and observe the principal reason behind their development: language. Put simply, when it comes to composing, we are what we speak.

CHAPTER 7

National Styles

Italy and Germany (or Why German Music Will Never Hit Your Eye Like a Big Pizza Pie and Italian Music Will Never Go from Best to Wurst)

The German-born Ludwig van Beethoven's Symphony no. 5 of 1808 begins with what is without a doubt the single most famous and recognizable four-note thematic idea in the entire concert repertoire, a musical idea with all the punch, power, and precision of the German language itself: dot-dot-dot-dash!

There's not an Italian composer on the planet who would have considered that musical idea as being long enough, expressively substantial enough, or attractive enough on which to base an extended theme; not a *one*, no *way*, no *how*.

During the course of an aria entitled "Siam navi all'onde algenti" ("We are ships on silver waves" in English) from his opera *L'Olimpiade* of 1734, the Italian-born composer Antonio Vivaldi sets the words *tutta la vita è un mar,* "the whole of life is a sea." The Italian word for sea is *mare*. Because of the nature of the Italian language, with its long and rich vowels and clear consonants, Vivaldi manages to sustain the word *mar* for an incredible seventy-four notes!

Crazy. There's not a German composer on the planet who, in setting German-language words to music, would (or could) ever have seriously considered sustaining a single syllable for that many notes; the German language is simply not given to that sort of elongation, no *way*, no *how*.

Where and when we grow up, how we grow up, and the native language we speak while we grow up are, for all of us, our formative heritage, the very backbone of who we are and how we perceive the world around us. It was during the Baroque era that powerful regional differences emerged in European music, differences that were to color the sorts of music composed in different places. The "Italian style," the "French style," the "Russian style," the "German style": there are, indeed, differences that go far beyond the individual personalities of the composers and have to do with the language and culture with which those composers grew up.

Opera was born and initially evolved in Italy. North German composers cultivated rigorous, highly technical sorts of vocal and instrumental music. French composers reveled in the sound of wind instruments and highly embellished musical textures. These sorts of national musical differences, difficult though they are to define, are still no less important for that difficulty. The Italian and German styles were the predominant compositional styles of the Baroque era, and being able to identify these styles, and their cultural regionalism, is part of learning to perceive them.

Here is the key statement as we begin our look at national styles: the nature of the language set to music will determine the nature of the melody that results. In the beginning, there was the liturgical music of the medieval Church: Latin-language plainchant created for prayer and ritual. Latin is a language of smooth, long vowels, few sharp consonants, and even fewer explosive articulations. Melodies set to Latin will mirror the characteristics of that language, and such melodies will likewise tend to be smooth and generally unmarked by harsh or explosive articulation.

The medieval Church's insistence on *vocal music* as the only viable music for worship helped to ensure its development above all other types, a cultivation that would continue particularly in Italy due to, one, the nature of the Italian language and, two, the fact that the Church was based in Rome.

Composed secular music in vernacular languages (that is, languages other than Latin) began to appear during the High Middle Ages. The creation and popularity of such music increased exponentially during the Renaissance, at a time when human expression was increasingly considered as important as religious expression.

Italy was the center of the Renaissance. The cultivation of the arts by the wealthy, combined with the power and wealth of the Rome-based Church, and Italy's physical proximity to so much ancient art and architecture, all contributed to making Italy the place to be during the fifteenth and sixteenth centuries. It was certainly the musical place to be; by 1500, the Italian peninsula had emerged as the musical capital of Europe.

The Italian Baroque Style

Of all the Romance, or "Roman," languages, Italian is closest to Latin. Of all the Romance languages, Italian was the easiest to adapt to the tradition of Latin vocal music. It was during the Renaissance, particularly as a result of the cultivation of the madrigal, that the

Italian language replaced Latin as the "indispensable" language of vocal music.

A few points regarding the Italian Baroque style:

- It was an outgrowth of Latin vocalism and the equally vocal character of the Italian language.
- The Italian Baroque style was essentially a homophonic tradition: it consisted principally of melody and accompaniment, the perfect example of which is opera, the dominant musical art form of the era.
- The Italian Baroque style exhibited a preference for melodic directness, as opposed to the ornamental complexity of the French style and the polyphonic and harmonic complexity of the Baroque German style.

MUSIC BOX

Antonio Vivaldi (1678–1841), *The Four Seasons* (*ca.* 1720), Concerto No. 1 in E Major: "Spring," First Movement

The four three-movement violin concertos known collectively as *The Four Seasons* are among the most frequently heard Baroque era works in the repertoire.

Please note the following:

- Vivaldi was a virtuoso violinist who composed forty-nine operas. His many concertos—particularly his violin concertos—reflect his operatic style and his experience in writing for the soprano voice with orchestral accompaniment.
- Typical of Vivaldi specifically and the Italian Baroque style in general, this music is for all of its many notes melodically direct and, particularly given all of its imitation of birdsong, most ingratiating.
- Typical of Vivaldi specifically and the Italian Baroque style in general, the music is homophonic in texture.

Trouble in Wittenberg and the Emergence of a
Distinctly German Musical Style

Through the High Middle Ages and the Renaissance, the principal cities of the Italian peninsula and their aristocrats, merchants,
and traders grew chubby, fat, *porcine* with wealth. One of the chief
beneficiaries of this wealth was the Rome-based Christian Church
and the popes, clergy, and bureaucrats who ran the Church like the
multinational corporate entity that it was. This state of affairs was
satisfactory in Italy but increasingly unsatisfactory for those living
in Switzerland, the Netherlands, and Germanic and Scandinavian
lands, where harsher climates and darker winters bred a different
sort of population. By the early sixteenth century, the working poor
of these northern lands had come to perceive the Church as a feudal institution and the functionaries of the Church as but another
wealthy, oppressive ruling class. The middle classes of the principal
northern cities wanted more control over their religious affairs, while
northern kings and ruling princes—who for decades had bickered
with the Church over taxation and legal jurisdiction—each wanted
to be master in his own territory. By the early sixteenth century,
much of northern Europe had become an anti-Roman powder keg.

The match that set it off was an intensely spiritual but deeply
troubled Catholic priest named Martin Luther.

Martin Luther was born in 1483 and died in 1546. Fairly early in
his life he decided that faith alone justified one in God's eyes. It was
a conclusion he reached by reading St. Paul, Romans: "The just shall
live by faith alone." With this potentially heretical idea in the back
of his mind, Luther lived, taught, and ministered quietly until an
incident brought him out of the cloister.

In 1517 he posted his Ninety-five Theses on the door of the Castle
Church in Wittenberg, where he taught. Among many other things,
he claimed that a sinner is freed of his guilt not by priestly absolu-
tion but by inner grace and faith. Luther questioned whether the

priesthood served any real spiritual function at all, and asserted that it was up to each individual to read and interpret the Bible according to his own conscience.

All of this (and much more!) went over like the proverbial lead balloon in Rome. Threatened by a papal bull with excommunication unless he recanted, Luther publicly burned the bull and was promptly excommunicated. As someone who had wanted to reform the Church from within, without recourse to violence, he watched in despair as an anti-Roman revolution swept across

Martin Luther's Ninety-five Theses (October 31, 1517) Library of Congress, Prints and Photographs Division, LC-USZ62-75127

Northern and Central Europe. It's a long and terrible story capped by the Thirty Years' War of 1618 to 1648, by which time much of Central Europe lay in complete ruin.

Out of this struggle came a new religious dogma, Lutheranism, which developed during the sixteenth and seventeenth centuries.

Among the elements of the new Lutheran dogma was the increasing use of vernacular language in place of Latin in church, something that would have a profound impact on the developing music of the Protestant Church.

A consequence was that German-language religious songs, or hymns, came to replace Latin plainchant as the basic religious music in the Lutheran community. These German-language church hymns, or chorales, became the backbone of the music in Lutheran communities across Europe, due in no small part to Martin Luther himself.

Luther attributed a semi-magical quality to music, claiming that it had the power to convey ideas, to steer the will, to fortify faith. (This should sound familiar: it comes right out of the ancient Greek view of music.) According to Martin Luther, the art of music was "a most wonderful and glorious gift of God, which has the power to drive out Satan and to resist temptations and evil thoughts."

The long-term impact of Luther's conception of music on the development of German music cannot be underestimated. Since all music was, according to Luther, "a gift of God," the act of writing or performing music was a godly act, irrespective of whether that music was secular or religious.

In opposition to the Roman Church, which traditionally claimed that only through vocal music could the word of God be taught and understood, the Lutheran Church embraced instrumental music as being capable of inspiring the same sort of devotion to God as vocal music. This Lutheran embrace of instrumental music would have a gigantic impact on the development of Northern European music.

By the seventeenth century, thanks in large part to Martin Luther's attitudes toward music and the role of music in the new Lutheran liturgy, music composed by Protestant German composers began to diverge significantly from Latin/Italian models. The primary influence on the emerging German musical style was the vernacular German language itself.

Because of the nature of the German language, melodies set to German words will be very different from melodies set to Italian words. For example, let's imagine that we're going to set the following phrase to music in Italian and German: "What a lovely evening." We will end up with two very different sounding melodies, as each language has a different cadence, vowels, and consonants.

Spoken or sung in Italian, the phrase gives us five incredibly juicy vowels, and a variety of colorful consonants to separate them: *che bella sera* (kay-bel-la-se-ra). My goodness, sung in Italian, the phrase could be sustained for days, and the words still understood. When it comes to beauty of vowel and clarity of consonant, Italian is indeed the "chosen language."

And in formal German? *Welch ein schöner Abend* (Velk-ein-cher-nar-ah-bent). The German version is much more about guttural, explosive consonants than vowels. German-language melodies tend to be syllabic, meaning that they feature one pitch per syllable: *Welch ein schöner Abend*. But a setting of the Italian *che bella sera* could feature multiple pitches on virtually every syllable. Big difference.

We say that Italian is a *melismatic language*: a language that by its nature allows for long, soaring melismata (multiple notes per syllable) when set to music. We say that German is a *syllabic language*: a language that, generally, allows for but one pitch per syllable when being set to music.

Thus, German-language melodies will tend to be syllabic, with one pitch per syllable. The sharp, sometimes guttural articulations of the German language will be reflected in the sharp, clearly articulated rhythms of the melody. A sharply articulated, compact language such as German will tend to create, when set to music, sharply articulated, compact melodies. Taken all together, this is the essential nature of music in German, a language not exploited musically until the Protestant Reformation.

As we move through the Baroque, we will observe two often very different musical traditions that developed side by side, one of them in Protestant Europe and one of them in Catholic Europe. A composer growing up in Lutheran Saxony perceived music differently, spiritually and linguistically, from an Italian growing up in Catholic Florence. The Lutheran Saxon would perceive melody more syllabically, not only because he spoke German at home but also because he sang in German at church and was surrounded by a municipal culture that played and celebrated German-language melodies at every occasion. In Lutheran Europe, complex polyphonic and instrumental music was cultivated on a par equal to that of vocal music.

MUSIC BOX

Johann Sebastian Bach (1685–1750), Brandenburg Concerto No. 2 (ca. 1720), Third Movement

This brilliant movement, scored for clarino (soprano trumpet), flute (or recorder), oboe, solo violin, string orchestra, and basso continuo, puts Bach's awe-inspiring Germanic craft in high relief. Note the following regarding Bach's concertos in general:

- The genre of concerto came into being in Italy during the 1660s and '70s.
- Bach learned to compose concertos primarily by studying those of the Italian composer Antonio Vivaldi.
- Nevertheless, Bach's concertos are fundamentally different from his Italian models. In terms of their length; dramatic intensity; harmonic, melodic, and formal complexity; and their dazzling polyphonic intricacy, Bach's concertos (and the concertos of such other German composers as Georg Philipp Telemann and George Frideric Handel) go far beyond the Italian models.

The next chapter will examine fugue, a compositional procedure that was named in Catholic Italy but brought to its artistic apogee by composers in Protestant Germany, the multinational musical equivalent of a pizza topped mit bratwurst und kraut (to further compound the sin of this chapter's subtitle).

CHAPTER 8

Fugue It!

F ugue is the single most representative musical procedure (or "form") to emerge from the Baroque era, as it epitomizes the Baroque musical duality of melodic extravagance governed by systematic organization and control.

Before we move on, please note that in defining *fugue*, we used the word *procedure*. Later in this book we will encounter and use the word *form* as in "musical form." "Musical form" is a terminological phrase that's been in use for over a century, and it's one we're stuck with. But we don't have to be happy about it. In truth, *procedure* offers a much better description of how a piece of music is put together. *Form* implies that musical structures are molds: pour in the notes, and out comes a uniform and correctly shaped musical composition. But in reality, each piece of music is different. Musical form, then, is *not* a mold but rather a series of guidelines on how to go about using thematic material. Composing, like writing a poem, short story, or novel, is not an act of filling "molds" but rather a *process*.

How a Fugue Works

By definition, a fugue is a polyphonic composition. By definition, a fugue is the systematic examination of a single thematic melody, called the fugue subject. (This means that a work called a fugue features only one principal melody, making it a *monothematic* work. A fugue that features two or even three subjects will be called a double fugue or a triple fugue.) By definition, a fugue will feature three structural elements: an exposition, in which the fugue subject is stated in each of the fugue's component voices; restatements of the subject across the span of the fugue; and episodes that transit between those subject restatements.

Fugue subject is a term worth unpacking. The terminological issue of theme versus subject is not one of pedantic protocol but rather a most important matter of conception. A fugue subject is a special sort of thematic melody, one made to be dissected, manipulated, and, ultimately, sewn back together. In fact, the entire point of a fugue is to see how many different ways the subject can be dissected and reconstituted: how many different ways it can overlap with itself and other melodies generated from it; how it might be broken down into its constituent motives; how it can be compressed, expanded, inverted, and so forth.

A fugue subject is to a regular thematic melody what an Olympic gymnast is to the rest of us. Olympic gymnasts can bend and torque their bodies in ways that both inspire us and give us the willies. A fugue subject is the musical equivalent of an Olympic gymnast. A fugue subject is designed to do all sorts of extraordinary and arcane things, because the whole point of a fugue is to codify and demonstrate the polyphonic capabilities of the fugue subject!

This is why fugue is considered the quintessential Baroque procedure: because it so beautifully illustrates the duality of Baroque art, of melodic extravagance tempered by iron-fisted procedural control. Even more, fugue embodies the Baroque predilection for systematic examination. In a fugue, the thing we're systematically investigating is the fugue subject itself. During the course of a fugue, the subject is observed and its capabilities are catalogued and demonstrated. It's real Baroque stuff, this thing called a fugue.

The most expressively intense and technically complex fugues came from the quills of composers in central and northern Germany, where sheer compositional technique and polyphonic complexity were considered aesthetic qualities unto themselves. Johann Sebastian Bach was the great master of fugue, a composer who combined an Italian melodic sensibility (Baroque extravagance) with the German intellectual rigor and craft (Baroque control) that great fugue writing requires.

There are three basic structural elements common to any fugue: the exposition, episodes, and subject restatements.

Exposition

The exposition is the first part of any fugue. During the course of the exposition, the subject is stated successively in each individual part until all the parts have entered. For example, in Bach's Fugue in C Minor from Book One of the *Well-Tempered Clavier* (see the following Music Box), the three constituent parts of the fugue enter with the subject in the following order:

Soprano————

Alto————

Bass————

The individual parts in a fugue are referred to as its "voices," and once all the voices have entered, we will hear an equal balance among them all. This is important. We live today in a homophonic musical age and are accustomed to perceiving what is on top as being more important than what is in the middle or on the bottom. But when we listen to a fugue or any polyphonic composition, we must try to hear in layers, so that we can perceive each voice as being of equal importance.

Once a voice has entered and "sung" its version of the fugue subject, it will continue with a complementary melody, called the countersubject, a melody generated from the fugue subject itself. In the voice entry chart that follows, the bold lines indicate the fugue subject, dotted lines indicate the countersubject, and the sawtooth line indicates "free" (meaning "nonthematic") material.

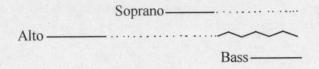

The successive entries that characterize a fugal exposition sound a lot like the beginning of a round, a piece of music employing strict imitative polyphony. Appearances notwithstanding, a fugal exposition is an example not of strict imitative polyphony but rather of nonstrict imitative polyphony.

The order in which the voices enter must ensure that each newly entered voice is either the highest or the lowest voice. Here's why: Let's say that we choose to array our entries as soprano (that's the top voice), followed by the bass (the bottom voice) and, last, the alto (the middle voice).

Houston, we have a problem. By not putting the alto voice in high relief by making it the highest or lowest voice when it enters, we make its entry difficult, if not impossible, to hear.

Thus, each new voice, as it enters, must be either the highest or the lowest voice. In a three-voice texture there are four possible voice-entry permutations: soprano-alto-bass, bass-alto-soprano, alto-soprano-bass, and alto-bass-soprano. That's it: in a three-voice fugue, those are the only permutations that permit each new voice to enter as either the highest or lowest voice, and thus in high relief.

Episodes and Restatements

Following the exposition, a fugue will consist of a number of transitions (called episodes) that pave the way for restatements of the fugue subject. In a standard fugue, the episodes and restatements will alternate until one final statement of the fugue subject is heard, after which the fugue concludes.

The episodes are perceived as transitional for two reasons. The first is that they typically consist of melodic fragments: of motives drawn from the fugue subject and its countersubject and sequences of those motives. The fragmentary nature of such a passage ensures that it will not sound as important as one in which the fugue subject is heard in its entirety. The second reason why episodes are perceived as transitional has to do with the fact that they modulate—that is, they effect a change of key—with the result being that the subject restatements that the episodes transit to are heard in a variety of different keys before the music returns to the original, or home, key for the conclusion of the fugue.

MUSIC BOX

Johann Sebastian Bach, Fugue in C Minor, *Well-Tempered Clavier,* Book One (ca. 1722)

This "garden variety" fugue is a picture of fugal precision and brevity. Listen for the following:

1. The fugue subject itself is as memorable as your first kiss. It features a motive that is heard, in some form or another, three times (see numbers 1, 2, and 3).
2. The fugue is cast for three voices, and the voices are, as indicated previously, alto, soprano, and bass (see figure on the preceding page).
3. Five subject restatements follow, each preceded by an episode (a transition).
4. The rock 'n' roll–steady rhythm and overlapping of the voices typical of polyphony preclude us from easily distinguishing the

continued on next page

beginnings and endings of the fugue's constituent parts. This is as it should be; good polyphony means not hearing the zippers, not noticing the seams. Bach's genius is apparent in the continuous, seamless curve of polyphonic sound in which the fugue subject, in different keys and different voices, alternately rises and falls from view.

Fugue might rightly be considered the musical poster child for the Baroque era artistic and intellectual aesthetic, considered as broadly as we please. Its multiplicity of voices ensures an exuberant surface of intertwining melodies. However, its structural ritual—consisting of the exposition, episodes, and subject restatements—ensures a logical and orderly presentation of materials that acts to control the fugue's melodic exuberance. Finally, the ongoing processes of subject restatement, fragmentation (in the episodes), and polyphonic overlapping of all sorts are a direct manifestation of the Baroque intellectual predilection for observation and codification. Fugue is a brilliant reflection of the intellectual and artistic spirit of the Baroque era, of music as a mirror.

CHAPTER 9

Opera

The Baroque Expressive Revolution in Action

We return to opera, which at once capped the ancient Greece–inspired Renaissance quest for magnified expression in music and opened the door to an entirely new musical/expressive world.

Opera. To know thee is to love thee. Yet many fine and upstanding lovers of music perceive opera as a strange and artificial construct in which large people in horned helmets scream God-knows-what in each other's faces from a distance of half an inch. For such opera-sensitive folks, I must counsel patience. Because whether we are fans or not, opera *is* the ultimate musical art form. It combines *everything*, and offers thrills that are still illegal in certain parts of Massachusetts. Let us not be afraid. Opera is good.

I would ask those who think of opera as "unnatural" to observe a group of three- or four-year-old children at play. As often as not, they singsong their words to each other or themselves while they play. Kids understand instinctively what every songwriter and opera composer knows: by adding musical inflection to words, one interprets and intensifies the meaning of those words a gazillion-fold.

In opera, the composer is the dramatist. In opera, the music interprets, crystallizes, and intensifies the expressive meaning of the words far beyond anything the words alone are capable of doing. This is the basic premise of opera: that music has the power to interpret and intensify the feeling and spirit behind the word.

An opera is a stage play set to music, a spectacle that combines scenery, action, literary drama, and continuous or almost continuous music into a whole greater than its parts. Spiritually, opera's direct forerunner was ancient Greek drama. Renaissance artists and thinkers came to believe that the reason why the ancient Greeks were able to evoke the sort of response to their dramas that they claimed they evoked was because their dramas were sung, or at least chanted, and thus they combined the best of literature and music.

According to our textbooks, another forerunner of opera was the medieval liturgical drama. These were Latin-language plays, based on religious texts, which were sung to plainchant-like music. The vast majority of these liturgical dramas were written to be performed at Christmas and Easter. (With all due respect to our textbooks, I would suggest that the medieval liturgical drama was not a forerunner of opera but rather an extension of a plainchant-dominated medieval liturgy that, by the late Renaissance, was considered, even in a Catholic territory such as Italy, hopelessly outdated.)

We've already discussed the keen desire of Renaissance composers to capture in their music the same sort of expressive power they attributed to the music of the ancient Greeks. Lacking any actual ancient Greek music to look at and listen to, Renaissance composers based their view of the power of Greek music entirely on written accounts by the Greeks themselves. That's okay, because what the Greek philosophers said about the power of music was enough to ignite the imaginations of the Renaissance artistic and intellectual communities.

The impact of the humanist Greek ideal on the music of the Renaissance was huge. We've talked about how Renaissance composers cultivated clear vocal articulation so that the meaning of the words would be clear to their listeners. We've discussed word painting as a technique meant to create more expressive music by using musical gestures to illustrate the literary meaning of the words being sung, and we've discussed the madrigal as an experimental vocal genre that employed word painting as its primary expressive vehicle.

Even as the madrigal evolved and flourished during the late six-teenth century, another musical genre developed that would lead directly to the invention of opera.

This immediate precursor to opera was the intermezzo.

The late Renaissance and early Baroque saw a huge rise in the pro-duction and popularity of secular stage drama. Performances of secular drama in late sixteenth-century Italy were punctuated, increasingly, by musical interludes inserted between the acts of the plays. Such a musical interpolation was called either an intermedio or an intermezzo (intermedi or intermezzi in the plural); both these terms mean, liter-ally, "in the middle." These intermedi (intermezzi) were sung com-mentaries placed between the acts of otherwise spoken Renaissance plays, and they commented on the action of the play up to that point. As such, they were inspired by the choruses of Greek drama.

By the 1580s, these intermezzi were often so substantial that they had become virtual plays within the play. They were increasingly spectacular in their staging and in the musical forces they required, and became very popular in their own right.

This is akin to the halftime show becoming more popular than the football game. The Italian playwrights of the late sixteenth cen-tury came to hate the intermezzi: they were too long, they got in the way of the play, and they were a huge distraction.

But not for the audiences; the audiences loved them! The inter-mezzi had music, they accentuated the dramatic and emotional con-tent of the play in which they were interpolated, and all the leading Italian composers wrote them.

Many of the most important surviving intermezzi were created by poets and composers based in the great Tuscan city of Florence. The wealth and patronage of Florence's leading citizens had made the city an artistic Mecca for hundreds of years. By the late sixteenth century, it had become a musical Mecca as well, due in no small part to an organization called the Florentine Camerata, which counted among its members poets and composers who created contempo-rary intermezzi. The Florentine Camerata was an intellectual club:

a *ridotto*. These clubs were common in Italy during the Renaissance, consisting of groups of men who would band together to research and discuss topics of common interest. The Florence-based Camerata on which we're going to focus was a group of scholars, poets, musicians, and amateurs who met, in some form or another, for nearly thirty years, first at the home of Count Giovanni Bardi, a distinguished patron of the arts and letters, and then at the home of Jacopo Corsi, an aristocrat and amateur composer. What the members of the Camerata were interested in was ancient Greek and contemporary drama and music.

The Camerata based its work on that of a Florentine scholar named Girolamo Mei. While working in Rome as the secretary to a cardinal, Mei did extensive research into ancient Greek music and the role of music in ancient Greek theater. Mei was convinced that Greek tragedy had to have been sung. It was, in his mind, the only way the Greeks could possibly have gotten the kind of emotional jolt from their drama they claimed to have received.

And what was the character of this ancient Greek theatrical music? Mei concluded that "The Greeks were able to obtain powerful effects with their music because it consisted of a single melody. This melody could affect the listener's feelings, since it exploited the natural expressiveness of the rises and falls of pitch and the register of the voice and of changing rhythms and tempos" (Grout, Palisca, 4th ed., 359).

Based on Mei's ideas, the Florentine Camerata developed a theory of new music based on both their vision of ancient Greek music and theater and on what they themselves wanted their music to express in their own time. The Camerata developed what we refer to as the "three corollaries of modern music," derived from what they considered the Greek expressive ideal:

• Corollary number one: The text must be clearly understood. This can be achieved only in a homophonic texture, by a solo singer supported by the simplest possible accompaniment.

- Corollary number two: The words must be sung with correct and natural declamation, as they would be spoken; textual repetitions should be avoided, except for rhetorical reinforcement.
- Corollary number three: The melody must not depict mere graphic details, as in word painting, but rather, must interpret the feelings and emotions of the character singing them. (We've mentioned this before, when discussing the differences between madrigals and opera.)

Ultimately, the Camerata advocated music that expressed emotional, not literary, meaning.

Now, all this would have been just a pile of "highfalutin' howdy-do"—a bunch of guys sitting around and talking about how the world would be if they were in charge—if not for the fact that among the Camerata were three very good composers and a number of very good writers. Those three composers were Emilio de' Cavalieri, Giulio Caccini, and Jacopo Peri. Peri was also a singer, an organist, and director of the Duco, the de' Medici chapel; he was an important musician of considerable influence. Taken together, the Camerata had among its members writers and musicians who did not just talk the talk, but also walked the walk.

As an example of the ideas and innovations of the Camerata in musical action, we turn to Jacopo Peri and his *dramma per musica*, a stage play with music entitled *Euridice*.

Jacopo Peri

Jacopo Peri (1561–1633) wrote the earliest surviving work that we call an opera. Titled *Euridice*, it premiered on October 6, 1600, at the Pitti Palace in Florence, where its production was part of the wedding festivities of Henry IV of France and Marie de' Medici. Peri's *Euridice* celebrates, as all opera celebrates, the single emotion, expressly portrayed by solo singers. For all intents and purposes, the

Baroque era began there at Florence's magnificent Pitti Palace on October 6, 1600.

Euridice

Peri's *Euridice* was a fully sung stage work that employed three distinct musical elements. Two of these elements were old, but one of them was new and spectacularly innovative.

First, the old. In *Euridice*, Peri employed a smallish chorus, which sings madrigal-like commentaries in the style of a Greek chorus.

The second element Peri used was simple, rhymed songs as lyric interludes to the action, to end scenes and for transitions between scenes.

It was with the third musical element that Jacopo Peri revolutionized Western music, with something he called the *stile rappresentativo*, or the "representative style." It is something we now call recitative, or recitation, and it became the heart and soul of the new Florentine style. Peri created a sort of half-sung, half-spoken recitation, or recitative, to carry the essential dramatic substance of his opera. He used it for narration, for dialogue, and for action. No one before him had managed to figure out a way to write music that would allow large amounts of text—as in dialogue and action sequences—to be articulated clearly and still be sung.

Peri solved the problem, and in doing so created the first surviving, fully sung stage drama we can comfortably call an opera.

Peri wrote of his *stile rappresentativo*:

> I believe that the ancient Greeks and Romans, who, according to the opinion of many, sang their tragedies throughout, used a kind of music more advanced than ordinary speech but less so than melody singing, thus taking a middle position between the two. (Grout, Palisca, 4th ed., 365)

More musically advanced than ordinary speech but less so than melody singing—this is what Peri created in his *stile rappresentativo*, a "speech-song" that adheres absolutely to the natural rhythms, accents, and inflections of the literary text.

Peri's *stile rappresentativo* takes place entirely in the present and future tenses. Such passages do not reflect but take place in real time and are understood as "action music." Frankly, to our modern ears, Peri's *Euridice* sounds rather stiff, though I can confidently assure you that the audiences were weeping in their seats when the work was first performed. Stiff or not, Peri's solo-sung recitative provides an emotional jolt far beyond anything possible in a madrigal. It was an emotional jolt that would become an expressive paradigm shift just seven years later, with the composition and production of the first operatic masterwork, Claudio Monteverdi's *Orfeo* of 1607.

Claudio Monteverdi (1567–1643)

Claudio Monteverdi was neither a Florentine nor a member of the Camerata. He was from Cremona, the great northern Italian city of violins, where Niccolò Amati, Giuseppe Guarneri, and Antonio Stradivari, among many others, built stringed instruments that remain the standards to this day.

Monteverdi was trained by Marc'Antonio Ingegneri, the head of music at the cathedral in Cremona. In 1590, at the age of twenty-three, he entered the service of Vincenzo Gonzaga, the Duke of Mantua. In 1602, Monteverdi became master of the Ducal Chapel in Mantua, and it was there that he composed his first opera, *Orfeo*, in 1607. Between 1613 and 1643, Monteverdi was the choirmaster at St. Mark's Basilica in Venice, the single most prestigious musical job in what was the single most happening city in all of Europe.

Monteverdi was as adept at writing Renaissance-style madrigals as he was at writing the "new style" opera. He made a distinction in his own music between writing in the "old" and "new" styles, what he called, respectively, the *prima prattica* and the *seconda prattica* ("first practice" and "second practice"). Among his *prima prattica* works are seven "books," or collections, of madrigals numbering in total nearly two hundred madrigals. Among his *seconda prattica* compositions are nineteen works for the stage of which, most sadly, only six have survived in their entirety. Among those survivors are Monteverdi's first and last operas, *Orfeo*, of 1607, and *The Coronation of Poppea*, of 1642. *Orfeo* and *The Coronation of Poppea* are, simply, the best operas written during the first half of the seventeenth century.

Orfeo

Like Peri's *Euridice*, Monteverdi's *Orfeo* is based on the legend of Orpheus and Eurydice. For the early composers of opera, the golden-voiced demi-god Orpheus was the very embodiment of how they saw themselves with regard to the new operatic art: as purveyors of music capable of changing the face of nature, and hearts of animals, men, and gods with their song.

It was in Monteverdi's hands that opera passed out of its "experimental" stage.

Orfeo is a spectacular synthesis of pretty much every expressive device, musical genre, and musical instrument available to Monteverdi at the time. During the course of the opera we hear madrigal-style choruses, popular-style rhymed songs, and popular dances. Most important, though, Monteverdi's *Orfeo* features the most melodically interesting and dramatically effective recitative ever written by anyone, before or since. Monteverdi also calls for what was by far the most massive instrumental ensemble ever seated for an opera up to that time, one of more than forty different instruments (as opposed to the four instruments Peri called for in *Euridice*).

Just seven years after the de facto "invention" of opera, Claudio Monteverdi, in composing his first opera, managed to create the first operatic masterwork. His *Orfeo* opened a lot of eyes and ears: it made clear that opera was not just a fad (like *intermezzi* and chia pets), not just an entertainment for rich peoples' weddings, but a revolutionary new medium with unlimited musical and expressive potential. Soon enough, opera—and the celebration of the individual person and individual emotion opera represented—would come to dominate Italian musical culture, and from there, European musical culture as well.

The Next Big Thing: Enter the Aria

The word *aria* translates, literally, as "air." An air is generally defined as a tune or melody; a more specific definition would be an accompanied song dating from Elizabethan or Jacobean England, roughly 1560 to 1625.

If we are to understand what constitutes an opera aria, we must first purge those definitions from our minds! An operatic aria is not a song. A song is a short rhymed poem accompanied by music that is usually as simple and direct as its text. Obviously, we're not referring here to the so-called art songs of the nineteenth century, such as the German lieder of Schubert, Schumann, Brahms, Wolf, and Mahler. No, we're referring to your basic "popular song," which, with all due respect to the great songs of George Gershwin and Cole Porter and Richard Rodgers, is still as far away from an operatic aria as a Chevy Nova is from a Ferrari FXX (which is one fine set of wheels). But to the point: an operatic aria is a lengthy, substantial, and often highly complex piece of vocal music in which the essential character and dramatic information are transmitted via the music itself. The same Baroque innovations in harmony, rhythm, motivic manipulation, and melodic construction that led to the development of purely instrumental music provided the technical grist for the invention of the operatic aria as well.

Unlike recitative, in which the words carry the essential expressive message, in an operatic aria, it is the music that carries the expressive message. Oh, the words might initially inspire the creation of an aria, but once the aria is complete, its words float on top, in plain sight, while the great bulk of the expressive message is carried on out of sight, by the abstract elements of the music itself.

By 1660 or so, the two basic aspects of operatic dramaturgy were both firmly established: recitative and aria. Recitatives were used for narration, action, and dialogue: real-time situations where the words carried the essential expressive message. Arias were used for reflection, for character development, for the expression of feeling. During an aria—just as during a soliloquy, the theatrical equivalent of an aria—time stops and reflection begins.

Good News and Bad News

So, the good news: the invention of the aria added a wonderful new element to the vocabulary of opera. The bad news: recitative was reduced to the obligatory, if tedious, filler that one had to sit through between arias. The magnificent and substantial art of recitative that Monteverdi cultivated was lost entirely, as the aria became the focal point of Baroque opera.

After roughly 1660, recitative is usually performed *secco*, or "dry": that is, accompanied only by the basso continuo (usually a harpsichord and a cello). On occasion, we will hear something called recitative *accompanato* or recitative *obbligato* or recitative *strumento*, which is when the whole orchestra accompanies a recitative. However, in Baroque opera, only royal or aristocratic characters will be favored with such orchestrally accompanied recitatives. The recitatives of a common character will always be accompanied *secco*.

Conversely, arias are always accompanied by the orchestra, no matter who sings them.

The impact opera exerted on other types of Baroque music, vocal and instrumental, was singular. The next two chapters will deal with the impact of opera on Baroque sacred music, as "opera goes to church."

CHAPTER 10

Opera Goes to Church

I n this chapter, we will begin to look at Baroque sacred music, taking a quick tour through the many genres composed during this time. We'll then examine the oratorio and, in the next chapter, the Lutheran Church cantata, two sacred genres born from Baroque opera.

There was no dearth of sacred music written during the Baroque era. Here's a roundup of the principal genres of sacred music composed during the time:

Oratorio: An oratorio is an extended work for chorus, soloists, and orchestra based on a dramatic story drawn from scripture. We might think of an oratorio as a multi-act religious opera performed as a concert piece without acting or staging.

Cantata: A cantata is a dramatic work that, like oratorio, uses the resources of opera—chorus, soloists, and orchestra—but is performed as a concert piece, outside of a religious service. Both sacred and secular cantatas were written during the Baroque era. Lutheran Church cantatas were part of the Sunday worship service—an important difference between oratorio and church cantata.

Mass: Masses continued to be composed during the Baroque era. Catholic composers continued to set the traditional

five sections of the musical Mass: the Kyrie, Gloria,
Credo, Sanctus, and Agnus Dei. The so-called Lutheran
Mass consisted of only the Kyrie and the Gloria.

Magnificat: A magnificat is a Latin-language cantata based
on the Canticle of the Virgin, from Luke (1:46–55).

Passion: A passion is an oratorio based on one of the Gospel
accounts—Matthew, Mark, Luke, or John—of the events
culminating in the crucifixion of Christ. These were
written for Holy Week services (that is, the week before
Easter) for both Protestant and Catholic audiences.

Motet: A motet is a cantata featuring an unaccompanied
a cappella chorus.

All of these sacred Baroque genres make heavy use of the chorus.
Typically in such sacred works, the chorus portrays either the people
or Christianity itself. The use of the chorus is an element that distin-
guishes these sacred genres from the Baroque opera, which, by the late
seventeenth century, had done away almost entirely with the chorus.

I offer this mini-glossary of Baroque sacred genres for a number of
reasons. First, it reminds us that despite the increasingly humanistic
intellectual climate of the seventeenth and early eighteenth centuries, religion and religious faith continued to play a singular role in
European life and culture. Second, it reminds us that religious institutions, both Catholic and Protestant, were still major patrons of
music during the Baroque era. Finally, and most important for our
purposes, each of these Baroque sacred genres, to some degree or
another, was powerfully influenced by opera.

Baroque sacred music in Catholic Europe, particularly in Italy, was
a mix of old style and new style. By the mid-seventeenth century—
the mid-1600s—the provisos of the Counter-Reformation regarding
music had come to be considered ancient history, and were being
treated rather flexibly in many locations. In Italy they were outright
ignored.

As a result, Baroque Italian sacred music was a mix of just about everything. Old-style Masses continued to be composed, although many of them contained elements of the "new" Baroque Italian style.

These new elements were drawn from opera. For example, the basso continuo had been invented in order to accompany recitative in early Baroque opera. But it was adapted to fill an even greater need, and that was to supply the rock-steady harmonic and rhythmic materials that together became the "control" element in so much Baroque music. The basso continuo came to be used universally during the Baroque, in both secular and sacred music.

Then there was the issue of instruments in church. The Counter-Reformation demanded that the use of "noisy" instruments in church should cease. But the new "concertato" style, mixing voices and instruments, proved to be irresistible to Baroque Italian composers of sacred music.

Solo singing, with its increased emotional content, was adapted for use in Italian Baroque Masses, as were multiple choirs with soloists, and orchestras featuring instrumental soloists.

The most explicitly operatic sacred genre to emerge in Baroque Italy was also the most important new genre of Catholic music to evolve during the Baroque, and that was the oratorio. For all intents and purposes, an oratorio is an opera about a religious subject, a work that employs recitatives and arias, a narrative plot, several acts, real characters, and implied action. Compare this to the musical Mass in which the same words are set over and over again. The difference between oratorio and the Mass is, in a nutshell, the difference between Renaissance ritual and restraint and Baroque expressive exuberance.

Oratorios evolved from something called sacred dialogues, which were late Renaissance and early Baroque Roman religious productions that combined narrative, dialogue, and exhortation. By 1650, sacred dialogues had come to be known as oratorios because they were performed in small chapels or houses of prayer called oratories. Thus, the word *oratorio* actually refers to the performing venue in which these musical/dramatic religious works were originally performed.

By 1660, these sacred dialogues, or oratorios, had taken on the trappings of opera: recitatives, arias, and orchestra. However, unlike opera, they featured a chorus, and used someone called a *testo*, a "narrator"—a feature we will not find in the opera house.

What Happened to the Chorus?

There were three reasons why the chorus, which had been such an integral element of early opera, disappeared from the Baroque opera house. First of all, a professional chorus of twenty or thirty singers was expensive to maintain, dental coverage notwithstanding. More important, opera producers didn't want a chorus, because, reason number two, with the invention of the aria, audiences came to the opera house to hear solo singing; the more virtuosic, the better. Reason number three: if you wanted to hear a chorus during the late seventeenth century, you could always go to church, where the chorus was a metaphor for the "body of humanity." By the 1680s, the Baroque opera chorus was a thing of the past.

By the late seventeenth century, oratorios had become a hugely popular form of entertainment in Italy. The popularity of oratorio in Baroque Italy might strike us as odd: after all, why in a country where you could go to a different opera every night did these non-staged, non-costumed oratorios become so incredibly popular?

The answer is Lent, the forty days of abstinence and devotion prior to Easter. Theatrical performances, including opera, were considered profane and were banned during Lent. Forty days without an operatic fix? What's an Italian opera addict to do? And in a place like Venice, where tourism and the opera houses were the city's life blood, the show, *some* kind of show, had to go on.

Theatrical performances might have been banned during Lent, but oratorios were not. Performed as concert works—without costumes, acting, or scenery—and based on religious subjects, they were deemed as being Lenten-friendly, and their performance was permitted.

The Oratorio in England

A great trivia question: What is the only Baroque composition that has been performed continuously since its premiere? The answer: George Frideric Handel's oratorio *Messiah*, composed in 1741 and premiered in Dublin, just prior to Easter, on April 13, 1742.

Oratorios became a substitute for opera in Protestant England as well as in Catholic Italy, but for completely different reasons. The man responsible for the phenomenal popularity of the English-language oratorio was the German-born, Italian-trained George Frideric Handel, who lived from 1685 to 1759.

George Frideric Handel (1685–1759)

Some background on Maestro Handel will help us understand how and why he came to compose the most famous oratorio in history.

Handel was born and raised in Lutheran Germany just a few weeks apart and a few miles away from Johann Sebastian Bach. That is where the resemblance between these two composers ends. Where Bach spent his entire life in his native central and northern Germany, working for either the Church or local municipalities and courts, Handel was a cosmopolitan with an international career. He trained extensively in Italy, and when he

George Frideric Handel (1685–1759)
Library of Congress, Prints and Photographs Division, LC-USZ62-59925

completed his training in 1710, at the age of twenty-five, he accepted a job working for the Elector of Hanover. Almost immediately, he took a leave of absence to go to London in 1710, and then another in 1712. In 1714, Handel was *still* in London (on that extended "leave of absence") when his boss, the Elector of Hanover, was crowned King George I of England upon the death of Queen Anne.

For a while Handel was afraid to show his face at court. According to the legend, he got himself back into the king's good graces by composing and conducting a group of pieces played as a surprise for the king during a boating party on the Thames: the *Water Music*. Some sources would have us believe that it was actually an earlier composition that Handel played for the king, but I say, let's not let the facts get in the way of a great story.

An extremely savvy businessman, Handel was a natural-born entrepreneur and marketeer. He made his fortune composing and producing Italian-language operas for the London stage. Between 1715 and 1740, he composed more than thirty operas. They were all the rage, hugely popular with the English aristocracy and the upper classes.

We shouldn't think for a minute that these English "people of quality" spoke Italian any more than the folks today who fill up trendy French restaurants speak French. Back then, one went to the opera to be seen, to do business, to flirt, to gamble, to eat, and, on occasion, to listen to the music. During the recitatives, food vendors came through the aisles selling their wares. If you had a favorite singer, you would hush everyone around you so that you might hear that singer's arias; and if you were part of the singer's clique, you would applaud him or her loudly and then hiss during the other singers' arias. The opera house in 1730 was a very different sort of place from what it is today: equal parts theater, stadium bleachers, restaurant, and casino. This was the environment for which Handel composed his operas.

Handel was a big, strong man, and he was known to take a singer by the scruff of the neck and hold him outside the window of his upper-story office until the singer agreed to toe the line, accept the contract, or just behave, whatever the issue was. Handel knew how to deal with singers, and the wise singer—no oxymoron intended—gave him a wide berth.

Around 1740, Handel's opera audiences began to dwindle. Handel had no way of knowing that he was experiencing the first tremors of a huge social shift, and that it was nothing personal: Italian Baroque opera began falling out of favor universally in the 1740s and '50s. A new, middle-class public was emerging, and it had no interest whatsoever in the overinflated Italian-language operas the aristocracy so adored.

Handel might not have known that the Enlightenment was having an impact on his finances, but he darn well knew that he was going to have to start thinking outside of the box or else he might soon be living in one. Handel the entrepreneur thought long and hard about what sort of music would entice the new, middle-class audience to the theater. He decided to try his hand at writing oratorios: English-language oratorios, Protestant in flavor, musical dramas that any English speaker could follow.

The long story short? Pay dirt. Gold mine. The mother lode. Handel's twenty-six English-language oratorios number among some of the most famous and beloved works of all time, including *Saul*, *Solomon*, and of course *Messiah*. Handel was vaulted back to the top, and that's where he stayed until he died in 1759.

(FYI: Don't tell an English musician that Handel was German. The English embraced him as their own, and rightly so. He is buried in the South Transept of Westminster Abbey along with, among others, Robert Browning, Geoffrey Chaucer, John Dryden, Charles Dickens, Samuel Johnson, and Laurence Olivier. Good company.)

Messiah

Let's get this out of the way: it's not *The Messiah*; it's just *Messiah*.

As oratorios go, *Messiah* is an exception to the rule, as there are no characters per se. Instead, narrators relate the story of Christ's life in recitative. Along the way, commentators interrupt the primary narrative to react with recitatives and arias of their own. The chorus is extremely important in *Messiah*. It represents the people generally or Christianity specifically.

There are fifty-plus separate numbers in *Messiah*. Almost all of them are gems, and it remains something of a miracle that the entire two-hour oratorio was composed, start to finish, in twenty-four days. That's absurd.

No mention of *Messiah* would be complete without a reference to the brilliant "Hallelujah Chorus" that concludes the second of the oratorio's three parts. George II of England, attending the first London performance of *Messiah*, was so moved by the "Hallelujah Chorus" that he stood up in tribute to the "King of Kings" evoked in the text. Or perhaps he stood up in tribute to Handel, whose music was so inspirational. Then again, maybe he stood up in tribute to himself, assuming that the evocation of the "King of Kings" was a veiled reference to his monarchy. (Of course, once he stood up, everyone in the audience had to stand up; and to this day, it is customary to stand during the "Hallelujah Chorus.")

In the "Hallelujah Chorus," Handel gets a tremendous amount of mileage out of relatively few words; and like an aria, the words themselves are infinitely less important than the mood and spirit evoked by the music. Handel captures a celebratory joy and ecstasy rarely equaled in religious music.

MUSIC BOX

George Frideric Handel, *Messiah* (1741), "Hallelujah Chorus"

Handel employs three different sorts of writing during the course of the "Hallelujah Chorus," each of which serves a different dramatic function. Listen for the following:

- Homophony. When the chorus begins, the voices—a metaphor for the "voice of all humanity"—are united in their singing of the word *Hallelujah*.
- Imitative polyphony. Handel sets the words "And he shall reign forever and ever" in imitative polyphony. The effect is stunning, as one segment of humanity after another enters, cheering the peace brought by Christ.
- Responsorial singing. Finally, Handel employs responsorial singing creating a sort of "prayer meeting" effect. The sopranos sing "King of Kings, Lord of Lords," and the altos, tenors, and basses respond, "Forever, Hallelujah."

CHAPTER 11

A New Liturgy Comes of Age

Lutheran Baroque Sacred Music

Thirty Years Europe Could Have Done Without

The violence and strife triggered by Martin Luther's posting of his Ninety-five Theses in 1517 saw a terrible denouement a hundred years later. The series of horrific wars that devastated Germany between 1618 and 1648 are collectively referred to as the Thirty Years' War. More than just a German war, the Thirty Years' War was a pan-European struggle in which politics and national interests became inextricably intertwined with the religious issues that, presumably, had given rise to the conflict in the first place. Before the Reformation, the area of Germany that went on to Lutheranism had been part of what was called the Holy Roman Empire, a political conglomerate created in 800 CE.

The Holy Roman Empire was founded for two reasons: one, to consolidate the power of the Church across a vast stretch of only slightly civilized Europe, and two, as a defensive bulwark against non-Christians, which included everyone from Vikings to Muslims. The Holy Roman Empire was, by definition, a Catholic empire. If a substantial part of it should cease being "Catholic"—which is what happened during the Protestant Reformation—it no longer had any reason to exist. This was not lost on the empire's chief ally and supporter, the Catholic Habsburg Empire based in Austria.

The Habsburgs saw Protestantism as an intolerable threat to their national interests. In 1618, Austrians declared war on Protestantism, and soon brought the tremendous resources of their empire to bear on the Protestants of Germany.

Meanwhile, to the west, the French perceived a resurgent Habsburg Empire as extremely dangerous to France's national interests. As a result—and talk about strange bedfellows—Catholic France allied itself with the Protestant northerners, so that it could fight the Catholic Habsburgs on German soil, which sure beat fighting them on French soil.

The English, who were always at odds with the French, nevertheless allied themselves with the French during the Thirty Years' War, not just because the English were Protestant and it was in their best interest to keep part of Germany Protestant, but because they feared the growing power of the Austrians more than they did the French.

The Spanish, who were related to the Austrians through marriage, allied themselves with the Habsburgs against the French and the English. The Dutch and the Danes allied themselves with France and England; the Lutheran king of Sweden, Gustavus Adolphus, invaded Germany; entire armies of mercenaries and criminals roamed Central Europe, changing sides at will depending upon who had the upper hand and where the loot was. It was a terrible war, one that left Central Europe devastated.

When the war ended in 1648, peace and Protestantism were firmly established in what today is central and northern Germany, and energies could turn, in the Lutheran community, to creating a uniquely Lutheran liturgy. It was during this period, from about 1650 to 1680, that the most important new style of Lutheran Church music emerged: the Lutheran Church cantata, a one-act religious opera intended for performance as part of the Lutheran Sunday service.

The Lutheran "Chorale," or Congregational Hymn

At the very heart of the new Lutheran liturgy was congregational singing in the vernacular language. The congregational hymns sung in Lutheran churches are called church chorales, or simply chorales. A Lutheran Church chorale is a direct, songlike setting of a text from the Bible. As these chorales were set primarily in German, the chorale melodies reflect the idiosyncrasies of the German language to which they were set.

But even more than religious songs, these hymns came to constitute the core of municipal culture in Lutheran towns. Every burgher knew his Lutheran chorales as well as he knew his Bible, and he sang them at home as well as in church. On top of that, these hymns were heard at every civic occasion. The city pipers, the *Stadt* pipers, the guild of professional wind players, played them daily from the towers of churches and from the balconies of public buildings. These hymns, and the particularly German melodic sensibility they embody, became, for Central and Northern European composers, as important a musical and spiritual resource as plainchant had been for southern European composers.

Any Given Sunday: The Lutheran Church Cantata

The high point of the Lutheran Sunday service is the sermon: an interpretation of the prescribed Bible reading for that particular Sunday. This reading also dictated which chorale would be sung that day; the appropriate chorale was one whose words reflected that same Bible reading.

In Baroque Lutheran practice, the cantata was performed immediately *before* the sermon. The cantata was based on that day's prescribed chorale. Since a cantata interpreted, musically, the same biblical text the minister would interpret and teach in his sermon, the Lutheran Church cantata came to be called the "sermon in music."

With the emergence of the Lutheran Church cantata between

roughly 1650 and 1680, there arose two conflicting philosophies regarding the role of music in the Lutheran Church. The so-called orthodox party favored using all available musical resources. The more conservative Pietist party, on the other hand, distrusted "high art" and opulence in worship. The orthodox party won out; and by the early eighteenth century, the Lutheran Church cantata had come into being as a one-act religious opera.

The first great cantata librettist was a gentleman named Erdman Neumeister of Hamburg, who lived from 1671 to 1756. He was an orthodox theologian, an excellent poet, and the first cantata librettist to structure his libretti along the lines of secular Italian opera. Herr Neumeister declared his artistic intentions in 1704, when he wrote, "If I may express myself succinctly, a cantata appears to be nothing but a piece out of an opera put together from recitative style and aria" (Grout, Palisca, 4th ed., 438).

Johann Sebastian Bach, who, if he'd been born in Italy would undoubtedly have been one of the greatest opera composers of all time, agreed entirely with Neumeister's operatic conception of the Lutheran Church cantata.

Johann Sebastian Bach
(1685–1750)

Bach, who lived from 1685 to 1750, was a devout Lutheran who passed his entire life in his native central and northern Germany. He was a composer and keyboard player of the greatest genius—an indispensable member of our species.

Bach held five principal positions during the course of his career. Two of these were "court" positions; the other three were Lutheran Church/municipality gigs.

Johann Sebastian Bach (1685–1750) Library of Congress, Prints and Photographs Division, LC-USZ62-9033

As far as Bach was concerned, the best job he ever had was as court composer to Prince Leopold of Anhalt-Cöthen, a position he held from 1717 to 1723, when he was between the ages of thirty-two and thirty-eight. Bach loved his prince, and the prince loved Bach. The only person Bach was answerable to was the prince. He had few killer deadlines to meet and few job responsibilities above and beyond writing and making music, which is, after all, exactly what a composer wants to do.

Unfortunately, nothing lasts forever, and personal and financial circumstances forced Bach to move on. He became cantor and Kapellmeister—that is, music director for the churches and municipality—for the city of Leipzig. It was a difficult job. He had more than two dozen bosses overseeing his activities in Leipzig, from the rector of the church school to the town council to an "ecclesiastic committee." Bach was not the easiest man in the world to get along with; proud and intelligent, he knew his worth, and he found the meddling and ignorance of his so-called superiors intolerable.

Bach's job description in Leipzig was crazy. He had to supervise the music at Leipzig's four churches; he had to write and perform music for worship and for municipal occasions; he had to keep the church's organs in working order; he had to oversee the musical education of roughly fifty-five choirboys; he assumed the position of music director of the Collegium Musicum at Leipzig University; the list goes on. Bach augmented his income by writing music and performing for weddings and funerals, working as an organ consultant, taking on the odd commission, and so forth. He also fathered twenty children. He must have consumed a lot of coffee; it's our best explanation.

Bach's Cantatas

Altogether, Bach composed roughly 350 cantatas, the overwhelming majority of which are sacred cantatas. By far, the great bulk of his sacred cantatas were composed between 1723 and 1728, during his first five years on the job at Leipzig. There were years, for example, 1724 and 1725, when Bach, along with all his other duties and responsibilities, composed one cantata per week. Be still our hearts; how was it possible?

Perhaps the biggest single conflict Bach had with the ecclesiastic authorities in Leipzig was over the operatic nature of his cantatas and passions. He believed completely in the orthodox assertion that a cantata should be "like an opera," and should employ the resources of opera. Unfortunately, the authorities in Leipzig were Pietists through and through, something Bach knew when he signed his contract with the city in May of 1723. Article seven of that contract reads as follows:

> To the end that good order may prevail in those churches, I should so arrange the music that it may not last too long and also in such ways that it may not be operatic but, rather, incite the hearers to devotion.

Bach was not the first, nor the last, person to sign a contract he had no intention of honoring. And thank goodness, because his cantatas are among the great masterworks of the Baroque. They are also responsible for no small bit of heartbreak. You see, of the roughly 350 cantatas Bach composed, only 209 have survived. After he died, and his library was broken up, his cantatas were far more valuable as paper than music. They were sold off in bulk and used to wrap meat, fish, and cheese; or tarred and wrapped around fruit trees in Leipzig to protect them from the winter cold.

That hurts. Still, we have 209 of them, and in terms of sheer number, these cantatas comprise the greatest and most significant of all of Bach's compositions.

Johann Sebastian Bach, Cantata No. 140, *Wachet auf* ("Awake") (1731)

Bach's cantata is based on a Lutheran Church chorale entitled "The Sacred Bridal Song," which was composed around 1599 by German Lutheran pastor, poet, and composer Philipp Nicolai. The text of the chorale is based on Jesus' parable of the ten virgins from Matthew 25:1–13, in which five virgins are prepared for the arrival of the bridegroom and are thus "married," while five are not prepared and are thus not "married." The meaning of the parable is clear: be ready for the day of reckoning, for only those thus prepared will receive the eternal blessing of Christ "the Bridegroom."

Nicolai's chorale has three verses.

Note the following when you listen:

- Bach's cantata is cast in seven discrete parts.
- Parts one, four, and seven are built around, respectively, the first, second, and third verses of Nicolai's chorale.
- Parts two and five are recitatives.
- Parts three and six are both duets, and are the operatic "core" of the cantata. In part three, a bass represents the "Bridegroom"— the Savior. He assures a worried soprano, the "Bride," who represents the Christian soul, that she has nothing to fear. In part six, all fear has passed, and the Bridegroom and the Bride, the Savior and the Christian soul, engage in a most romantic duet, sounding more like contented newlyweds than penitent Christians.

Take a moment to consider that between 1723 and 1735, a parishioner at Leipzig's St. Thomas Church would have heard the performance of a seemingly endless stream of works by Bach: more than 325 cantatas, as well as motets, passions (including the epic and amazing *St. Matthew Passion*), oratorios, all sorts of organ works, and more. Bach himself would have participated as a performer—either as conductor, keyboard player, or string player—in almost every one of those performances. If a parishioner chose to, he could hang out and shoot the breeze with Bach after the service or arrange to go out for some brewskies and schnapps.

Did those blessed worshippers have *any* idea what they were hearing week after week? Did they appreciate the transcendent genius that fate had placed in their bourgeois midst? Did they have a clue as to the lasting, universal greatness of the music they were ear-witness to? With just a few exceptions, the answers are no, no, and no. It is incredible, and just a small bit heartbreaking.

CHAPTER 12

Instrumental Form in Baroque Era Music

What do these words all refer to? *Rondo, scherzo, ritornello, minuet, trio, fugue, sonata allegro, passacaglia, binary, ternary, chaconne, ground bass, theme and variations, rhapsody, toccata, prelude, double exposition, caccia, kanon, ricercare, round,* and *fantasy.* They are all names of instrumental musical forms or processes: ways of organizing thematic material in a given movement of music.

We've observed that the Baroque era saw the development of a tradition of instrumental music, and we've discussed one instrumental musical form, fugue, in chapter 8. We've gone far enough in our story that we can now loop back to pick up this formal thread.

It's not by accident that certain musical forms evolved. It's not by accident that composers of a given period employed the same forms. Musical form is a given, a common point of departure between a composer and his or her audience. More than any other single factor, it is musical form that determines the overall expressive content of a piece of instrumental music, and more than any other single factor, it is musical form that mirrors the environment in which a piece of instrumental music was created.

Up to now we've defined musical form very generally, as "a way of using thematic material." Let us now be a bit more specific: musical form refers to how many large sections of music there are within a movement, and how those sections are related to one another.

An essential step in the emergence of instrumental music during the Baroque era was the development of instrumental musical forms. Some of these instrumental forms were based on the ritualized phrase structures of Renaissance and Baroque social dancing, but many were not: they were abstract structures that had to make sense, of themselves and by themselves, through some logical and consistent process of variation, development, contrast, and return.

In vocal music, it's the poetic structure of the words being set that almost invariably determines the form, the structure, of the piece of music that results. For example, the Agnus Dei—the fifth and final section of a standard Mass—consists of this line, heard three times: *Agnus dei, qui tollis peccata mundi, miserere nobis.* This translates as "Lamb of God who taketh away the sins of the earth, have mercy upon us."

By definition, then, a musical setting of the Agnus Dei will have three parts: one part or section for each of the three lines of text.

But instrumental music has no a priori literary structure on which to base its form; in instrumental music, form is the result of compositional processes: repetition, variation, contrast, and development. Unlike vocal music, which is bounded by its words, instrumental music is bounded only by time. It is the composer's job, then, when writing instrumental music, to coherently organize, to structure, time.

One might think that when it comes to instrumental music, anything is possible; that a composer can sit down and just go with the inspirational flow and write whatever comes to mind. In actuality, the opposite is true: the abstract nature of instrumental music demands tremendous compositional discipline and rigor to create musical and expressive clarity and coherence in the absence of words.

Starting with the Baroque, the instrumental musical forms of any particular era became part of the fabric of the culture, standard compositional procedures (such as fugue) that offered a shared, comprehensible common ground between composers and their audiences. In our world, we have many such forms, such ritual procedures, that are part of the fabric of our culture. The plots of certain movies and television shows, for example. There's the buddy movie, the television

police drama, the hospital medical show: these are the same archetypal stories, played over and over again. Disaster/horror/stranded-
in-space, *Alien*-type movies? The only mystery in those movies is in
what order the characters will be killed off. And when it comes to a
pure, communally shared ritual, nothing beats a baseball game. At
the macro level you've got the game itself. Then there's the large-
scale form, the nine distinct parts, or innings, in a professional or
college game. Then there's a midi form: each half of an inning, each
team's at bat. Then there's a mini form: three outs per half inning.
Then there's a micro form: each individual at bat, which could lead
to an out or a hit or any number of other results. And then there's the
micro-micro form: each pitch. And this is, of course, where the real
action takes place. And that real action, despite the formulaic nature
of the structure, is completely unpredictable.

To paraphrase the architect Le Corbusier, God is in just such
details. But I would also like to think that God is in the structure,
because without a structural context, the details cannot be contex-
tualized. In order, then, to contextualize the details and understand
the expressive message of a movement of instrumental music, we
must first comprehend its structure, its *form*.

Now, having said all of this, we must point out that there are some
musical compositions that do not ascribe to a preexisting form. Such
works are essentially improvisatory in nature, and are likely to be given
a title that indicates that fundamentally "improvisatory" conception:
fantasy or fantasia, toccata or rhapsody, prelude or impromptu.

Such improvisatory, stream-of-consciousness musical procedures
are in the distinct minority. In general, composers will willingly, even
happily, adhere to the structural parameters of the musical forms of
their age. The issue is not one of originality, but of coherence.

In short, if we are to understand, at a gut level, what a composer is
saying to us, then we must know something of what that composer's
audiences knew. Among other things, this means we must have a
working knowledge of a given era's instrumental musical forms.

We can do that!

Baroque Instrumental Forms

As we have discussed, it wasn't until the Baroque era that the parts of musical speech—pitch, rhythm, melody, texture, harmony, and so forth—were sufficiently developed to create a large-scale instrumental tradition. And it wasn't until the Baroque era that instrumental forms and procedures truly began to develop in their own right, divorced from vocal models. We've already discussed one Baroque form or process, and that is the fugue.

As a reminder, a fugue features three basic structural givens: an exposition, followed by a series of episodes and subject restatements. Bach's contemporary audience recognized these "givens" as easily as we do the seventh-inning stretch.

Hearing Is Believing

The next time you hear the familiar sound of a fugal exposition— be it by Bach or Mozart or Beethoven or Stravinsky—say to yourself, "Hey, that's a fugal exposition! I hear it! I recognize it!" It's a great moment when this happens, when we suddenly realize we've consciously recognized something we might not even have noticed before. And it gets better still, because by noticing the fugue, we make the visceral experience of the music a hundred, a thousand times more powerful than it would have been had we not noticed it. At such a moment, we're no longer passive observers but rather, active participants in the music's unfolding. We're hearing the piece the way the composer's audience heard it or, even better, the way the composer heard it while it was being created.

It is what a composer does with the given that sets his or her music apart from that of other composers. Johann Sebastian Bach's fugues are transcendent, but we still perceive them as fugues. To invoke a tiresome cliché, we can't go outside the box unless we first perceive the existence of the box.

Across the remainder of this chapter, we are going to discuss forms based on an ongoing process of variation (passacaglia, ground bass, chaconne, and ciaccona). In chapter 13, we will discuss ritornello form, a form based on an ongoing process of contrast.

Baroque variations procedures are those musical forms—those movements of music—based on an ongoing process of variation. Such a movement will state a theme of some sort, after which subsequent sections will vary that theme to some degree or another. There are a number of interchangeable terms for this Baroque variations procedure: *passacaglia*, *ground bass*, *chaconne*, and *ciaccona*. For the purposes of our discussion, we will not attempt to differentiate among these terms. Suffice it to say that these terms all refer to the same generalized procedure: the statement of a theme and, in subsequent sections, some sort of variation on that theme.

Here's how a Baroque era variational procedure works, and for ease of use, we'll just call it a passacaglia.

The theme in a passacaglia is a bass line or a harmonic progression built upon that bass line. That bass line or harmonic progression will then be repeated, over and over again, cyclically. As soon as that bass line is completed, it will be played again and again and again—on the same pitches—until the piece is over. In a passacaglia, this cyclical repetition is the given, that formal element that's shared between the composer and the audience. What changes are the upper voices, which are layered atop the cyclical repetitions in the bass. Each new cycle of the bass line is called a "variation" because of the changing nature of the material above it.

Passacaglia is the essence of the Baroque era duality of exuberance and control: the theme, the control element, the invisible "hand of God," is a structural, below-the-surface element, its cyclical repetitions controlling the changing and complex surface of the music.

To the casual observer, this process may seem absurdly rigorous. For example, what if a composer doesn't want to keep repeating the same bass line over and over again, what if halfway through the piece he decides to do something different? It would never occur to him, any more than it would occur to a batter in a baseball game to step up to the plate with a lacrosse stick. Without discipline there cannot be art, and the art of the Baroque is, at a structural level, about control, about logic, about discipline.

Johann Sebastian Bach, Passacaglia in C Minor for Organ (ca. 1715)

Bach's Passacaglia in C Minor is a magnificent, artistic tour de force that is, nevertheless, built with the structural precision of a particle accelerator.

Note the following:

- The theme is eight measures long. (See the figure that follows.)
- The theme is initially presented monophonically, so that we as listeners have a chance to hear it before the upper voices begin to be layered atop.
- After its initial statement, the theme is repeated 20 times in succession. Consequently, the theme is played 21 times in total. The movement is 169 measures in length (8-measure theme x 21 repetitions = 168 measures), as Bach adds an extra measure to the end for a few closing chords.
- While listening to this passacaglia, try to follow (or even sing along with) the theme notated below as it is played, in some form or another, 21 times in succession. Even a brief attempt to follow the theme will give you a sense of the iron-clad formal discipline that lies at the heart of passacaglia.
- This passacaglia is "about" expressive magnificence rigorously controlled—Bach and the Baroque aesthetic at their very best!

CHAPTER 13

Baroque Era Musical Genres

Instrumental genre refers to different categories of works for instruments. The broadest and most generic instrumental genres are solo compositions, chamber music, and orchestral music.

A solo composition is a piece of music composed for a single instrument.

A chamber work is a piece of music written for two or more players, with one player per part. For example, a string quartet is an instrumental ensemble consisting of four strings, each playing its own part: a first violin, a second violin, a viola, and a cello.

An orchestral composition, on the other hand, is a work in which one or more of the parts are doubled. For example, a typical modern orchestra will seat between sixteen and eighteen first violinists. They all play the same part, and thus we say that the part is being doubled (technically, eighteen-tupled; but we still call it doubled, whether there are two first violins or fifty). We'll see between fourteen and sixteen second violinists (first violin and second violin are two entirely different instrumental parts; think of them as dueling sopranos onstage together); likewise, the fourteen to sixteen second violinists are doubling the same part, and playing the same notes at the same time. The same will be true for the roughly twelve violas, ten cellos, and eight basses: the instruments in each of those sections will be playing the same part.

It wasn't until the late 1600s that the distinction between music composed specifically for a chamber group and music composed specifically for an orchestra first came to be perceived.

Up to that point of the Baroque era, only rarely were works composed specifically for orchestra outside of the opera house. Most commonly, chamber works were simply arranged for orchestra. For example, a church or court might have five or six instrumentalists in full-time employ: a violin, a viola, a cello, a flute, an oboe, and a harpsichord. But on certain special feast days or municipal occasions (Midnight Mass at Christmas or a royal wedding, for example), a larger ensemble might be required. What typically happened under such circumstances was that extra players would be hired to double up the parts played by the house band, thus converting a chamber work into an orchestral work simply by adding more players to the parts. It wasn't uncommon for the composers of late seventeenth-century chamber music to include instructions on how to properly double the parts in order to convert such a piece into an orchestral work. More often than not, this is what passed for orchestral music in the late 1600s, with one important exception: the opera houses of Europe, which did maintain standing orchestras.

In terms of sheer size and quality, the most important orchestra in all of Europe during the late 1600s and early 1700s was that of the Opéra, the French National Opera Orchestra. This was the opera, and the orchestra, that served the persons and propaganda of Louis XIV and Louis XV. It was in the opera house where orchestras performed music written specifically for them, for "the orchestra." As Baroque opera became more popular and, in Paris, more magnificent, instruments were modernized and added to the opera orchestra to expand the timbral resources of the ensemble. As we have observed, it was at this time the flute, oboe, English horn, bassoon, clarinet, natural horn, and trombone came into being, more or less as we know them today, for use in Baroque opera orchestras.

The orchestra as we know it today is by and large a creation of Baroque opera.

Even the word *orchestra* comes from the opera house. The semi-circular rim between the stage and the benches in a Greek theater was called the orchestra, and it was in the orchestra that the chorus stood during the performance of a Greek play. The Renaissance theater took the word *orchestra* as its own, and it was there—in the orchestra: the lip, the gap between the edge of the stage and the seats of the spectators—from which the small ensembles that accompanied early opera played. These instrumental ensembles then came to be known by the name of the location from which they played.

Many of the most important types of Baroque orchestral music grew directly out of operatic practice, including the overture, the orchestral suite, and the concerto. Let us take a closer look at the concerto.

The Baroque Concerto

The concerto appeared around the year 1680.

A concerto consists of one or more instrumental soloists accompanied by—and sometimes pitted against—the body of the orchestra. At its core, the concerto is a theatrical construct, contrasting the individual (the soloist or soloists) against the collective (the orchestra).

The concerto adapted the operatic model of a virtuosic, dramatic vocal soloist accompanied by the orchestra to the medium of orchestral music. By the high Baroque, the concerto had become the single most important type of orchestral music. The great composers of the high Baroque—Antonio Vivaldi, Georg Philipp Telemann, George Frideric Handel, and Johann Sebastian Bach—were also the great composers of the high Baroque concerto. Indeed, concertos by these masters of the high Baroque are the earliest orchestral works that we will hear performed on a regular basis today. Thus, in discussing the

Baroque concerto, we have crossed something of a Rubicon, because from here on out, we'll be talking about music that is part of the standard repertoire.

The Baroque era saw the creation of three different types of concertos. They are the orchestral, or *ripieno* concerto; the concerto grosso; and the *solo* concerto.

An orchestral, or ripieno, concerto is a high Baroque orchestral work scored for strings and continuo alone, in which there are no particular soloists and in which the first violins, collectively, play the principal melodic material. Bach's Brandenburg Concertos nos. 3 and 6 are just such orchestral concertos.

The solo concerto is the type of concerto with which we are most familiar today, one that features a single soloist accompanied by—and, perhaps, pitted against—the orchestra. The great Baroque composers of solo concertos were Arcangelo Corelli, Antonio Vivaldi, and Johann Sebastian Bach.

A concerto grosso is a Baroque concerto that features more than one soloist. (In later ages, such a work might be called a double or triple concerto.) What is *grosso* ("big") about such a work, then, is the number of soloists.

There's a Word for Everything: Concerto Terminology

There are a number of important concerto-related terms we need to know before we can continue our discussion of Baroque concertos in general and the concerto grosso specifically:

Tutti. In a concerto, the entire ensemble—orchestra and soloist or soloists—is referred to as the *tutti*. *Tutti*, in Italian, means "everything." When we refer to tutti in a concerto, we're referring to all the players involved in a concerto performance, including the soloists.

Ripieno. In a concerto, the term that refers to the accompanying ensemble—meaning the orchestra but not the soloists—is *ripieno*. *Ripieno* in Italian means, literally, "full," as in the "full ensemble."

Concertino. *Concertino* refers to the soloists in a concerto grosso. Like many Italian words that end with the letters *i-n-o*, *concertino* is a diminutive. It means, literally, "little concerto," or "little ensemble." Along with *ripieno*, the word *concertino* implies something very important about the basic nature of a concerto grosso.

Ripieno: the full ensemble. Concertino: the little ensemble. A concerto grosso, by its nature, pits two different ensembles, of two different natures, against each other. On the one hand, there are two different "groups of instruments" coexisting in a single composition: a large ensemble and a small ensemble. But more subtly, a concerto grosso features two different *instrumental genres* vying with each other in the same composition: an orchestral ensemble (the ripieno) and a chamber ensemble (the concertino).

By the high Baroque, most Baroque concertos were three movements in length, which remains the standard length of a concerto to this day. Also by the high Baroque, the first movement of almost all concertos was structured in ritornello form.

A ritornello form movement is one in which the opening musical idea returns periodically, like a refrain. Ritornello form is just that sort of formal construct that imbues a piece of instrumental music with a sense of logical "inevitability." In such a movement, every time we hear the ritornello theme return—every time we hear the refrain—we know we've come back home; and each time we depart from it, we know we will eventually return.

Ritornello is one of the most commonly used instrumental musical forms of the Baroque era. We see it employed in almost every kind of composition because it creates a sense of departure and return, and in doing so, renders coherent long spans of music.

Typically, the first movement of a Baroque era concerto will be cast in ritornello form. The second movement of a Baroque era concerto will be a slow movement meant to provide a lyric respite from the rigors of the first, and the third movement will typically be fast and fuguelike in character.

Let's take a close-up look at the first movement of Johann Sebastian Bach's Brandenburg Concerto no. 5. In doing so, we'll familiarize ourselves with ritornello form, learn something of Herr Bach's life, and gain some insight into why he is considered among the handful of greatest composers ever to have lived.

Johann Sebastian Bach, Brandenburg Concerto No. 5 (ca. 1721); First Movement

Ritornello Form

Bach's Brandenburg no. 5 is scored for the following: The concertino (the "little ensemble" of soloists) consists of a flute, a violin, and a harpsichord. The ripieno is a string orchestra. The basso continuo consists of a cello and harpsichord (which does double duty as a soloist).

The ritornello theme—fussy, note-filled, extravagantly ornate, and thus in all ways "Baroque"—is presented homophonically. The theme:

Typical of ritornello form in a concerto grosso, there is a built-in contrast between the ritornello theme and its various reappearances and the episodes that occur between those reappearances. Statements of the ritornello theme will be played homophonically by the ripieno. The episodes played between the thematic restatements of the ritornello theme will be played polyphonically by the concertino, with light accompaniment provided by the ripieno. (A request: go back, read this paragraph again, and be proud, dear reader, be *proud*. Dollars to doughnuts says it made sense when you first read it, and it still makes sense after being reread: it's a testament to your new-found familiarity with music terminology!)

Typical of ritornello form, the ritornello theme is heard in its entirety only at the very beginning and very end of the movement. The other statements of the ritornello theme are but partial and are perceived as momentary touchstones between the much longer solo episodes.

Not typical of ritornello form, the final solo episode is dedicated entirely to a lengthy and virtuosic harpsichord solo that Bach undoubtedly composed to be performed by himself. It is the first such keyboard solo in the history of the concerto, an episode that many music historians credit as having given birth to the keyboard concerto!

The Brandenburg Concertos

In March of 1721, Bach put together a package containing what he considered six of his best court orchestra compositions—six concertos—and mailed it off to the newly appointed Margrave of Brandenburg in Berlin. The cover letter, which was written in French, the courtly language of the day, is as perfect an illustration of the social status of a Baroque era musician vis-à-vis the aristocracy as any we are likely to find. Here's an excerpt from Bach's painfully obsequious letter:

To His Royal Highness, Christian Ludwig, Margrave of Brandenburg, etc. Sire, since I had the happiness a few years ago to play by command before your Royal Highness and observed at that time that you derived some pleasure from the small musical talent that Heaven has given me, and since when I was taking leave of your Royal Highness, you did me the honor to request that I send you some of my compositions, I have therefore, in compliance with your most gracious demand, taken the liberty of tendering my most humble respects to your Royal Highness with the present concerti arranged for several instruments. . . .

Grovel, grovel, grovel. We've all written cover letters of some sort, but I trust never one quite like this. What does Bach want from the margrave? It's a letter of application: the thirty-six-year-old Bach is looking for a job.

At the time he wrote the letter, Bach was the music director for the court of Prince Leopold of Anhalt-Cöthen. As we've previously observed, Bach loved this job and he loved his prince. But the prince began having financial problems and had to start cutting back his musical establishment. Then, in May of 1720, Bach's beloved wife, Barbara, died suddenly, leaving him crushed, bereft, and with four young children. Finally, the last straw: Prince Leopold became engaged to Princess Frederica Henrietta von Anhalt-Bernburg. The princess did not approve of the amount of money her husband-to-be was spending on his musical hobby, and she was jealous of the relationship between Bach and the prince.

So Bach assembled what amounted to a musical résumé consisting of six concertos, wrote a cover letter, and sent the package off to the Margrave of Brandenburg with the hopes of getting a job in Berlin. The margrave did not write back. Nevertheless, the six concertos Bach sent to him were dubbed in the nineteenth century the Brandenburg Concertos, and the name has stuck.

Whether or not Bach's contemporaries were aware of it (and, for the most part, they were not) his music capped an age. It was an age shaped and conditioned by the expressive exuberance of opera, which itself recognized the expressive primacy of human emotions as no other musical genre had since the ancient world. It was also an age shaped by science, rational thinking, and common sense, a shared sensibility that would, in the second half of the eighteenth century, be focused on religious institutions and institutions of the state. This tilt toward humanism in Western society—which can be traced back to the shattering events of the fourteenth century and which gathered such tremendous steam during the Renaissance and Baroque era—will continue unabated into the art (and music) of the Enlightenment, the great social evolution that marks the second half of the eighteenth century. The music of the Enlightenment is referred to as that of the Classical era, which is the next stop in our story.

CHAPTER 14

Enlightened Is as Enlightened Does

An Introduction to the Classical Era

The Classical era is understood as running from 1750 to 1827, from the death of Bach to the death of Beethoven. Even as period dates go, these are awful, and here's why.

While Johann Sebastian Bach's death in 1750 affords us a serviceable year to end the Baroque era, it's a fairly useless year with which to begin what we now call the Classical era. Those musical stylistic elements that we will soon enough define as being "Classical" reached their first real flower in Italy in the early 1730s. For at least twenty-five years, stylistically Baroque and stylistically Classical era music coexisted, like the Neanderthal and Cro-Magnon. In reality, it isn't until the 1760s that those stylistic elements we would identify as Baroque had become a thing of the past.

Concluding the Classical era in 1827 with Beethoven's death is absurd. Instead, we should end it in 1803, the year Beethoven composed the bulk of his Symphony no. 3 and, in so doing, rendered classicalism obsolete in one outrageous act!

But who asked me?

The evolution from the high Baroque to the Classical musical style was a mirror of an extraordinary social evolution that we, today, call the Enlightenment.

The Enlightenment, circa 1730 to 1780, was a period that saw the institutions of Europe—religious, political, social, educational, industrial, financial, and artistic—slowly but inexorably lower their

focus from the aristocracy and the high clergy to a new class of people then emerging from the bowels of the new European mercantil-
ism and the beginning of the Industrial Revolution. For lack of a
better name, we call this new and growing class the middle class, and
the Enlightenment marked their initial entry into the mainstream of
European society. A new brand of humanism, philosophical humanism, evolved, one that asserted that all people were important, not
just representatives of the Church and the state.

Since the beginning of recorded time, European class structure
and wealth had been based upon hereditary land ownership. But by
the early eighteenth century, new patterns and methods of trade and
manufacturing had contributed to creating a *nouveau* wealthy class
whose wealth was based not on inherited real estate, but rather on
accumulated cash.

This new middle and non-aristocratic upper class, by the sheer
weight of their numbers, buying power, and growing political influence, began to assert terrific pressures on their respective societies to
meet their needs and desires.

The nouveau riche wanted to be educated and consequently, it
was during the Enlightenment that the concept of universal education first emerged. They wanted at least a modicum of political
power and a greater degree of control over their own lives.

The new middle class also wanted an end to social and religious
injustice. People in the middle and upper classes began to believe
that an institution was "good" to the extent that it did the greatest
good for the greatest number of people. The faith in reason that had
inspired the scientific community during the seventeenth century
was steered, in the mid- and late eighteenth century, toward the
social sphere, with the result that social institutions and mechanisms
were put under the scrutiny of common sense. The middle class
wanted quality of life, comfort, and upward mobility.

From a purely social point of view, Enlightenment humanism
was, perhaps, the most important of all the intellectual currents of
the time. Enlightenment humanism stated that life on earth and the

quality of that life were as important as the afterlife promised by religion. Making the best out of an earthly life became a basic desire for the new middle class.

For the most part, the hereditary monarchies and aristocracies that still ruled Western Europe were grudgingly willing to oblige. In the 1760s, '70s, and '80s (up until the advent of the French Revolution), most such bigwigs were, to some degree or another, "enlightened": that is, concerned for the well-being of the "little people" to a degree unheard of in previous European history.

Cosmopolitanism

The ideal of international brotherhood as espoused by Enlightenment humanism was partly realized in a trend that we now refer to as cosmopolitanism. Cosmopolitanism saw national differences downplayed in favor of a vision of the common humanity of all people.

The ideal of cosmopolitanism also applied to the music of the late eighteenth century. In 1752, J. J. Quantz, the court composer and flute teacher to Frederick the Great of Prussia, opined that the ideal musical style of his enlightened time was a composite of the best features of all European nations, writing, "A music that is accepted and recognized as good not by one country only, but by many peoples must, provided it is based, as well, on reason and sound feeling, be beyond all dispute the best."

Enlightenment musical cosmopolitanism refers to a common international style, a style that will come to be known as the Classical style. As it turned out, this pan-European, cosmopolitan music was one that combined the melodic fluency of the Italians; the rigor, craft, and spiritual profundity of the Germans; and the instrumental techniques and technology of the French. It was a music also profoundly influenced by the "Every Person" spirit of the Enlightenment.

The Enlightenment doctrine that asserted that the institution that does the greatest good for the greatest number is good had as its artistic analog that that music that is accessible and pleasing to the greatest number is good. (As contrasted with the relatively more complex musical surfaces and politically elite music of the Baroque.) In the end, a musical style evolved that resonated with the spirit of Enlightenment humanism and cosmopolitanism: an attractive, accessible, tuneful music that obscured the national origins of its composers.

MUSIC BOX

Something Else to Try at Home!

Play the first movement of any symphony by Joseph Haydn (1732–1809). (One hundred and four of Haydn's symphonies have survived, so you have a rather wide range to choose from.) Then listen to the first movement of a symphony by Jan Stamitz (1717–1757; fifty-eight of Stamitz's symphonies have survived) followed by the first movement of a symphony by Luigi Boccherini (1743–1805; twenty-one of Boccherini's symphonies have survived). Note that there is no "national signature" to any of this music. Its relative "quality" notwithstanding, the style, the sound, the expressive content is very much the same, despite the fact that Haydn was born and raised in Austria, Stamitz in Bohemia (the present-day Czech Republic), and Boccherini in Italy. Their countries of origin aside, these are three cosmopolitan composers writing in a single, pan-European style.

My Kind of Town, Vienna Is . . .

The Classical style reached its zenith in and around the great Habsburg capital of Vienna between roughly 1770 and 1800. In honor of the city, the mature Classical style is often referred to as the Viennese Classical style.

There are five reasons why Vienna became the locus of classicism.

First, Vienna stands at the crossroads of four very musical nations: Germany, Bohemia, Hungary, and Italy.

Second, Vienna stood smack-dab between the two dominant musical traditions of eighteenth-century Europe: the operatic vocal tradition of the Catholic south and the more instrumental, polyphonic tradition of the Protestant north.

Third, Emperor Joseph II of Austria, the most enlightened of all the Habsburg rulers, cultivated the musical arts big time, and thus presided over a golden age in Viennese music.

Fourth, as a capital city, Vienna was filled with rich and powerful people who had money and time to burn. Vienna also had a large and financially well off middle class: the bureaucrats who manned the government and municipality, and the merchants and contractors who served the needs of the city and its population. For the Viennese aristocratic and middle classes, then as now, music was *the* leisure time consumable. One would have to look long and hard (and likely in vain) to find a more music-friendly environment.

Which explains the fifth and final reason why Vienna was the capital of the Classical style: it became the adoptive home of a majority of the most important composers of the time, including Joseph Haydn, Wolfgang Mozart, and Ludwig van Beethoven.

Music to All Our Ears: The Doctrine of Accessibility

The new middle class wanted what the founding parental units of the United States called the "pursuit of happiness," what I like to refer to as "the pursuit of entertainment." The new middle class had something their grandparents never had: free time, leisure time.

For the new, Enlightenment era middle class, music became the indispensable leisure time consumable, their primary form of entertainment. The sort of music they chose to consume—the sort of music that resonated with the "every person" spirit of the time—was music in which melodic beauty and directness were of primary importance.

Both the new middle class and the Enlightened aristocracy came to reject the music of the high Baroque, which they considered to be unnecessarily complicated and elitist. The listening public of the Enlightenment preferred to consume music that emphasized vocal lyricism: accessible, homophonic music, which became a metaphor for the spirit of individuality abroad in contemporary society.

The New Vocally Conceived Melody

Play, back to back, the opening of the first movement of Bach's Brandenburg Concerto no. 5 and of Mozart's *Eine kleine Nachtmusik*. Bach's thematic melody is a brilliant example of high Baroque art: exuberant, complex, and filled with detail (notes, notes, and more notes). Mozart's thematic melody has just enough notes to create a virtually unforgettable melody, no more and no less.

Next, do your best to *sing* each melody. Bach's theme is not particularly "singable"; its range is too great and it contains too many notes (too much information) to fall naturally in the voice. It is an *instrumentally conceived melody*. Mozart's thematic melody, on the other hand, is eminently singable. Despite the fact that it was written to be played by musical instruments, it is a *vocally conceived melody*. In an era when accessibility and expressive directness were considered aesthetic qualities, direct and engaging melodic surfaces were cultivated above everything else. The so-called doctrine of accessibility of the Enlightenment demanded a music that was vocal, tuneful, and thus accessible.

The opening theme of Mozart's *Eine kleine Nachtmusik* evoked in the previous Music Box is an example of what Jean-Jacques Rousseau—the Swiss-born hippie whose ideas so helped to shape the Enlightenment—would have called "natural" art. *Natural* became an Enlightenment buzzword; natural was good. Art that was perceived as being contrived and complex (such as Baroque music) was considered "unnatural": not good.

All too often, the difference between Baroque era music and Enlightenment (or Classical era) music is erroneously described as being "more complex" (Baroque era music) versus "simpler" (Classical era music). In reality, Mozart's *Eine kleine Nachtmusik* is not musically simpler than Bach's Brandenburg Concerto no. 5. That Mozart's piece appears simpler than Bach's is an illusion, a product of the two works' respective styles and aesthetic, not their musical content.

Comparing two images can help us grasp this stylistic and aesthetic difference. The first is an image of the Nymphenburg Castle and gardens, located outside of Munich. Typical of Baroque design, the garden sees nature ordered and controlled by the hand of the landscape architect. There's a tremendous amount of stuff: plants, hedges, flower gardens, fountains, paths, and so forth, yet everything is carefully trimmed, potted, and symmetrically arrayed. Visual exuberance and symmetrical control, typical of Baroque era design.

Our second image is of a Classical era garden at Stourhead Estate in Wiltshire, England, constructed during the Enlightenment,

Nymphenburg Castle Hemera/Thinkstock

Stourhead Park iStockphoto/Thinkstock

between 1741 and '80. We see a placid lake with an arched footbridge at one end. Beyond the lake is a neoclassic building of great elegance nestled among the trees. Trees, shrubs, and plants grow in profusion, through which curving paths gently wend their way. "Pastoral calm" is written all over this park. Compared to the Baroque era park, this Classical era park seems so much "simpler" and more "natural."

In reality, this Classical era park is as calculated and complex as the Baroque era park. The lake, buildings, bridge, and foliage were designed and built to look natural. Just so, the apparent "simplicity" of Mozart's *Eine kleine Nachtmusik* is a product of its design aesthetic. In truth, there's nothing simple about it. But like the park at Stourhead House, the complexities of Mozart's *Eine kleine Nachtmusik* lie out of plain sight, below the musical surface. These design "complexities" have to do with such things as phrase structure, accompanimental textures, harmonic motion, thematic contrast, motivic development, and the differentiation of thematic music from transitional music. Bach's Brandenburg Concerto no. 5, like the Baroque garden, wears its complexity on the surface. The riot of information that is the essence of Baroque design demanded to be seen in all its profuse detail, shaped and controlled by the hand of the artist.

The role and function of music in society came to be viewed quite differently during the Enlightenment relative to the Baroque era. Music came to be perceived as a decorative art, rather than as a spiritual and intellectual pursuit, an assertion supported by none other than Charles Burney, the greatest writer on music of the age. In 1779, Burney described music as being a condiment—mayonnaise, perhaps—for the ears. "Music is an innocent luxury, unnecessary to our existence but a great improvement and gratification of the sense of 'hearing.'"

Idle speculation. What if Mozart's and Bach's birth years were reversed, and Mozart had been born in 1685 and Bach in 1756? Would Bach have composed a piece like the Brandenburg Concerto no. 5 in the 1780s? Would Mozart have composed *Eine kleine Nachtmusik* in the 1720s? No, they would not have. The greater cultural environment creates the sound, the "style" of a given era's music. Bach and Mozart would still have been great composers, but the expressive content and syntax of their music would have mirrored their world and experience, and thus would have been completely different had they been born at different times.

Classicism and Cadence

The Enlightenment's impact on musical style was profound. The melodically ornate and intellectually complex music of the high Baroque was rejected as being out of touch with the spirit of the time, and a new, more melodically and expressively flexible musical style evolved, one that resonated with the new spirit of individualism that lay at the heart of Enlightenment doctrine. It was a musical style that celebrated melodic beauty and clarity above all else. This musical style eventually became known as the Classical style because, like "classical art"—ancient Greek art—this music celebrated: one, clarity and beauty of line (melody); two, balance and purity of form (clear phrase structures and carefully wrought musical forms); and, three, expressive restraint and good taste (purity of conception and expression).

The increased emphasis on lyric melody characteristic of Classical era music placed a new degree of emphasis on the beginnings and endings of those melodies. Such beginnings and endings are recognized as such because they are marked by cadences, musical punctuation marks. A cadence is a harmonic or melodic formula that occurs at the end of a phrase, section, or movement, a formula that conveys a momentary or permanent sense of conclusion.

This is not to say that there are no cadences in the music of the Baroque era; of course there are. But rhythmic continuity— meaning a rock-steady beat and almost constant forward motion— was a basic stylistic element of most Baroque era music, particularly instrumental music, and that rhythmic continuity tends to steamroll cadences, which in such a rhythmic environment pass by in the blink of an eye.

Conversely, the music of the Classical era tends to be rhythmically discontinuous, as its tune-dominated music allowed for cadential flourishes and extensions, and thus for a movement to *breathe*—to start and stop—in a way that Baroque instrumental music rarely does.

The Classical era cultivation of cadence and the impact of cadential cultivation on the musical forms of the Classical era require that we identify and discuss the four principal types of cadences: open (or half) cadences, closed (or authentic/standard) cadences, false (or deceptive) cadences, and plagal (or amen) cadences.

Open or Half Cadence

In any given key, there is a chord that creates tremendous dissonance— tremendous tension—and thus needs to resolve. That chord is the one built atop the fifth pitch (or "fifth degree") of any major or minor collection (or "scale"). If we're in the key of C major, the pitch C is the home pitch, or "tonic" (the word *tonic* should be thought of as a contraction of the phrase *tonal center*). The fifth pitch of a C major collection is G. In the key of C major, then, the pitch G is called the dominant pitch, and the chord built atop that G is called the dominant chord: the "chord of tension."

An open, or half, cadence is one that stops on this tension-producing chord, the dominant chord. An open cadence creates dissonance, which, properly defined, means a state of irresolution. (A word of encouragement, dear reader: as with all of the notational examples in this book, the following examples of cadences want to be seen and heard. If you cannot play them on an available keyboard yourself, find somebody who can play them for you. These are formulaic chord progressions with which you are already familiar: the average listener already knows what these cadences sound like. What we want to do now is give names to these harmonic progressions and, in doing so, make ourselves consciously aware of their musical function. It's the same way we learned our native language: first by "ear" (by speaking it), then by recognizing it in notated form (reading it), and finally by learning the rules of grammar (becoming conscious of function and structure).

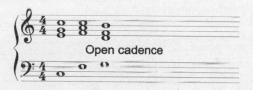

Open cadence

An open (or half) cadence like the one above is the musical equivalent of a comma. Like a comma, an open cadence demands that a musical sentence continue in search of a period: in search of resolution.

Closed, Authentic, or Standard Cadence

A closed (or authentic or standard) cadence is one that resolves from the dominant chord to the tonic chord, and in so doing, creates resolution and thus rest.

That sense of rest might be temporary if we're in the middle of a movement or permanent if we are at the very end of a movement.

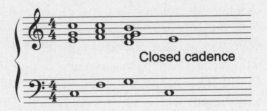

Closed cadence

A closed (or authentic or standard) cadence is the musical equivalent of a period.

Deceptive or False Cadence

A deceptive, or false, cadence is one in which the dominant chord resolves, but not to the tonic. As such, deceptive cadences are used to prolong phrases by avoiding the tonic, and are the musical equivalent of a colon or a semicolon.

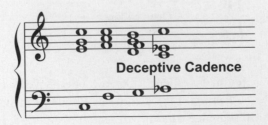

Deceptive Cadence

Plagal or Amen Cadence

A plagal, or amen, cadence is one that sees the chord built on the fourth degree of a major or minor collection (called the subdominant chord) resolve to the tonic. The plagal cadence is often referred to as an amen cadence because it is the harmonic progression that underpins the word *amen* in the great majority of Protestant church hymns.

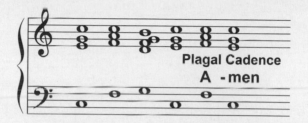

A plagal cadence is not a substitute for a closed, open, or deceptive cadence. Rather, it will typically follow a closed cadence at the very end of a passage as a sort of add-on, one that reinforces the tonic harmony at the end of that phrase or passage.

We'll return to the use of cadences in the next chapter, where we'll explore their expanded role in the musical forms of the Classical era.

CHAPTER 15

Putting It All Together:
Classical Era Musical Form,
Part One

A
s we have discussed, hand in hand with the development of instrumental music during the Baroque era was the development of instrumental musical forms. These compositional procedures with which composers could shape their ideas, and through which an audience could anticipate certain types of musical discourse, changed the development of Western music, rendering coherent the otherwise abstract medium of instrumental music. From the Middle Ages through the mid-Baroque, vocal music was far and away the most important type of music. But from the mid- to late Baroque onward, instrumental music first equaled and then displaced vocal music as the primary vehicle for musical discourse.

With the coming of the Enlightenment, and the evolving belief that music should be accessible to a sort of idealized Every Person, a musical style evolved that gave pride of place to direct, vocally conceived melody. Concurrent with the development of what we now call the Classical style was the development of instrumental musical forms that could exploit the narrative possibilities inherent in this tune-dominated musical style.

What developed were the Classical era forms, the so-called homophonic forms. These forms continued to be used through the nineteenth and well into the twentieth century. That's an amazing shelf life for a set of musical forms, and it speaks to just how superbly conceived and adaptable they are.

A musical form pep talk: No single aspect of a movement of music is more revealing of its expressive message than its musical form. Formal perception creates a context for detail, and allows us, as listeners, to follow a piece of music the way we'd follow a great raconteur telling a story. The process of variation will create one sort of story. The process of contrast will create an entirely different sort of story, one informed by conflict. The process of development will, likewise, create yet another sort of story. In summary, when it comes to listening—really hearing what's going on in a piece of music—nothing is more important than a knowledge of musical form. Nothing. Is. More. Important.

We will examine the four principal Classical era forms progressively, in order of increasing complexity. First theme and variations form, then minuet and trio form, rondo form, and finally, sonata form.

Theme and Variations Form

Theme and variations form is the Classical era adaptation of Baroque era variations procedure (passacaglia, for example).

As we observed in chapter 12, the Baroque era model put the theme in the bass, where it became a structural rather than a surface aspect of the music. In a Classical era theme and variations form movement, the opposite is true: the theme will be a tune and, therefore, the principal surface element of the movement. As for this tune, the more memorable the better. It is not unusual for a composer to use a preexisting melody as a theme for such a movement, as the overriding artistic challenge in theme and variations form is not the creation of the theme itself but rather how cleverly a composer can recast, reinterpret, and reclothe the theme during the course of the variations. It's actually to a composer's advantage to use as a theme a melody his audience is already familiar with; it will be that much easier to follow the variations as they progress. Thus, when we see such titles as Beethoven's *Diabelli Variations*, Chopin's variations on Mozart's *La ci darem la mano*, and Brahms's *Handel Variations*, *Haydn Variations*, and *Paganini Variations*, we are being told, one, that the piece is cast in theme and variations form, and two, who was the composer of the theme.

For the non-composer, such thematic borrowing reeks of plagiarism. In fact, the co-opting of one composer's melody by another for a theme and variations form movement is considered a gesture of respect, even an act of homage. Full credit is given to the composer of the theme, whose name typically appears in the work's title. And that theme will be lavished with all the imagination and craft at the disposal of the co-opting composer. The theme will be given new life and breadth through his efforts, perhaps even immortality. (Would anyone remember Anton Diabelli if not for Beethoven's masterful variations on Diabelli's theme? I think not.)

A hugely important point. The optimistic thematic statement in a theme and variations form movement will conclude with a closed cadence and a brief pause. With but the rarest exception, each variation that follows will *also* conclude with a closed cadence and a brief pause. These closed cadences punctuate the structure, separating the theme and each of the variations from each other. Thus, these closed cadences *articulate the form*, as the theme and each of its variations are perceived as separate entities. A theme and variations form movement is therefore a discontinuous structure, one that starts and stops regularly over its course.

The opposite is true for a Baroque era passacaglia (or chaconne or ground bass). The cadences, the punctuation marks, between the iterations of the bass theme are not "cultivated," that is, brought to the fore and used as moments of repose. Instead, the rhythmic momentum never flags, and consequently we perceive such a movement as being a continuous structure.

Like Baroque era passacaglia, theme and variations form is a rigorous, highly disciplined procedure. Each variation will have the same phrase structure and cadences as the theme. (On those rare occasions when a composer takes structural liberties, she will typically call her piece "Fantasy Variations," or a "Rhapsody on a Theme by So-and-So," or employ some other such "qualifying" title.)

The only limit to the variational techniques that may be employed is a composer's imagination. The theme can be embellished; its accompaniment can be varied; a theme originally set in major can be reset in minor, and vice versa; the speed (or tempo) can be varied; and so forth. The one thing a composer will not do is alter the phrase structure and cadence structure of the theme during the course of a variation. This could render a variation unrecognizable as a variation, and is thus antithetical to the rigor and discipline of theme and variations form.

There is no limit to the number of variations a composer can write beyond his own ambitions for the movement. In the second movement theme and variations form of his String Quartet in E-flat Major, op. 74 (1809), Beethoven composed a theme and two variations. In his *Diabelli Variations* for piano (1823), Beethoven appends *thirty-three* variations to Diabelli's theme.

A theme and variations form movement will conclude with a coda, an extra section of music added at the end of a movement to create a convincing sense of conclusion. A coda is essentially an expanded final cadence. As such, it plays an important structural role in theme and variations form, as its presence tells us that the ongoing process of variation is over and the movement is about to end.

The coda is a Classical era phenomenon, because codas are all about cadence; about expanded, rhetorical final cadences that create a satisfying and often emphatic sense of conclusion.

Theme and variations form is based on an ongoing process of variation: a theme is stated, and each subsequent section of the movement (until the coda) constitutes a variation on that theme. There is no departure in theme and variations form; rather, it is a monothematic construct based entirely on the opening thematic statement. On those rare occasions when a composer does introduce a contrasting theme in the course of theme and variations form, such a movement will be called double variations.

Theme and variations form is understood to be the least complex of the Classical era forms because it features no departure. You might say that the music never leaves the house. It might walk from room to room, but it never goes outside. As a result, there is no departure, contrast, or conflict inherent to theme and variations form.

Another way to think about the theme and variations form is as a fashion show in which the "theme" is a model constantly reclothed. We recognize the "model" (the theme) as the "constant," but we also recognize that, at each appearance, the model has been reclothed, and through that reclothing, some new aspect of the model's (theme's) personality has been brought to our attention.

MUSIC BOX

Mozart's Twelve Variations on *Ah vous dirai-je, Maman,* K. 265 (1782)

For this theme and variations form work for piano, Mozart chose a familiar folk song he knew under the French title of "Ah vous dirai-je, Maman," which translates as "Whatever you say, Mom." English speakers know the tune as both "Twinkle, Twinkle, Little Star" and "Baa, Baa Black Sheep."

Note the following:

- Mozart initially presents the theme as directly as possible, with but the simplest of accompaniments. His intention here, at the beginning of the piece, is to make sure we hear the thematic melody and its phrase and cadence structures with absolute clarity.
- Twelve variations follow. They run the gamut from simple reharmonizations to elaborate embellishments that obscure the thematic melody almost entirely. However, since the phrase structure and cadence structure of each variation are the same as the theme, we recognize the theme's structure in each variation whether we hear its melody or not.

- The theme and each variation that follows are set off from the next by a closed cadence.
- Following the twelfth variation, a coda briefly but convincingly brings the process of variation and the piece to its conclusion.

Minuet and Trio Form

Most four-movement Classical era works—be they symphonies, string quartets, or other chamber works—will feature a movement cast in minuet and trio form. That minuet and trio form movement will be one of the "middle" movements, most frequently the third, but sometimes the second.

The upshot: minuet and trio form is ubiquitous in Classical era instrumental music. In concert program notes and CD booklets: any movement called a menuetto is a minuet and trio.

Minuet and trio form—like theme and variations form—has its roots in the Baroque era, specifically in the courtly dance music of seventeenth-century France.

Suites and "Stylized Dance Music"

The French love dance, and we will see extensive dance episodes not just in ballet proper but in almost any French musical stage entertainment. French opera, for example, has always been distinctive for its lengthy episodes of dance, something only rarely seen in Italian or German opera.

The dance music that appeared in Baroque French operas was typically condensed into "suites" and published and performed separately from the stage entertainment in which those dances originally appeared. The word *suite* means, literally "a sequence" or "a series," and a "dance suite" is therefore a sequence or series of dances extracted from a larger production and packaged and sold separately. For example, Peter Tchaikovsky's *Nutcracker Suite* is a sequence of dances extracted from the ballet, a sort of *Nutcracker's Greatest Hits*.

The incredible popularity of Baroque French dance music inspired the composition of stylized dance music. Stylized dances are instrumental works based on the characteristic rhythms and moods of various dances, intended for listening rather than dancing. Collections of such stylized Baroque dances for keyboard, cello, violin, or lute were called partitas or suites, and those scored for orchestra were called orchestral suites.

With just a handful of exceptions, Baroque era dance music, whether real or stylized, is homophonic in texture, something that made it a natural model for the tune-happy, homophony-dominated music of the Classical era. If you think about it, the group dance music of the Baroque had to be a homophonic musical tradition. Simply put, trying to coordinate the ritualized steps of group dance to polyphonic music could have disastrous results: different dancers would follow different voices, which would result in choreographic mayhem. Consequently, Baroque dance music, real or stylized, will almost invariably be homophonic in texture.

Almost all Baroque era dance types, whether of folk or courtly origin, were brought to their peak of sophistication in seventeenth-century France. No matter where these dances originally came from—Italy, Spain, Sicily, Germany, or England—it was the French who perfected them.

Given their brevity, shorter dances such as the minuet were paired by type: in both the ballroom and in stylized dances, two minuets would be played back to back in order to stretch things out. Such a pairing triggers a fascinating formal phenomenon: the need for thematic closure, to return to the melodic material and harmonic area that began the piece.

This principle of thematic closure is operative in any dance that is paired by type. If, for example, we hear two contrasting minuets played back to back, the demands of thematic closure require a return to the first minuet. Consequently, any dance that's paired by type in performance will conclude with a return to the first dance, creating a large-scale structure of A (dance one), B (contrasting dance two), A (dance one, return), or A-B-A.

During the seventeenth century, it became traditional to score the contrasting dance, the B section, for but three instruments. As a result, this B-section dance came to be called the trio.

These three-part, A-B-A dance movements were called minuet and trio, or gavotte and trio, or whatever and trio. The sticklers among us would rightly point out that the form should properly be called minuet, trio, and minuet form. Well, the sticklers are going to have to give it a rest, because when we say "minuet and trio," the reprise of the opening minuet (referred to as the minuet da capo, the "return to the top") is understood.

Thanks to its incredible popularity as a social dance, the minuet has the distinction of being the only Baroque era dance to survive into the multi-movement instrumental genres of the Classical era. As a social dance, the minuet remained popular well into the nineteenth century, and for the composers of the Classical era, its moderately paced triple meter offered an excellent contrast to the fast duple-meter movements that were standard in Classical era genres such as symphonies and string quartets.

Classical era minuet and trio form maintained the large-scale, three-part structure of the Baroque era model while extending the length of the individual minuet and trio sections. Much as I'd love to explore these small phrase extensions with you—and in doing so, introduce such killer-fun terms as *binary form*, *rounded-binary form*, and *ternary form*—the scope of this book precludes such detailed analysis. And that's just as well, because the large-scale formal and dramatic point of a minuet and trio form movement is contrast—departure and return—that is, A-B-A, with each of these large sections ending with a closed cadence.

Joseph Haydn, Symphony No. 88 in G Major (1788), Movement Three: Minuet and Trio Form

This is a big, brilliant minuet and trio form movement, an example of the Viennese Classical style and its *numero uno* proponent, Joseph Haydn, at their best.

Note the following points while listening:

- The minuet sections are bold and pomp-filled, and scored for full orchestra, including brass and drums. This is royal and urban music, music that smacks of the imperial ballroom!
- The rustic trio, on the other hand, evokes the countryside. A bagpipe-like drone accompanies a team of country fiddlers (the violins), whose melody wanders just a bit. The nature of the contrast in this movement, then, is between citified, urbanized, imperial music and this rustic, fun, fiddling music.

(A word about the instrumentation of Haydn's trio. In a Baroque era minuet and trio, the trio was indeed scored for three instruments; thus the designation "trio." In a Classical era orchestral minuet and trio, that second, contrasting minuet is still called the trio, but we can no longer assume that it will be scored for just three instruments. What we can assume of a Classical era trio is that it will be scored for *fewer* instruments than the minuet sections: a "reduced" instrumentation, but not necessarily as few as three.)

- When listening to this (or any) minuet and trio form movement, what is of primary importance is to perceive the large-scale form of the movement: the departure to the contrasting music of the trio and then the thematic closure that comes with the arrival of the minuet da capo. As for following the small-scale phrase structure and its repetitions, detailed hearing comes only once we're comfortable with the broader context of the large-scale form.

Joseph Haydn

Joseph Haydn (1732–1809) was just about the nicest person ever to be a major composer. Everybody seems to have liked him—from the humblest fiddle player to the king of England. He had no chip on his shoulder and was self-confident without being arrogant. He was small, spry, and energetic; a loving and thoughtful friend who was moved to tears easily. He had a legendary sense of humor and was something of a practical joker.

Joseph Haydn (1732–1809)
The Teaching Company Collection

Haydn was a wonderful boss to the players who worked for him, and they began calling him Papa when he was still in his thirties, because he took such good care of them. He was a loyal friend and mentor to Mozart, and somehow he managed to tolerate Beethoven, who, though thirty-eight years Haydn's junior, showed him little respect when he studied with him in the early 1790s.

We hear Haydn's personality in his music: his joie de vivre, his emotional balance, and especially his marvelous sense of humor.

Rondo Form

If minuet and trio form is the most formulaic of the Classical era forms, then rondo form is the least formulaic of the bunch. Rondo is a "refrain" form, and all a movement has to do to be called a rondo is feature periodic thematic return. A rondo form movement will begin with a clear and unambiguous statement of the theme: the "rondo theme." Subsequent sections of the movement represent departures from and returns to that theme. Like theme and variations form, a rondo form movement will end with a coda, which tells us that the ongoing alternation of departure and return is over.

Rondo Form and Baroque Era Ritornello Form

While rondo and ritornello are both refrain-type musical forms, there's a huge difference between the two. It's a difference that has to do with the treatment of the theme across the span of the movement and the subsequent locus of the dramatic weight of the movement.

In Baroque era ritornello form, the theme, once stated, is only rarely heard again in its entirety, typically only at the very end of the movement. As a result, the core musical and dramatic "substance" of a ritornello form movement lies not in the appearances of its theme but rather in the contrasting episodes the theme punctuates.

The opposite is true of Classical era rondo form. In a rondo form movement, the rondo theme represents the core musical substance of the movement. The contrasting episodes, no matter how interesting, have as their ultimate goal a return to the rondo theme, which is typically heard in its entirety (or very nearly so) at every appearance. This is utterly typical of the Classical style, in that the "rondo theme" is a tune, and that "tune" is the preeminent musical element in the movement.

MUSIC BOX

Beethoven, Piano Sonata in G Major, Op. 49, No. 2 (1795), Movement Two: Rondo Form

- The movement presents a modest, Irish–crystal clear rondo form movement that can be schematicized as A-B-A-C-A-coda. The A sections represent the rondo theme, a dancing, minuet-like tune set in triple meter and G major:

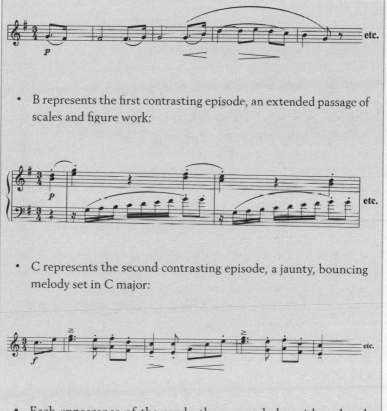

- B represents the first contrasting episode, an extended passage of scales and figure work:

- C represents the second contrasting episode, a jaunty, bouncing melody set in C major:

- Each appearance of the rondo theme concludes with a closed cadence, which effectively seals the theme from whatever follows. Conversely, the contrasting episodes each end with a lengthy open cadence, which creates tension that is resolved only with the arrival (whew!) of the rondo theme.
- A brief coda brings the ongoing process of departure and return to its conclusion and provides the sort of extended final cadence so typical of the Classical style.

Beethoven, Piano Sonata Opus 49

*O*pus is a word we encounter constantly.

In Latin, it means "work," as in "a work of art." Starting around the late 1700s, it became increasingly common for publishers to assign "opus numbers" to a composer's works to indicate the order in which they were published. Note well: opus numbers do not tell us the order in which works were composed, only the order in which they were published. For example, Beethoven's Opus 49 consists of two piano sonatas that were published together, as a set, in 1805; that's why we call them op. 49, nos. 1 and 2. However, the pieces themselves were composed ten years earlier, in 1795, and if they had been published then, they would have been published as Opus 3.

Not all of a composer's music will be published in his or her lifetime. Works published for the first time after the death of a composer are often designated as Opus posthumous. In Beethoven's case, such works are designated WoO, meaning "Without Opus."

On to sonata form, the most substantial and artistically significant of the Classical era forms.

CHAPTER 16

Classical Era Musical Form, Part Two

Sonata Form

The word *sonata* has been used, over the centuries, to mean many things musical, perhaps too many things musical, so before we begin our exploration of sonata form, it behooves us to get a handle on the various meanings of this overused term.

Sonata means "sounded piece," implying a work that is played, or "sounded," on an instrument or instruments. In its earliest usage (during the Renaissance) the word *sonata* was a generic term, synonymous with "instrumental music." (For our information, the complementary term to *sonata* is *cantata*, a "sung piece" of music.)

By the Baroque era, the word *sonata* began to be applied to various multi-movement instrumental works for both solo instruments and chamber groups. It wasn't until the Classical era that the term took on the two meanings for which it is still understood today.

First, sonata is an instrumental genre: a multi-movement work for solo piano or piano plus one other instrument. Since the Classical era, a piano sonata has been understood to be a multi-movement work for piano, and a designation such as *violin sonata* or *cello sonata* or *clarinet sonata* is understood to mean that instrument plus a piano.

Second, *sonata* as we understand it today refers to a specific musical form, sonata form. We will often see sonata form referred to as sonata allegro form, in order to further differentiate it from the instrumental genre of sonata.

In order to establish what makes sonata form special, we would step back for just a moment and observe what all the Classical era forms we've examined thus far have in common, and that is a *single, principal theme*.

Theme and variations form (unless entitled "double variations") features one theme only—no contrasts, departures, or returns. In minuet and trio form, the opening minuet is perceived as the principal theme. It is departed from and contrasted by the trio; it then returns to create thematic closure. Rondo form features one principal theme; it is departed from, contrasted, and returned to multiple times. Sonata form is that formal process that evolved to accommodate the presentation, interaction, and reconciliation of *multiple principal themes*, most typically two in number. Our first job, then, is to *deconstruct* sonata form. (We try, in this business, never to use the word *decompose*.)

Technically, sonata form evolved from something called Baroque binary dance form. Spiritually, sonata form was *inspired* by dramatic procedures inherent in opera. Let us discuss these dramatic procedures and, at the same time, observe their parallels in sonata form.

In the first act of an opera, we meet the principal characters and encounter the situation on which the drama will turn. In the first large section of a sonata form movement—a section called the exposition—we meet the (typically two) principal themes that become the characters in the musical drama. The expressive nature of those themes, and the degree of contrast between them, create the situation on which the musical drama will turn.

As an opera progresses, stuff happens: action and interaction between the characters, drama, comedy, pathos, bathos, whatever. In the second large part of a sonata form movement, called the development section, the themes interact in passages characterized by great harmonic instability and expressive interest to create drama, comedy, pathos, bathos, whatever.

The closing scene of an opera sees the denouement—the moment of truth—during which the dramatic situation plays itself out; the characters learn something of themselves and thus reconcile themselves to the events that have taken place. In the third part of a sonata form movement—called the recapitulation—the themes return in their original order but with important changes, changes that reduce the degree of contrast (and conflict) between them and that, as a result, allow the themes to be reconciled to one another. An opera will typically conclude with finale and curtain calls. A sonata form movement, much more often than not, will conclude with a coda, there to create a convincing sense of conclusion.

Exposition

It is in the exposition, the first large section of a sonata form movement, that the two principal themes of the piece are first heard.

In a typical sonata form movement, theme one is generally the more dramatic of the themes. It is followed by a modulating bridge, the transitional passage, or "bridge," that lies between themes one and two. It is called a *modulating* bridge because it effects a modulation, that is, a change of key, from the conclusion of theme one to the beginning of theme two. (Contrasting keys are a crucial element of contrast between the themes in a sonata form exposition.) We perceive a modulating bridge as a transition because it is built from fragmentary melodic ideas—from motives and sequences of those motives, scales, and passage work—and will not feature anything resembling a complete thematic melody with a beginning, middle, and end. Modulation is an aspect of harmony, and learning to perceive the subtleties of harmony takes years of study. So let's put it this way: We are not aware of the rotation of the earth on its axis; we're not holding on for dear life, stretched horizontally as the planet spins beneath us. But we'd be very aware of it if the earth stopped spinning on its axis. The dark side would freeze and the bright side would cook up rather quickly, and that would be that for us bipeds.

So it is with modulation. We might not notice it when keys are changing, as they do constantly in the course of a piece of tonal music, but we would certainly notice it if the modulation stopped. Modulation is the grease that lubricates the skids of tonal music. Without it, music would seem frozen and immobile. When modulation is properly used, a movement will soar through harmonic space, its propulsion supplied by a subtle and constant use of harmonic departure and return.

Theme two is generally the more lyric of the two principal sonata form themes.

MUSIC BOX

Mozart, Symphony in G Minor K. 550 (1788), Fourth Movement: Themes

The degree of contrast (and therefore implicit conflict) between Mozart's two principal themes is stunning, and looks forward to the sort of thematic confrontations typical of Beethoven's "heroic" music, still twenty years in the future.

• Theme one is usually the more dramatic of the themes and that is certainly the case here. Theme one is cast in G minor, and in terms of its melodic contour, it is nothing less than bi-polar, alternating between disjunct leaps and conjunct twitching (marked, respectively, as A and B here):

Likewise, the dynamics shift suddenly and disconcertingly from loud to soft, from soft to loud. The theme is underlain by a harmony long on dissonance and is played by the entire orchestra.

- Theme two is as sweet and smooth as a baby's bottom. In fact, it's hard to imagine a greater contrast than the one here between themes one and two. Theme two is set in the contrasting key and mode of B-flat major. The melody is uniformly conjunct and is played quietly by the strings and solo woodwinds.

If the themes are the musical "characters" in the drama that is sonata form, then the modulating bridge is "action music"; if the themes are more aria-like in their musical substance, then the modulating bridge is the recitative that connects those arias.

This exposition concludes with the cadence material, an extended bit of closing music. The cadence material will typically end with a closed cadence, clearly and unambiguously bringing the exposition to a close in the new, contrasting key of theme two.

Sonata form expositions are almost invariably meant to be repeated note for note. Consequently, following the closed cadence that concludes the cadence material, we should expect to hear the exposition repeated verbatim. Among other things, this repetition maximizes the listener's opportunity to know and recognize the themes and the key areas in which they are set (at least subliminally) before they're developed and recapitulated. In music, familiarity breeds perception.

The development section is an extended action sequence in which the themes are fragmented, recombined, transformed, re-dressed, undressed, cross-dressed, and generally treated according to the dramatic whim of the composer. There are only two generalizations we can make about development sections. One, they will be based on musical materials drawn from the exposition, and two, they will be characterized by thematic fragmentation and harmonic instability, meaning modulation.

The biggest difference between the exposition and the recapitulation has to do with effecting a tonal reconciliation between the themes. What this means is that theme two appears not in its own, contrasting key, but in the home key, the tonic key, of theme one. There are two reasons for this.

Reason number one: by reconciling the themes to each other tonally, the degree of contrast between them is reduced exponentially. Just as we would expect the characters in an opera to change, somehow, in response to their experiences across the span of the drama, so we must expect thematic change in sonata form as well. This change manifests itself in theme two, which will be heard in the key of theme one in the recapitulation.

Reason number two is purely practical. If a sonata form movement is to end convincingly in the home key, the key of theme one, then theme two and the ensuing cadence material will now, in the recapitulation, have to be set in the home key.

A sonata form coda can be quite substantial, as befits a musical form of such length and dramatic breadth. Looking slightly ahead, I'd point out that the codas in Beethoven's sonata form movements often take on the length and dramatic character of a second development section! It is therefore all the more unusual that the fourth movement of Mozart's G Minor Symphony K. 550—the themes of which we sampled in the preceding Music Box—does not include a coda, but rather, it concludes at the end of the recapitulation.

It's time to meet and greet the composer who took the Classical era forms to a level of beauty, expressive depth, invention, clarity, and charm that awed his greatest contemporaries (meaning Joseph Haydn and Ludwig van Beethoven) and continues to leave us breathless today: Wolfgang Mozart.

Wolfgang Theophilus / Gottlieb / Amade ("Don't Call Me Amadeus") Mozart (1756–1791)

Mozart was born in 1756 in Salzburg, two hundred miles or so southwest of Vienna. He was an extraordinary child prodigy, the prodigy by whom we measure prodigies to this day: playing harpsichord and violin at four, composing dances at five, touring Europe at six. He was baptized Johannes Chrysostomus Wolfgangus Theophilus Mozart. Wolfgang, who adored word games and puns, loved to play with his name. In his letters, he refers to himself as De Mozartini, Mozartus, and Mozarty. Sometimes he shuffled the letters around and called himself Romatz or Trazom. On occasion, he messed with his common name, Wolfgang, rendering it into Wolfgangus (Latin), Wolfgango (Italian), and Gnagflow (retrograde).

(For our information: it was while Mozart was living in Paris in the late 1770s that he began to use the French version of his middle name, Theophilus: Amadé. He never referred to himself as Amadeus, except in jest, and then always in the combination Wolfgangus Amadeus Mozartus.)

Mozart settled permanently in Vienna in 1781, and died there ten years later, in 1791. It was a ten-year period of perhaps unparalleled musical creation. During those years, Mozart wrote seventeen piano concertos and a clarinet concerto, every one of them a certifiable masterwork. He also composed a huge amount of chamber music, including eleven string quartets, five string quintets, an oboe quartet, a horn trio and quintet, a clarinet quintet, two piano quartets, six piano trios, and ten sonatas for violin and piano. Hyperbole aside, every one of them was a certifiable masterwork. During this period he composed a Mass, a requiem, and a cantata; ballet music, dance music, marches, arias and scenes for voice and orchestra, and songs. Between 1781 and 1791 he composed seven symphonies, each of them a certifiable masterwork. Between 1781 and 1791 he composed six of the greatest operas in the repertoire: *The Abduction from the*

Harem, *The Marriage of Figaro*, *Don Giovanni*, *Così fan Tutte*, *The Mercy of Titus*, and *The Magic Flute*.

Along the way he got married; fathered seven children (two of whom survived into adulthood); performed as a pianist, violinist, and conductor; maintained a successful teaching studio; wrote thousands of letters; traveled widely; attended the theater religiously; played cards, billiards, and bocce; and rode horseback for exercise. Not bad for someone portrayed as a giggling idiot in the movies.

Mozart at the Summit: The Last Three Symphonies

July of 1788 was a bad time for Wolfgang Mozart. It was hot and humid. His wife, Constanze, was in poor health and away at the spa in Baden. Mozart's own health was not particularly good, and his infant daughter, Teresa, had just died on June 29. Mozart, deeply in debt, was in the process of begging money from anyone who'd listen to him. Given this information, many commentators have, over the years, fallen into the trap of attributing autobiographical substance to Mozart's dark and even violent G Minor Symphony. Are they right?

No. Because, back to back with his G Minor Symphony, Mozart composed two of his most brilliant and upbeat works. He composed the glowing and gorgeous Symphony no. 39 in E-flat Major between June 10 and 26. He then composed the G Minor Symphony, completing it on July 25, after which he wrote out the magisterial and magnificent Symphony in C Major, the *Jupiter*, completing it on August 10.

In fact, Mozart was among the least autobiographical composers in the canon. His music came from a source frankly divorced from the issues and worries of the everyday.

Without resorting to voodoo or a discussion of extraterrestrials, it's hard to say where Mozart's music *did* come from. Let us take these three (dare we say?) perfect symphonies as an example. There are no extant sketches for any of them; Mozart apparently sat down and wrote them out in full score, as quickly and as neatly as a copyist could copy them. There are no erasures or alterations on the scores: everything is written with a firm, confident hand. (Mozart referred to this process as "copying out"; he did not refer to it as "composing." The implication is that the symphonies were complete, to their every detail, somewhere in his noggin, and all he needed to do was write them down, "copy them out," something he could do while he was talking, drinking, playing billiards, bowling, whatever.) Referring to the apparent ease with which he composed, Mozart once wrote, "I write music the way cows piss," an inelegant if not inaccurate appraisal of his abilities.

Mozart was freaky. It's no wonder he scared the bejesus out of his contemporaries.

CHAPTER 17

Classical Era Orchestral Genres, Part One

The Symphony: Music for Every Person

You will allow me a momentary contemplation of the joys and sorrows of terminology.

Sometimes terminology is our friend; but often it is not. The problem with musical terminology is that we have so much of it, literally thousands of years worth, in a Tower of Babel–like glut of Western languages from ancient Greek and Latin to Italian, French, German, Spanish, and English. It's not just the synonymous terms like *polyphony* and *counterpoint* that make us crazy but, worse, those seemingly synonymous terms that almost describe the same thing but not quite. For example, we tend to use the word *opera* to describe a sung stage play composed by a dead Europerson (and the occasional live non-Europerson as well). But there are sometimes subtle, sometimes huge differences between different types of opera. Only the most ardent of opera fans would be willing to attempt to differentiate between opera seria, dramma giocoso, opera buffa, opera verismo, bel canto opera, tonadilla, singspiel, grand opera, pocket opera, lyric opera, opera comique, and operetta.

Some terms imply distinctions that are almost impossible to recognize, while others—such as sonata and cantata—are extremely general, and mean different things depending upon when they were used.

Which brings us to the topic at hand. This chapter and the next are dedicated to the two most important orchestral genres of the Classical era: the symphony and the concerto, which are two very different sorts of music. And yet the words *symphony* and *concerto* mean *exactly the same thing*. *Symphony* comes from the Greek word *sumphonos*, meaning "sounding together, in agreement or in concordance with." The word *concerto* comes from the Latin word *concertare*, which means "sounding together, in agreement or in concordance with." Let's sort this out!

Symphony

The Romans appropriated the Greek word *sumphonos* and converted it to the word *symphonia*. The Latin word *symphonia* became the Italian word *sinfonia*.

It was during the late 1500s and very early 1600s—during the last years of the Renaissance and the first years of the Baroque era—that the Italian word *sinfonia* began being used to identify instrumental introductions, episodes, and interludes in otherwise vocal compositions. After 1630 or so, the word *sinfonia* (along with the word *sonata*) was used with increasing frequency to designate specifically instrumental compositions, the usage implying that multiple instrumental melodies were sounding together, in concordance, in agreement, in "symphony" with each other.

By the late 1600s, the word *sinfonia* had come to represent—in Baroque Italy—a particular type of opera overture now referred to as an Italian overture.

By the Classical era, the Baroque Italian-style overture had evolved into the Classical era *sinfonia*, or symphony. In doing so, it became the single most important genre of orchestral music of its time. In the hands of its greatest practitioners—Joseph Haydn and Wolfgang Mozart—the Classical era symphony became a transcendent art form.

Another Terminological Rant

Very often, the large instrumental ensemble that performs symphonies is itself called a symphony. But this is a misnomer. A symphony is a musical composition for orchestra; it is not a performing ensemble.

The great people of Cleveland got it right when they called their ensemble the Cleveland *Orchestra*. The citizens of the City of Brotherly Love got it right when they named their ensemble the Philadelphia *Orchestra*. An orchestra is a performing ensemble.

Many ensembles try to have it both ways: the CSO, the Chicago Symphony Orchestra; the LSO, the London Symphony Orchestra; and so forth. This particular designation is generally understood to mean "an orchestra that plays symphonies," which is accurate provided the orchestra plays *only* symphonies (no concertos, suites, symphonic poems, etc.).

Finally, there's a wonderful French word that has become synonymous with "large musical organizations," a word that means, literally, "loving harmony": *philharmonique*, or philharmonic. When we shorten the names of the great orchestras of Berlin, Los Angeles, and Vienna to the Berlin Phil., the LA Phil., and the Vienna Phil., what we're saying, literally, is "Berlin Love," "Los Angeles Love," and "Vienna Love." Love it.

Our understanding of what constitutes a symphony dates to the Classical era: a multi-movement work for orchestra designed to explore a range of moods. While many Classical era symphonies are three movements in length, we will focus on the more substantial four-movement template, a template that by the last third of the eighteenth century had become the symphonic standard.

Like sonata form, with which it co-evolved, the symphony has proved to be among the most substantial, artistically important, and long lived of all musical genres. Symphonies have been composed continuously from the 1740s to the present day. The orchestral repertoire is dominated by symphonies, and it is a rare orchestral concert that does not feature at least one. Many, if not most, listeners "cut their musical teeth" on the symphonic repertoire, as the symphonies of Haydn, Mozart, Beethoven, Schumann, Brahms, Dvořák, Tchaikovsky, Bruckner, and Mahler have attained iconic status as a uniquely popular canon within the concert repertoire. The symphony—like its chamber music cousin, the string quartet—is a Classical era genre that transcended the Classical era. All in all, the symphony demands our attention as do few other musical genres.

Four's the Charm: The Four-Movement Symphonic Template

The first movement—intellectually and emotionally challenging—addresses the mind: the intellect and the soul. The first movement of a Classical era symphony will usually be the most complex, both in terms of its structure and range of emotional expression. Almost invariably, this first movement will be in sonata form. Beethoven composed nine symphonies. Every one of them begins with a first-movement sonata form.

The second movement of the Classical era symphonic template is a lyric respite from the rigors of the first. It addresses the heart, and will generally not be characterized by the degree of contrast we were witness to in the first movement.

The third movement of a four-movement Classical era symphony is almost invariably cast as a minuet and trio: a stylized dance meant to reactivate the pelvic region of our bodies after the lyric respite of the second movement.

The fourth movement is typically fast and playful, more often than not in rondo form. It's a movement that's meant to leave us with a smile on our faces and a bounce in our steps.

This four-movement symphonic template did not appear from a vacuum. Let's examine some of the musical and social events that led to the creation of the four-movement symphony and its growing popularity among the middle class of the Enlightenment.

The musical genre most responsible for the invention of the symphony was Baroque era opera.

Oh opera, what would we have done without you?

Early in its development, opera composers created for opera a distinction between lyric singing and action singing. As we observed in chapter 9, by the 1660s and '70s the two basic aspects of Baroque operatic dramaturgy had been firmly established: aria and recitative.

Aria is the operatic equivalent of a soliloquy: a moment when time stops and a character reflects, emotes, and explores his or her inner world. The expressive essence of an aria lies in its music, not in its words. In an aria, the music focuses, crystallizes, and finally deepens the emotions beneath the words to a degree far beyond where the words by themselves can go.

Recitative (or recitation) is employed for real-time situations— for narration, dialogue, action—for any dramatic circumstance that requires rapid movement through a large amount of text. Recitative is by its nature a syllabic musical construct, and its rhythms and melodic contour follow those of the words being set. As such, the expressive essence of recitative lies in its words, not in its music.

Baroque era opera created a double precedent for the Classical era symphony. Not only did the symphony, in both name and substance, grow out of Baroque Italian-style opera overtures, but sonata form— with its opera-inspired contrasts, conflicts, reconciliation, and its differentiation between thematic music (aria) and developmental music (recitative)—lay at the dramatic heart of the Classical era symphony. Like dogs and humans, the symphony and sonata form coevolved; you can't have one without the other.

The new Enlightenment musical style crystallized in and around the multi-ethnic, multinational Habsburg capital of Vienna between about 1750 and 1780. As we observed in chapter 14, the Classical style is a cosmopolitan style, a synthesis of various national musical styles. Most conspicuous in this synthesis was the melding of south and north: the Italian tradition for vocal melody and lyric fluidity with the German traditions of compositional rigor and instrumental music.

Just as the Enlightenment celebrated the individual as the essential unit in society, so the evolving Enlightenment, or Classical, musical style celebrated the individual melody: the tune as the essential musical element. Economics also played a major role in creating what we now call the Classical style, as the growing middle class, whose particular needs and desires brought about the Enlightenment in the first place, became conspicuous consumers of music during the second half of the eighteenth century. They constituted a body of musical hobbyists and amateurs the size of which the Euro-music industry had never before seen. This new music-consuming class demanded music that was tuneful, direct, accessible, and entertaining, and the composers and publishing houses of the time were more than happy to oblige them.

In 1748, one hundred and ten years after the first public opera house was opened in Venice, the first public concert hall threw open its doors in Oxford, England, a testament to the growing financial power of the middle class and the growing popularity of instrumental music among that class.

Increasingly, symphonies played by orchestras became a favored entertainment for the middle class of Europe, so much so that by the early nineteenth century, middle-class tastes had come to be considered equal to those of the aristocracy, which had for so long been the essential musical patrons of Europe.

Joseph Haydn

Oh Haydn, what would we have done without *you*?

Joseph Haydn did not invent the genre of symphony. But he so redefined what a symphony was and could be that he is known, rightfully, as the father of the Classical symphony. Haydn's

symphonies—104 of which have survived—were the essential repertoire on which the growing popularity of the symphony was based.

In 1761, Prince Paul Anton Esterhazy, one of the richest men in all
of Europe, offered the twenty-nine-year-old Joseph Haydn the position
of vice-director of music at his court. Haydn took the job. Within a
year he was promoted to music director, a position he held until 1790.

In March of 1762, less than a year after Haydn had signed on with
the Esterhazys, his benefactor died at the age of fifty-one. Prince
Paul's successor, his younger brother Nicholas, was an even bigger
music freak than Prince Paul. And he was wise man: Prince Nicholas
treasured Joseph Haydn. Haydn later wrote:

> My prince was always satisfied with my works. Not only did I
> have the encouragement of constant approval, but as conductor
> of an orchestra I could make experiments, observe what produced
> an effect and what weakened it, and was thus in a position to
> improve, to alter, make additions or omissions, and be as bold as I
> pleased. I was cut off from the world; there was no one to confuse
> or torment me, and I was forced to become original. (Geiringer)

As music director for the Esterhazy family, Haydn had to conduct the court orchestra, which meant daily rehearsals and, almost
as frequently, orchestral performances. In addition, he was expected
to write the great bulk of the music the orchestra performed, and to
hire, fire, and take care of the musicians under his direction.

Haydn composed at least eighty-eight symphonies while
employed by the Esterhazy family; there were probably more, but
they have been lost. More than any other of his compositions, these
symphonies made Haydn famous, and by the late 1780s he wanted
to be free from what he increasingly considered his servitude to his
"master." Prince Nicholas was a good master, but, yes, master he was.

Fate intervened. The prince died on September 28, 1790. He was
succeeded by his son, Prince Anton Esterhazy, for whom music was not
an important thing. Haydn was granted a pension and his freedom.

From there he went to London, under the sponsorship of Johann Peter Saloman.

Haydn's first visit to England lasted from January of 1791 until July of 1792, and his second from February of 1794 to August of 1795. It was during his two English visits that he composed his last twelve symphonies, which are collectively referred to as his London Symphonies.

The London Symphonies

Haydn's London Symphonies were molded to what he perceived as being English taste and style. In them, Haydn struck an equal balance between intellect and feeling, between rhythmic energy and gentle lyricism; music that he believed would appeal to both the aristocratic and middle-class English listener. In reality, what he produced in his London Symphonies was the capstone of what he had always sought to achieve in his music: a perfect balance between head and heart, dance and song, a balance we hear and admire and resonate with to this very day.

Haydn's twelve London Symphonies are masterworks, each and every one of them, and they have been appreciated as such since the moment they were premiered.

As it turns out, the first of Haydn's symphonies to be performed in London during his first stay was one he had composed two years before, Symphony no. 92 in G Major. It is nicknamed the Oxford symphony because Haydn chose to have it performed in Oxford in 1791, when he was awarded the honorary degree of Doctor of Music.

Though not one of Haydn's London Symphonies, for two reasons we will use the Oxford as an example of Haydn's mature symphonic craft and the Classical symphonic template he did so much to standardize. First of all, it is also a great masterwork, characterized by the same sort of balance as the London Symphonies. And second, the London premiere of the symphony, on March 11, 1791, received a glowing review that demonstrated the breathless hero worship with which the mature Haydn was regarded by the European musical public.

(Please note: typical of the English at the time, the reviewer refers to the work not as a symphony but as a "grand overture," or simply an "overture.")

> The first concert under the auspices of Haydn was last night, and never was there a richer musical treat.
>
> It is [no wonder] that to souls capable of being touched by music, Haydn should be an object of homage, and even of worship; for, like our own Shakespeare, he moves and governs the passions at will.
>
> His new grand overture was pronounced by every scientific ear to be a most wonderful composition; but the first movement in particular rises in grandeur of subject, and in the rich variety of [theme] and passion, beyond even any of his own productions. The overture has four movements—an Allegro, Andante, Minuet, and Rondo. They are all beautiful . . . (Weiss/Taruskin, 1984, p. 315)

MUSIC BOX

Symphony No. 92 in G Major, "Oxford" (1789)

Haydn's Symphony no. 92 is a brilliant example of the Classical symphonic template, a four-movement design that traces a downward progression from head, to heart, to pelvis, to toes. The first movement, cast in sonata form, is the most intellectually and spiritually challenging of the four movements (head); the second, lyric movement offers a respite from the rigors of the first (the heart); the third movement, a minuet and trio, reactivates the body through dance rhythms (the pelvis); and the fourth movement, fast and upbeat in mood, leaves us with a bounce in our step (toes).

Haydn composed his first symphony in 1759, at a time when the symphony was a three-movement construct performed in private concerts for the aristocracy. By the 1780s, Haydn's symphonies were being created for public concerts. More than any other single factor, it was Haydn's symphonies themselves that elevated and popularized the genre, particularly with the middle class, who found his music—as we still do today—beautiful, brilliant, deeply felt, perfectly crafted and paced, and completely accessible.

The numbers tell the story. In 1777 the Concert Spirituel, late eighteenth-century Paris's most important public venue for orchestral music, devoted 3.5 percent of its programming to Haydn. In 1780 it devoted 21 percent of its programming to Haydn; in 1782, 39 percent; in 1784, 66 percent; and in 1790, an incredible 78 percent!

At a time when audiences were accustomed to hearing new works at every sitting, Haydn's symphonies demanded and received repeated performances. In the process, they became the first large body of orchestral music by a single composer to become a "canon," to become basic repertoire.

Thanks in equal part to the opera-inspired co-evolution of the symphony and sonata form, the rise of the public concert hall, and the brilliant example of Joseph Haydn, the symphony became—and remains to this day—music for every person.

CHAPTER 18

Classical Era Orchestral Genres, Part Two

The Solo Concerto

Along with the symphony, the solo concerto was the most important orchestral genre of the Classical era.

The solo concerto—featuring, as it does, the voice of the individual (the soloist) heard with and sometimes against the collective (the orchestra) became an almost perfect metaphor for the Enlightenment view of the individual in society. With this in mind, it should come as no surprise that the Classical era was a golden age of the solo concerto.

The primary instrumental beneficiaries of the Classical era solo concerto were the violin and the new-fangled "fortepiano." This is not to say that other instruments were ignored when it came to the Classical era concerto; in fact, solo concertos were composed for nearly every orchestral instrument during that era. Nevertheless, the greatest number of great concertos were written for violin and piano.

During the Baroque era the violin was brought to a state of technical perfection that has rarely been equaled and never surpassed. The era also saw the invention of the piano. For a moment, then, we return to the Baroque era.

The Violin Family

By the high Baroque, the viola da gamba family had been replaced by the viola da braccio family. Oh goody, new words to define!

First, the word *viola*. In its broadest meaning, a viola (or plural *viole*) would be any stringed instrument played with a bow, what in English is called a viol.

The viola da gamba family of stringed instruments developed in the fifteenth century, during the Renaissance. These are instruments played resting on (or between) *da gamba*, "on the gam" (i.e., on the leg). Da gamba instruments feature six or seven rather thin strings, a fretted neck (like a guitar), and a flat (as opposed to a rounded) back. They create an intimate, rather flat sound, perfect for accompanying Renaissance choruses and for playing the light dance music of the Renaissance and the early Baroque.

By the high Baroque, the viola da gamba family had been replaced by the viola de braccio, an entirely different family of strings. *Da braccio* means "on the arm," and the smaller of these instruments are played resting across the upper arm or shoulder. A viola da braccio has four relatively thick strings, a fretless neck, and a rounded back. Da braccio instruments also have something called a sound post, a rounded wooden peg that connects the treble side of the bridge to the back of the instrument, and a bass bar, a piece of wood glued directly underneath the bass side of the bridge that renders the top of the instrument rigid.

What the sound post and the bass bar do is transfer the strings' vibrations to the body of the instrument and then force the air inside of the instrument to circulate at a very fast rate of speed. Da braccio instruments have a much fuller, richer sound than do da gamba instruments, and they became increasingly popular as purely instrumental music developed during the Baroque.

Today, the viola da braccio family is known as the violin family, and it consists of four principal instruments, SATB (soprano, alto, tenor, and bass), violin, viola, cello, and bass.

The soprano instrument is the violin. It is the prima donna, the first lady of whatever ensemble it inhabits, something violinists never let us forget.

The alto instrument of the violin family is the viola, pitched a perfect fifth below the violin.

The tenor instrument of the violin family is properly named the violoncello. The reason why we sometimes see an apostrophe before the word *cello* is that 'cello is an abbreviation of the word *violoncello*.

The bass of the violin family is the contrabass or double bass. It was the last of the violin family to evolve, and did not become a regular member of the orchestra until the late eighteenth century.

The violin and viola are today played resting beneath the chin; if you'll look at a modern violin or viola, you will see that a chin rest has been added to them. You can always identify violinists and violists by the calluses on their necks. They affectionately refer to them as their hickies, but for the rest of us they're just kind of gross.

They Build 'Em Best in Cremona

A primary reason the violin became so overwhelmingly superior to earlier stringed instruments has to do with a series of violin builders (luthiers) living and working in the northern Italian city of Cremona. These luthiers created instruments that continue to inspire unadulterated awe (and astronomical prices) to this day. No matter how much computer modeling is employed, no matter what technology has been brought to bear on the subject of violin making, the instruments of Amati, Stradivari, and Guarneri are still considered the standard by which all other string instruments are measured.

Why are these Baroque era instruments so good? Why have they endured? For starters, they were made out of wood taken from trees that had grown during the so-called Little Ice Age of roughly 1400–1800 BCE. Trees grew much more slowly during this period, and the grain of their wood was correspondingly tighter and denser.

These trees lived in a preindustrial atmosphere, and thus they didn't ingest the industrial pollutants that trees have to breathe today. The exact formulas of the varnishes and glues these makers used are still unknown. The instruments have patinated over time, having been exposed to everything from airborne pollutants to the salts in performers' perspiration. They've also been modified: the necks have been made longer, the bridges made higher, and heavier bass bars have been added.

The oldest surviving violin—an instrument nicknamed Charles IX—was built in Cremona in 1564 by the founder of the Amati family dynasty, Andrea Amati. His grandson Nicolò Amati lived from 1596 to 1684 and was the greatest luthier of his clan. His most important student was Antonio Stradivari, who lived from 1644 to 1737. Stradivari's most important student was Giuseppe (del Gesù) Guarneri, who lived from 1698 to 1744.

(Hold the phone! Might I point out that despite the glue and varnish fumes they breathed on a daily basis, Amati lived eighty-eight years and Stradivari ninety-three! Could we be onto something here?)

The Piano

In discussing the piano, we again run into some rather confusing terminology, as we encounter the completely interchangeable words *pianoforte*, *fortepiano*, and *piano*. Generally, we use the term *fortepiano* to refer to early pianos, pianos made with wooden harps between about 1710 and 1830, and the terms *pianoforte*, or simply *piano*, for metal harped pianos, built from around 1825 to the present day. We'll run with this distinction with the understanding that, in reality, these three terms refer to the same instrument.

The first working drawings for what today we call a piano date to around 1700. They were drawn (and the first pianos were built) by a Paduan-born, Florence-based harpsichord builder by the name of Bartolomeo Cristofori. Cristofori's invention addressed a growing demand for a portable keyboard instrument that could accent certain notes over others and follow the dynamic contours of the human voice, something the standard portable keyboard instrument of the time, the harpsichord, could not do. (As its name suggests, a harpsichord is a mechanical harp. The player doesn't directly pluck the strings; instead, they are plucked by a plectrum activated by a keyboard. The resulting timbre is dry and brittle, what the great English conductor Thomas Beecham described as sounding like "two skeletons copulating on a tin roof.")

Cristofori created an instrument he called a *gravicembalo col piano e forte*. *Gravicembalo* means "big harpsichord"; *col* means "with"; *piano e forte* means "soft and loud": a pianoforte is therefore a "soft-loud."

In truth, a big harpsichord it was not. With his "soft and loud," Cristofori used touch-sensitive hammers to strike the strings, rather than picks to pluck them. In doing so, he created an instrument capable of playing graded dynamics that is, capable of getting progressively louder and softer.

By 1770, such fortepianos had become the preferred keyboard of choice, and by 1800 they had replaced the harpsichord almost entirely. By the 1840s, metal harps had replaced wooden harps, and by the 1870s, the "modern" piano as we know it had come into existence.

The expressive power of the violin and the piano made both the ideal vehicles for the Classical era solo concerto.

Nobody Does It Better: Mozart's Concertos

The same lyric and dramatic skills that made Mozart the greatest opera composer who ever lived also made him the greatest composer of concertos who ever lived.

A subjective statement? No, not really.

Wolfgang Mozart composed more than forty concertos, including more than twenty for keyboard, five for violin, four for horn, and concertos for flute, for flute and harp, for oboe, for bassoon, and for clarinet, among others. Pride of place must go to his keyboard and violin concertos, the overwhelming number of which he composed as performance vehicles for himself. The percentage of first-class, grade-A masterworks among Mozart's concertos very nearly approaches 100 percent, and for no subset of his concertos is this truer than for the seventeen piano concertos he composed during the years he lived in Vienna, between 1781 and 1791. What this means for us, as music consumers, is that we cannot go wrong by listening to, studying, and falling in love with Mozart's seventeen "Viennese" piano concertos, numbers 11 through 27. For sheer beauty, elegance, brilliance, and imagination, we would be hard put to find a more consistently glorious set of works.

Johanne Chrysostom Wolfgang Gottlieb Mozart (1756–1791) Library of Congress, Prints and Photographs Division, LC-USZ62-87246

Double Exposition Form

Mozart composed so many great concertos that he is often credited (wrongly) with having invented double exposition form; sonata form adapted to the peculiar needs of a solo concerto.

It's called double exposition form because instead of featuring one repeated exposition, as in sonata form, it boasts two separately composed expositions—neither of which is repeated—before moving on to the development section, recapitulation, and coda.

During the course of the first exposition, called the orchestral exposition, the orchestra plays the themes, typically two in number. During the course of the second exposition, called the solo exposition, the soloist plays the themes.

A Mozart double exposition form movement will typically include a third principal theme. This third theme will be played only by the soloist, and is therefore generally referred to as the solo theme. The idea of creating a theme exclusively for the soloist is brilliant. First, it establishes a degree of parity between the orchestra and the soloist by allowing the soloist to introduce at least one theme. Second, since the solo theme is played *only* by the soloist, it can be engineered specifically for the idiosyncrasies of the solo instrument. For example, in a violin concerto, the theme might include high, long-sustained notes; in a piano concerto, the theme might feature short, percussive, quickly repeated notes.

The Cadenza

There's one final feature of a double exposition form movement of which we should be aware, and that is the cadenza. During the high Baroque, it became standard for an opera aria to pause just before its end, in order to allow a singer the opportunity to improvise some short (or long) bit of virtuosic vocal fluff before the aria came to its conclusion (and thus inspire his or her audience claque to scream with delight while other singers' claques would hiss with derision; this, after all, was a time when opera was considered a contact sport).

By Mozart's time, it had become standard operating procedure to interrupt the final cadence of a double exposition form movement to allow the soloist to perform just such an extended solo. This solo was named for the harmonic progression—the cadence—it interrupted, thus the designation *cadenza* (*cadenza* being the Italian word for "cadence"). In Mozart's day, these cadenzas were typically provided by the soloists themselves. We often read that they were improvised, but in reality cadenzas were usually carefully prepared beforehand by the soloists, so as to dazzle the audience with their virtuosity and, at the same time, exploit their own particular technical strengths.

When it came to *his* piano concerti, Mozart would indeed improvise something on the spot just because he could. Mozart rarely notated a cadenza, which means that in performance today, it's up to the soloist to create a cadenza of his own or to use one of the many cadenzas written by other composers or pianists over the years.

MUSIC BOX

Mozart, Piano Concerto No. 1 in G Major, K. 453 (1784); First Movement: Double Exposition Form

Themes One and Two

Themes one and two are introduced by the orchestra in the orchestral expositions. The beginnings of these themes—which will be played by both the orchestra and the solo piano—are notated here.

Theme One

Theme Two

continued on next page

Theme Three ("Solo Theme")

This theme is played only by the piano and makes its first appearance in the solo exposition. With its graceful embellishments (the "turn" in measure 2, the grace-note in measure 3, and the trill in measure 4), and variety of articulation (note in particular the rising staccato scales in measure 7), it is "custom-built" for the light touch and clarity of nuance characteristic of a contemporary fortepiano.

Mozart composed this concerto for a student named Barbara ("Babette") Ployer. Because he composed the concerto for someone else, he wrote for it a couple of cadenzas. They may not be as long or as technically difficult as a cadenza he would have improvised, but they're his, for which we press them to our bosoms and say, thank you!

The Relationship Between Solo Piano and Orchestra

When we hear a Mozart piano concerto performed today, we're most likely to hear the piano part played on a modern concert grand. In the hands of a professional pianist, such a piano can bury the strings and the winds and hold its own against the brass. But Mozart wasn't composing for a nine-foot-long, thousand-pound piano; he was composing for a five-and-a-half-foot-long, hundred-and-fifty-pound piano built from balsa wood and dental floss. Such an instrument had no more chance of going toe to toe with even a small orchestra than I would against boxer Marvin Hagler.

Thus, in his piano concertos, Mozart accompanies the piano the way he would accompany a very light voiced soprano singer. He never, for example, puts the orchestral strings in the same range as the piano when the piano is playing a theme, because the theme would be drowned out, just as a light-voiced singer would be drowned out. When it comes to orchestral accompaniment, a Mozart piano concerto is about deftness and lightness of touch, and is, in this way, exceedingly operatic.

Taken all together, from a quantitative and qualitative point of view, Mozart's piano concertos are the greatest set of concertos ever composed. That is not an opinion; it is a fact. They are desert island stuff, and we cannot live without them.

CHAPTER 19

Send in the *Buffone*

Opera in the Classical Era

We return to the most influential of all musical genres, opera. In doing so, we step back in time, to late seventeenth-century Baroque Italian opera, which was, by far, the most important and influential operatic tradition of its time.

Late seventeenth-century Italian opera was the network television of its day: a medium with tremendous artistic potential but even greater profit potential. Sadly, *artistic potential* and *profit potential* are not generally synonymous, and this was as true in the seventeenth century as it is today. As it became increasingly popular, the Italian opera industry aimed lower and lower, broadening its common denominator in a successful attempt to attract an ever larger audience. The price of that success was dramatic integrity, literary quality, expressive veracity, opera that sacrificed art in favor of low farce, cheap titillation, and overblown spectacle. Such was the state of Italian opera around the year 1700.

During the first decades of the eighteenth century, a number of talented and like-minded Italian poets, disgusted by the literary vacuity of contemporary opera, decided to do something about it. Spearheaded by a Venetian-born poet and librettist named Apostolo Zeno—who lived from 1668 to 1750 (making him a contemporary of Johann Sebastian Bach)—these poets sought to reinvest opera with a degree of literary quality and dramatic truth by refusing to dumb-down their libretti.

Apostolo Zeno had ample opportunity to put his ideas about opera reform into action. In 1718, at the age of fifty, he moved to Vienna, where he was appointed imperial poet and librettist until 1729, when he was replaced by a thirty-one-year-old Roman-born poet/librettist named Pietro Antonio Domenico Bonaventura Metastasio.

Opera Seria

The operatic reform movement begun by Zeno was brought to its fulfillment by Metastasio (1698–1782), who was so highly respected by his contemporaries that he was actually compared to Dante and Homer. Through the strength of his example, Metastasio created a literary template that became standard operating operatic procedure for the next hundred years and more, an operating procedure that came to be known generically as opera seria, or "serious opera."

Metastasio's example rested on the twenty-seven libretti that he himself authored. (For our information: *libretto* means, literally, "little book" and constitutes the script, the words, of an opera. The plural of *libretto* is *libretti*, just as the plural of *spaghetto* is *spaghetti*, and the plural of *graffito* is *graffiti*. A playwright or poet who writes a libretto is called a librettist. Only in the rarest cases will opera composer and librettist be the same person; Richard Wagner is the most notable of all such operatic multitaskers. Pietro Metastasio was strictly a librettist, and one of the greatest in the history of opera.) Metastasio's libretti were set to music hundreds of times by more than three hundred composers, including Vivaldi, Handel, Gluck, J. C. Bach, and Mozart. (Mozart's final opera, *La Clemenza di Tito*, or "The Mercy of Titus," of 1791, is a setting of a Metastasio libretto.)

By 1740 or so, Metastasian opera seria had come to dominate European opera. These operas followed a template that typically featured two pairs of lovers, a "magnanimous tyrant," and a plot that turned on heroism and/or sublime renunciation of some sort or another. The musical structure was utterly formulaic. Cast in three acts, these operas mechanically alternated recitatives and arias with one another. The recitatives were used for dialogue and action, while the arias allowed principal characters to vent their emotions or reflect on current events. Only rarely was the alternation of recitative and aria broken up by duets, ensembles, and simple choral numbers.

As one wag put it, the recitative loaded the gun and the aria fired it.

Metastasio's attempt to secure and preserve dramatic integrity through standardization ultimately had the opposite effect. The clockwork alternation of recitative and aria reduced the dramatic impact of Metastasian opera seria to near-nothing. Most librettists were not talented writers like Metastasio, and their opera seria libretti were hopelessly stiff and predictable.

With the drama predictable and the recitatives tedious, the overwhelming interest in Metastasian opera seria lay in the arias, and the arias lay in the throats of the singers. Increasingly, opera seria audiences came to hear not a story or even the "music" per se, but rather, the singers sing arias.

Singers—including, first and foremost, the famed Italian castrati—made endless and arbitrary demands on the poets and composers who created the opera, compelling them to alter, add, embellish, and even substitute arias without any respect for dramatic or musical appropriateness.

Moreover, the melodic embellishments and cadenzas the singers added at will were all too often mere tasteless displays of vocal acrobatics. It was Baroque opera seria that led Samuel Johnson to write, "The Italian opera is an exotic and irrational entertainment."

Indeed it was.

Many contemporary artists, writers, philosophers, and composers began to question the relevance of opera seria in the developing age of Enlightenment. The upshot was that even as opera seria flourished, yet another operatic reform movement began in the 1730s.

Baroque opera seria and the elites who consumed it outside of Italy fell under increasing attack from artists and thinkers at the vanguard of the Enlightenment. No one was more "on the vanguard" of Enlightenment thought than the intellectual, philosopher, composer, and author Jean-Jacques Rousseau. Rousseau—who was born in Geneva in 1712 and died outside of Paris in 1778—was an alienated intellectual and a terrific pain in the aristocratic derrière of his time. Whatever the topic, he blasted the establishment: church, state, and king. If he'd been born just a few years earlier, he wouldn't have lasted very long. But in the 1740s and '50s, the spirit of the Enlightenment was such that he became a prophet.

Rousseau believed in what he called the "natural man": that humankind was inherently good but had been corrupted by civilization. He held that society was an artificial, unnatural construct that was, ultimately, detrimental to the well-being of individual humans.

Rousseau launched a devastating attack on opera seria. By criticizing its musical and literary conventions, he was not just calling into question many of the basic aesthetic assumptions of the high Baroque; he was also attacking the aristocracy who, outside of Italy, consumed and supported opera seria. Rousseau claimed that the genre's plots and characters were as hopelessly artificial as their complicated and overblown music. He insisted that only an operatic genre that portrayed real people in real life, singing "natural" music, could be relevant to the humanistic spirit of the Enlightenment.

Rousseau wielded the power of a visionary, and his ideas sparked a major controversy. We must keep in mind that in those days, opera, more than any other extant media, was at the vanguard of depicting European society's self-image, just as television, the movies, and the Internet are in the vanguard of depicting our society's self-image.

The *merde* hit the fan in 1752, when Rousseau's attacks on the old-fashioned, state-subsidized French opera exploded in a pamphlet battle called *La Guerre des Bouffons*, the "War of the Clowns." It was called thus because it was triggered by the presence, in Paris, of an Italian opera company that, for two seasons, had enjoyed fabulous success performing Italian comic operas, or *opere buffe*.

Opera Buffa

Italian opera buffa evolved not from the operatic tradition born of the Florentine Camerata but rather, from street theater: the Italian *commedia dell'arte*.

The commedia dell'arte was born in the sixteenth century and featured traveling theatrical troupes that improvised comedic and musical episodes around certain archetypal characters that anyone could recognize. The most significant character division in opera buffa—and this betrays its common roots—is that between the savvy, street-smart servants and members of the lower class and the blundering, pompous aristocrats, doctors, lawyers, and merchants, or members of the upper and aristocratic classes.

Given the directness of its music and plots, and the social criticism inherent in its commedia dell-arte archetypes, it's no surprise that Rousseau and his followers endorsed opera buffa as the ideal opera for the age of Enlightenment.

Specifically, Rousseau and his clique embraced an opera entitled *La Serva Padrona*, "The Maid as Mistress," composed in 1733 by Giovanni Battista Pergolesi. Pergolesi was born in Iesi, in central Italy in 1710. He spent his professional life—what there was of it—in Naples, where he experienced great success. His early death in 1736 due to tuberculosis robbed posterity of a prodigious talent.

La Serva Padrona

La Serva Padrona represents an attempt by certain Italian composers and librettists to change the operatic language. Specifically, their efforts were directed toward making the entire operatic design more "natural"—more flexible in structure; more "natural" in expressive content; and less laden with vocal virtuosity.

Typical of these early Enlightenment Italian reform operas—these *opere buffe*—*La Serva Padrona* features the following elements: One, its music is lively and catchy, and plumbs a middle ground between the sophisticated and the popular. Two, the opera follows no formula; the music and the text are entirely in the service of the story being told. Three: typical of early *opera buffa*, the opera features a small, portable cast of three, only two of whom have singing parts. (Serpina is a soprano. Uberto is a bass. Vespone is a mute. Great idea: have one of your principal characters in an opera be a mute! This is definitely going to keep production costs down.)

The story of *La Serva Padrona* revolves around a ruse by which a servant girl (Serpina, "the serpent," also known as "temptation") tricks an old bachelor into marriage. It features familiar characters behaving, and misbehaving, in familiar ways. Whether or not we are, ourselves, maidservants, we can identify with Serpina and her desire for domestic security. Whether or not we are, ourselves, aging bachelors, we can identify with Uberto's desire to be loved and his fear of commitment. This ability, for middle-class audiences to identify personally with the characters and dramatic situations of *opera buffa*, cuts to the heart and soul of what the genre is all about.

MUSIC BOX

Giovanni Battista Pergolesi, *La Serva Padrona* (1733); Recitative and Aria, "Son imbrogliato io"

This recitative and aria is Uberto's "big number." "Son imbrogliato io" means "I'm all mixed up," and all mixed up Uberto is, as he contemplates the pros and cons of giving up his bachelorhood for the slinky Serpina.

continued on next page

Note the following:

- The orchestra enters about halfway through Uberto's recitative. This would *never* happen in an opera seria, in which only royal or divine characters sing recitatives accompanied by the orchestra. But this is opera buffa, in which dramatic need—in this case, Uberto's growing distress—not ritual or convention, drives the music.
- Uberto's aria is set in "patter style," which means that Uberto sings quickly and syllabically. He is confused, his mind is racing, and he's working himself into a tizzy. The effect is both comic and extremely ingratiating; we, as an audience, like Uberto; we're rooting for him, and we want him to figure this out!
- This recitative and aria reveals to us a great truth: that comedy is often capable of imparting much more pathos than breast-beating and melodrama. So-called comic opera is about recognizing and portraying life's everyday absurdity and trying to negotiate it with some degree of dignity.
- The empathy we feel for Uberto is a creation of Pergolesi's music.

Mozart's Operas and the Operatic Ensemble

An operatic ensemble is a piece for three or more soloists, occurring most typically at the end of an act.

The ensemble became an integral part of the Italian comic opera tradition in the years immediately prior to Mozart's birth. Where opera seria generally consisted of alternating recitative and arias, opera buffa added to these elements ensemble, or group, singing, in which three or more characters sing at the same time. Because of the dramatic interaction inherent in such a group sing, ensembles tend to move the action ahead. The Classical era operatic ensemble transformed opera into a much more dramatically dynamic genre than was possible using the comparatively static procedures of opera seria.

A Classical era operatic ensemble will have the dramatic thrust and action of recitative, the melodic contour of aria, with all of it accompanied nonstop by the orchestra. We would emphatically observe: no one, before or since, has written better operatic ensembles than Mozart.

Mozart composed operas in every major style of his day. Of his twenty-two complete and incomplete operas, musical plays, and cantatas, nine are in the style of opera seria, seven in the style of opera buffa, and six are singspiels. Opera seria continued to be popular among a large segment of the opera audience well into the nineteenth century. Among Mozart's *opere serie* are *Idomeneo* of 1781, his first operatic masterwork and by consensus the single greatest opera seria ever composed, and *La Clemenza di Tito*, of 1791, his final opera.

Mozart also composed singspiels, German-language musical theater works that combine music and dialogue. It just so happens that he composed the two greatest and most enduring singspiels in the repertoire: *The Abduction from the Harem* of 1782 and *The Magic Flute* of 1791.

And Mozart composed *opere buffe*. His first complete opera, written when he was twelve, was an opera buffa entitled *La finta semplice*, "The Pretended Simpleton." Mozart composed the three greatest *opere buffe* of all time in collaboration with the librettist Lorenzo Da Ponte: *The Marriage of Figaro* of 1786, *Don Giovanni* of 1787, and *Così Fan Tutte* (which translates, roughly, "Thus All Women Do") of 1789.

Don Giovanni, K. 527 (1787)

Don Giovanni is Italian for Don Juan: a bipedal archetype for the male phallus unfettered by moral restraint or conscience.

In Mozart/Da Ponte's version of the story, "crime" and "punishment" bookend the opera. At the very beginning of act 1, the don kills a father attempting to defend his daughter's honor. At the very conclusion of act 3, the dead father, in the guise of a statue, appears at

Don Giovanni's castle. The statue offers the don a chance to repent his sins, and when the don refuses, the statue drags him down to hell.

For all his obvious flaws, Mozart's Don Giovanni is a most ingratiating character, for which much of the credit goes to Lorenzo Da Ponte. Without a doubt, the particularly dashing "Don Juan" of Da Ponte's libretto is based on one of his best friends, Giovanni Jacopo Casanova de Seingalt—*the* Casanova!

Nevertheless, *Don Giovanni* is Mozart's opera. A libretto is not a self-contained, self-standing "play," and a great librettist—and Da Ponte was a *great* librettist—knows he must leave room for the music to interpret and deepen the characters and the dramatic situations. In an opera, the composer is the dramatist, and Mozart was one of the great, if not the greatest of all, musical dramatists in history.

MUSIC BOX

Mozart, *Don Giovanni*, Act I, Scene 1

The opening scene of *Don Giovanni* consists of five distinct episodes, during which characters are introduced and a crime is committed. During the course of the opening scene, different characters come and go, comedy and tragedy stand side by side, the orchestra plays almost continuously, and the dramatic momentum never flags. Throughout it all, there is no sense of formula or predictability. Rather, everything is in the service of dramatic continuity and line.

Act 1, Scene 1, Part 1: Aria

The curtain rises on Don Giovanni's manservant Leporello, who is wrapped in a cloak and pacing back and forth in front of a house. Leporello's entrance aria, entitled "Notte giorno faticar" ("Night and day I slave away!"), is the stuff of all disgruntled domestics, during which Leporello bemoans his life as a servant.

Listen for: Leporello's machine gun–like diction, which instantly identifies this as a patter-style opera buffa aria and Leporello as the comic relief.

Act 1, Scene 1, Part 2: Trio

Don Giovanni and Donna Anna burst out of the house. He is trying to get away and usually wears a little mask as a disguise. She is trying to detain and unmask him. Meanwhile, a frightened Leporello observes and comments on the scene.

Listen for: the short, fast, dramatic musical phrases that Donna Anna and Don Giovanni sing at (and occasionally with) each other. The sense of physical action and danger is palpable in this episode.

Act 1, Scene 1, Part 3: Trio

Donna Anna's shrieking has woken her father, the Commendatore, who makes his entrance wearing his nightshirt and holding his sword. Donna Anna runs off, in search of help. In the meantime, Don Giovanni and the Commendatore men fight, and with a climactic dissonance in the orchestra, the don runs the Commendatore through with his sword.

Listen for: the Commendatore's deep, ponderous bass voice, which contrasts mightily with the agile baritone of the don. Their dual is portrayed entirely by the orchestra.

Act I, Scene I, Part 4: Trio

The Commendatore drops like a cast-iron cannoli, and a haunting trio ensues, during which each man onstage—Don Giovanni, the Commendatore, and Leporello—expresses an entirely different view of what has just happened. The Commendatore's is the voice of death as he contemplates his approaching demise. Don Giovanni's is the voice of thoughtless impulse; he casually dismisses his actions and wishes only that the Commendatore had put up a better fight. Leporello is mortified; his is the voice of conscience.

continued on next page

Listen for: the quiet, drooping, deathly mood projected by this trio, which contrasts so profoundly with the dual that preceded it and the recitative that follows.

Two long chromatic descents mark the Commendatore's death. There is no closed cadence, no pause to seal this episode off from what happens next. Instead, a modulation transits to:

Act 1, Scene 1, Part 5: Recitative

Without warning, a comic recitative between Don Giovanni and Leporello ensues. It is the first recitative of the opera, and it transports us from the deathly twilight of the trio back to the present.

Mozart's is the art of the Classical era, opera buffa–inspired ensemble at its best. We can only weep when we contemplate the further glories he would have created had he lived a full life. He died in Vienna, almost certainly of acute rheumatic fever, on December 5, 1791, age thirty-five years, ten months, and eight days. As it turned out, it was almost exactly a year later that a new guy rode into Vienna on the stagecoach from the Rhineland, a nearly twenty-two-year-old piano slinger with bad hair and a bad attitude: the bad boy from Bonn, Ludwig ("my friends call me Louis") van Beethoven. In the absence of Mozart, it was Beethoven who would soon enough become the enfant terrible of Viennese music. We'll meet him in the next chapter.

CHAPTER 20

A Revolutionary Artist for a Revolutionary Time

Ludwig van Beethoven

'm always fascinated to see where music histories and appreciation textbooks put Beethoven. Should he be considered an eighteenth-century man or a nineteenth-century man; a Classical era composer or a Romantic era composer?

When it comes to Beethoven, such artificial constructs of century demarcation and historical periods are useless. Like Beethoven's exact contemporary Napoleon Bonaparte, he was a man of his time who nevertheless changed the face of Western history (in Beethoven's case, the history of Western music). Consequently, we're not going to put Beethoven anywhere; he gets his own chapter.

We begin our examination of Beethoven and the age of revolution with a telling comparison between the first-movement sonata forms of two relatively contemporary works, Haydn's Symphony no. 88 of 1787 and Beethoven's Symphony no. 5 of 1808. We're going to compare and contrast the first half of their first themes, which are notated here.

First, Joseph Haydn's Symphony no. 88 (1787), first movement, theme one:

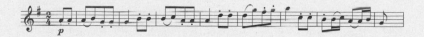

And now Ludwig van Beethoven's Symphony no. 5 in C Minor, op. 67 (1808), first movement, theme one:

Questions, questions, questions. Let's start by asking a subjective but absolutely necessary question: expressively, what are the themes about?

I would suggest that Haydn's theme is about "nice": nice, upbeat mood and expressive restraint, music that put the "C" in the *Classical style*.

I would further suggest that we hear Beethoven's Fifth Symphony the way his contemporaries heard it: as a fearsome, ferocious, cutting-edge piece of modernist art; gut-wrenching and explosive music written in an age accustomed to artistic good taste and expressive restraint. Whatever Beethoven's theme is about, it is most certainly not about "nice." Its jagged, dark character and discontinuous rhythm evoke violence and turmoil that would seem to be a metaphor for *something* above and beyond the music itself.

Haydn's theme begins in the key of G major, imbuing it with a bright sensibility, one that meets the listener 90 percent of the way. Beethoven's theme begins in C minor, and rarely will we hear the dark edginess of minor put to better use than in the opening of Beethoven's Fifth.

Next question: What is the nature of each thematic melody?

Both themes are highly motivic and compact, as befits two native

German-speaking composers. However, Haydn's theme is a tune, a vocally conceived melody with a clear beginning, middle, and end. Beethoven's theme is not a tune. Try singing it: you'll find that it doesn't fit the voice at all. Its range, its disjunct contour, and its nonstop sequencing of a single, four-note motive contribute to creating a theme that is utterly nonvocal.

In reality, Beethoven's theme is a mosaic. An examination of the orchestral score reveals that consecutive four-note motives are each played by a different group of instruments. The overall effect is a mosaic-like assemblage of motives rather than a vocally conceived tune. Beethoven's theme *is* the motive and its various permutations, unadorned by any embellishment or connective tissue.

Third: Are the phrases of the themes balanced or not balanced?

The melodic phrases in Haydn's theme are *rhymed*: balanced, predictable, and easily followed (like the phrases of "Twinkle, Twinkle, Little Star" or "Happy Birthday to You," for example). The melodic phrases in Beethoven's theme are open-ended and prose-like, neither balanced nor predictable. Haydn's theme is projected against a regular, steady, dance-like beat. Beethoven's keeps starting and stopping with rhetorical effect, as if some great and important story is being introduced replete with dramatic pauses and oratorical flair.

Rhythm in Haydn's theme is indivisible from pitch. But in Beethoven's theme, rhythm *is* divisible from pitch: Beethoven's thematic motive is, first and foremost, a rhythm and not a melodic idea. We don't need to hear a single pitch to recognize Beethoven's thematic motive: three short, hammering repeated notes followed by a longer note: DOT-DOT-DOT-DASH.

Last, what preexisting musical style does each piece represent?

Haydn Symphony no. 88 is a brilliant example of the Viennese Classical style. It exhibits the three basic aspects that together define classicism: clarity of line, meaning a clear, accessible, vocally inspired theme; beautiful proportions, meaning beautifully balanced musical phrases; and purity of conception, meaning artistic restraint and good taste.

What style is Beethoven's Fifth?

While Beethoven's Fifth is structured along the lines of a Classical era symphony, it doesn't sound like Classical era music. Point in fact, Beethoven's Fifth only sounds like Beethoven's Fifth; it is sui generis and adheres to no preexisting style. Beethoven's Fifth Symphony is a self-referential piece of art, and thus the essence of modernism.

This brief and telling comparison between themes by Haydn and Beethoven demands that we ask one more question: What gave Beethoven the temerity to compose music so far off the Classical era aesthetic track, a track that was perfectly good enough for the inexhaustible Haydn?

There were internal and external factors that shaped the development of Beethoven's music: personal issues on one hand, and environmental issues on the other. He was the right man in the right place at the right time, and his music gives voice and substance to his revolutionary age as does no other.

Let's take a look at some of the events that shaped Beethoven's life and music.

On July 14, 1789, a Parisian mob stormed the city jail, the Bastille, looking for weapons. The mob freed seven prisoners, killed the guards, killed the warden, killed the mayor of Paris, and then paraded around Paris with the heads of the murdered guards on pikes. (Who says you can't fight city hall?) Within three years, France was proclaimed a republic and the country was rallying against German invaders intent on returning their cousin, Louis XVI, to the throne. In the end, the problem of what to do with Louis XVI took care of itself. He tried to flee France and was captured. A revolutionary tribunal sentenced him to death, and he was guillotined in January of 1793. Nine months later, in October of 1793, Queen Marie-Antoinette was guillotined as well.

At exactly the same time, a young Corsican artillery lieutenant named Napoleon Bonaparte began his rise through the ranks of the French army.

It is hard for us to fathom today the impact of the French

Revolution on contemporary Europe. Unlike the Russian or Chinese revolutions of the twentieth century, the French Revolution occurred in what was the most advanced country of the time. France was the intellectual center of the Enlightenment. Europeans in the eighteenth century were in the habit of taking ideas from France. Therefore, they were, depending on their position, all the more excited (the promise of the Enlightenment fulfilled!) or alarmed (the anarchy of the mob!) when revolution broke out in Paris.

In July of 1789, Beethoven was an impressionable, energetic, testosterone-filled eighteen-and-a-half-year-old. He was inspired by the heady sense of individuality and change that the Revolution engendered, though, at the same time, frightened by the potential for chaos and anarchy that the revolution also seemed to represent. One way or the other, for Beethoven and his generation, it was clear that nothing was forever, including the Viennese Classical style.

Beethoven was born in the Rhineland city of Bonn on December 16, 1770.

His enormous talent was recognized early, and his father, Johann van Beethoven, a mediocre tenor in the employ of the city of Bonn, did his level best to beat his son into becoming a prodigy to rival Mozart. (Mozart was only fourteen years Beethoven's senior, and the legend of Mozart-as-prodigy was still contemporary when Beethoven was born.)

In this, Johann van Beethoven failed; there could be only one Mozart. What he succeeded in doing was to make his son hate his father pathologically and, by extension, anyone (or anything) he perceived as an authority figure.

Bernard Maurer, a cellist in Bonn and a friend of Johann van Beethoven's, described the ten-year-old Ludwig this way in 1780:

> Young Beethoven remained indifferent to all praise, retreated, and practiced best when he was alone, when his father was not at home. He was a lonely, withdrawn child. Outside of music, he understood nothing of social life. Consequently, he was

ill-humored with other people, did not know how to converse
with them, and withdrew into himself so that he was looked
upon as a misanthrope. (Solomon, 26)

During Beethoven's second decade he emerged from his shell,
thanks mostly to his musical talent. He began studying organ and
composition with a teacher named Christian Gottlob Neefe, the
newly hired Bonn court organist. Neefe was a Lutheran and a pas-
sionate devotee of the music of Johann Sebastian Bach at a time when
Bach's music had fallen into obscurity. More than any other music—
more than Mozart's, more than Haydn's—it was Bach's music that
was the decisive influence on Beethoven's.

A great opportunity came Beethoven's way in the spring of 1787.
At the age of sixteen, he was sent at the elector's expense to Vienna
so that the authorities there might judge his potential as a pianist
and also, perhaps, to study with Mozart. Sadly, the trip was cut short
soon after Beethoven arrived in Vienna when news reached him that
his mother was dying. Bitterly disappointed, he returned immediately to Bonn.

With his mother gone, the sixteen-and-a-half-year-old Ludwig
became, by necessity, the head of the Beethoven household, the
guardian of his two younger brothers and his drunken father. It was
an extraordinary amount of responsibility for a grieving teenager to
bear, but bear it successfully he did.

Vienna's Always Better the Second Time Around

In November of 1792, the nearly twenty-two-year-old Beethoven
again traveled to Vienna, presumably to finish his musical education
with the great Joseph Haydn. Perhaps even more important than
the letters of introduction he carried with him—at least in terms
of easing his way into Vienna's musical life—was his unique way of
playing the piano.

The Viennese had never heard anyone play like Beethoven. They were accustomed to the smooth, fluent, harpsichord-derived technique of Mozart. Beethoven reduced almost every piano he touched to kindling, aiming always for more sound, more sonority, and more power.

The lessons with Haydn were a travesty. Franz Joseph Haydn was thirty-eight years Beethoven's senior. He was responsible, more than any other composer, for creating the high Classical style, the Classical symphony, and the Classical string quartet. At the time Beethoven began his lessons with Haydn, Haydn had already composed at least ninety-seven symphonies, and was the most famous and popular living composer.

Beethoven was cocky, confident, and flush with self-importance. Thanks to his troubled relationship with his father, he also had a pathological problem with father figures, something that boded poorly for a teacher who went by the nickname of Papa. For his part, Haydn was an uninspired teacher at best, and was irked by Beethoven's attitude and quick success in Vienna as a pianist.

To make a long and extremely unsavory story very short: Beethoven lied to Haydn about all sorts of things, and Haydn, being the nice guy he was, believed everything Beethoven told him. But after about a year, the truth came out, as it usually does, at which point the lessons (and we use that word loosely) stopped.

It remains a testament to Haydn's extraordinary goodwill that Beethoven managed, in the end, to obtain his pardon.

Beethoven went on to take some counterpoint lessons with Johann Albrechtsberger, and vocal composition lessons with Antonio Salieri (yes, *that* Salieri!), but as with Haydn, the lessons were of limited value. Beethoven's friend and student Ferdinand Ries described Beethoven's attitude toward his erstwhile "teachers":

> I knew them all well; all three [Haydn, Albrechtsberger, and Salieri] thought highly of Beethoven, but they all were of one mind regarding his learning. Each one of them said that

Beethoven was so stubborn and self-willed that he had to learn from his own bitter experience what he had never been willing to accept in the course of his lessons. [They all agreed] the rules meant nothing to Beethoven. (Robbins Landon, 52)

Smokin' Hot—or Not?

By 1801, Beethoven was smoking hot. His first six string quartets had been published and were selling briskly. His first symphony had been publicly performed and acclaimed as a worthy successor to the great symphonic tradition of Haydn. His piano music and his own services as a pianist were in constant demand.

Unfortunately, all was not as well as it seemed.

Beethoven's hearing loss began around 1796, first manifesting itself as a ringing in both ears. It was oh so slowly disabling; it wasn't until 1818 that he could be considered clinically deaf: entirely deaf in one ear and with only limited, low-frequency hearing in the other.

Beethoven's great emotional crisis over his hearing loss came long before that, during the autumn of 1802, at a time when he was living and working in the Viennese suburb of Heilegenstadt. We're aware of this crisis because of a document discovered among Beethoven's effects when he died, a document that has come to be known as the Heiligenstadt Testament.

Part confession, part last will and testament, part rant against God and humankind, the document shows us a man enraged by his fate, deeply depressed, and borderline suicidal.

It's an amazing document, a dramatic composition in its own right, one that begins in despair, but then slowly, with ever greater conviction, catalogs Beethoven's determination to fight his fate and go forward through his music.

"Composing" the testament allowed Beethoven to articulate and contextualize some of his darkest thoughts and feelings, and helped him to determine his new artistic path. That the testament was important to Beethoven is clear, as he carted it around with him for the next twenty-five years, until the day he died.

Using for his model the heroic image of Napoleon—himself a middle-class man raised to the heights through the power of his genius—Beethoven molded for himself in 1803 a new, heroic self-image, one that allowed him to funnel his rage, alienation, passion, and imagination into a music the likes of which no one had ever imagined. In doing so, he was also able to give voice to his world: a world shredded by the French Revolution and the Napoleonic era that followed. Beethoven's mature music might have shocked its audiences, but part of it was the shock of recognition—the shock of truth, of relevance—that this music said something of its contemporary world that other music did not.

CHAPTER 21

Beethoven's Compositional Innovations

When the Going Gets Tough, the Tough Innovate

Beethoven's formative musical environment may have been dominated by the rituals and niceties of the Viennese Classical style, but his social and political inheritance was the age of revolution and Napoleon. Beethoven harnessed the grandiose, heroic, and turbulent spirit of this time even as he harnessed his own inner demons, and in doing so, he changed both the role of the composer and the language of Western music.

Beethoven's compositional life falls into four periods.

The first saw the creation of his juvenilia, the music he composed in Bonn before moving to Vienna in November of 1792.

The period between late 1792 and 1802 is referred to as his Viennese period, during which, we are told, he absorbed completely the Classical style of Haydn and Mozart. This is a half-truth because, even as he absorbed and mastered Viennese classicism, Beethoven was already his own man, often going uncomfortably beyond the Classical era envelopes of melodic grace, emotional restraint, and formal ritual. Beethoven's symphonies number one and two, his first six string quartets, and his first three piano concertos date from this period.

What is referred to as Beethoven's heroic compositional period runs from 1803 to 1815. It's a period that saw his expressive revolution in full swing, during which he composed, among many other works, his symphonies three through eight; the five so-called middle string quartets, his fourth and fifth piano concertos, the Violin Concerto in D, and the opera *Fidelio*.

Beethoven's "late" compositional period is understood as running from 1816 to his death in 1827, when he was clinically deaf, physically isolated, emotionally alienated, and not in the best of health. It was a period during which he once again reinvented himself, and having done so, composed music that confused the living daylights out of most of his contemporaries. Beethoven's late-period music includes his last five piano sonatas, the Ninth Symphony, the *Missa Solemnis*, the *Diabelli Variations* for piano, and his last six works for string quartet. These late works redefined their genres entirely. We stand humbled and awed by them.

Of all Beethoven's works, three particular sets stand out as musical diaries through which we can trace his development from his "Viennese" period through to the end of his life. They are the "nine," the "sixteen," and the "thirty-two."

The "nine," of course, refers to Beethoven's nine symphonies, composed between 1800 and 1824. When we say, the "sixteen," we can be referring *only* to Beethoven's sixteen string quartets, composed between 1798 and 1826. And when we say, the "thirty-two," we mean Beethoven's thirty-two piano sonatas, composed between 1796 and 1823.

All of Beethoven's mature compositional innovations are arrayed around a single, central belief: that music composition is a form of self-expression.

Heretical though Beethoven's attitude might have appeared to many of his contemporaries, the time was ripe for the development of such an egocentric attitude toward art.

Take, in equal parts, one, the Enlightenment's emphasis on the individual and the right of individuals to pursue happiness, meaning, to do their thing; two, the French Revolution and the spirit of accelerated, revolutionary change it provoked; and three, the social and economic upheavals engendered by Napoleon. Mix these societal events all together and sooner or later an artist (or a group of artists) was going to say something along the lines of "My art is for me, not for you. What I feel, see, and hear is *important*, and I/my art will express what I feel, what I see, what I hear. Take it or leave it."

Beethoven was not alone in his self-expressive attitude. In English literature, William Wordsworth, Samuel Taylor Coleridge, and Lord George Gordon Byron experienced the same environmental influences and put the same self-expressive ideal at the forefront of their work. In painting, it was the Spaniard Francisco Goya.

Beethoven's mature compositional innovations are five in number:

1. Contextual use of form: The mature Beethoven will use the Classical era forms only to the point where they serve his expressive needs. Beyond that, he will do what he pleases. For him, expressive context will determine the degree to which he adheres—or doesn't adhere—to preexisting form.
2. Pervasive motivic development: The manipulation, combination, and metamorphosis of motives lie at the heart of Beethoven's melodic language.
3. Ongoing dramatic narrative: Beethoven conceives of the individual movements of a composition not as self-standing entities related only by key but as individual "chapters" in a single, large-scale story.
4. The use of rhythm as a narrative element unto itself.
5. The ongoing pursuit of originality: Later in his life, Beethoven famously said that "Art demands of us that we never stand still." To that end, he placed a premium on continual artistic growth and development, something that strikes us, today, as being very modern.

Beethoven, Symphony No. 5 in C Minor, Op. 67

We are about to indulge in the most detailed musical analysis in this book.

This analysis is, truly, the centerpiece of our story, a single foray into real musical detail that brings together all the terminology and listening skills I've discussed to this point. It is also a "walk-the-walk" moment, as most of the literature out there, from textbooks and biographies to program notes and CD booklets, "talk" about Beethoven's innovations, but never demonstrate precisely what he actually did that was so innovative. Finally, the remainder of this book rests atop the spirit of innovation and personal musical expression that Beethoven brought to the compositional table. He was, truly, the first musical modernist, someone who placed originality and self-expression above the artistic rituals of his time and the personal taste of his audience. We must attempt to understand something of the essence of his mature music if we are to understand his profound influence, musical and spiritual, on the composers and music that followed him.

First Movement: Sonata Form

Exposition

All of Beethoven's mature compositional innovations can be observed in the first movement of his Symphony no. 5 in C Minor, op. 67 (1808).

During the course of the exposition, the music grows from violent melodic minimalism to lyric triumph.

Theme one begins with a statement of purpose in the home key of C minor. An orchestral unison (meaning that all the instruments play the same notes at the same time) intones a hammering, four-note motive, the so-called fate motive:

The opening fate motive is immediately sequenced downward to create a longer, eight-note unit set off from what follows by a long pause:

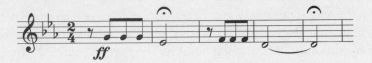

The remainder of theme one and the modulating bridge that follows are generated entirely by various repetitions, sequences, and permutations of the fate motive. It is an example of total motivic saturation, and given the hammering, rhythmic nature of the fate motive, our ears are ringing and our bladders are weak by the time the modulating bridge comes to its conclusion. It is a moment of almost singular relief, then, when we hear the horn call that introduces theme two in E-flat major. "Finally, something different!" or so we think.

The horn call functions analogously to the eight-note statement of purpose that began theme one. It calls us to attention and sets the mood for the theme to come. The theme to come, theme two, is everything we hoped it would be: a lyric, gentle tune set in the new key of E-flat major. Here's the opening phrase of theme two:

Motivic Development as an Expressive Metaphor!
We must now step back and observe the motivic development that lies at the heart of this thematic material and, in doing so, observe how this motivic development becomes an expressive metaphor for spiritual growth.

The first thing we hear at the beginning of the movement—asserted unequivocally by an orchestral unison—is this generative four-note "fate" motive:

That four-note fate motive is the first generation, the movement's basic DNA, the code from which everything will grow across the span of this movement.

Beethoven next sequences that motive downward to create the second-generation motive, an eight-note unit that outlines four pitch contour: G-Eb-F-D:

The horn call that initiates theme two represents generation three. To create the horn call, Beethoven elongated the distance between the first/second and third/fourth notes of the opening four-note contour just given, while leaving the inner pitches—Eb and F—the same.

Finally, Beethoven inverts the horn call contour, adds a few notes, and in doing so creates theme two:

The graceful, lilting theme two is in actuality the fourth-generation descendent of the fate motive. The fact that we do not consciously hear theme two as an outgrowth of the opening fate motive should bother us not a whit; by the time we hear theme two (generation four) we are too far removed from the fate motive (generation one) to perceive their relationship consciously. But the evolutionary process by which we've transited from the opening fate motive to theme two makes perfect sense. This is narrative, musical storytelling at its best, as one idea seems inevitably to lead to the next; this is music in which unity and variety paradoxically coexist.

Theme two and the cadence material that follows it are set in the "new" and contrasting key of E-flat major. Expressively, we've come a long way since the beginning of the movement, and when the exposition concludes—joyfully and brilliantly—we cannot help but feel that as it has matured, the music has triumphed over its dark beginnings. Certainly, there is a dramatic progression here that speaks to us of struggle and growth, achieved through Beethoven's extraordinary use of motivic development.

Development Section

In the development section, the thematic growth and transformation that marked the exposition are crushed by motivic fragmentation and disintegration. The section begins with a vicious return to the dark side of minor, pounded out in fate motive rhythms.

About halfway through the development section, two horn calls defiantly thunder forth:

A third horn call begins, but is brutally cut short as its final note is severed from the body of the motive:

Things go from bad to worse, as, in the next iteration of the horn call, its dismemberment continues; now only the middle two notes are heard.

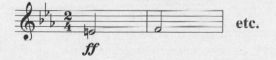

The dismemberment continues, because after a few moments, these two-note units dissolve, leaving only single, isolated "chords of despair," as they were referred to in the nineteenth century.

The rhythmic machinery of this movement, from the beginning powered by the hammering fate motive, grinds to a halt. A heart monitor hooked up to this music would indicate a near flat line.

The music has entered, virtually, the Valley of Death. Here in the development section, motivic fragmentation is used as a metaphor for physical and spiritual destruction.

The movement survives, but just barely, as the recapitulation begins back in the key of C minor.

The events of the exposition and development section are ripe with extra-musical meaning. It has been suggested that this music is autobiographical; that it describes Beethoven's brutal childhood, his flowering as a young musician, and then the struggle with fate brought about by the disintegration of his hearing. That's a tad literal for my taste, but if it works for you, then go for it. The larger point: metaphorical meaning here is a product of motivic development and fragmentation.

Recapitulation
A washed-out and melancholy version of theme one is heard, followed by a plaintive oboe solo. The near-death experience of the development section has traumatized this music, and that trauma is reflected in the downhearted mood of theme one. But the music

has survived, and this will be reflected in the unexpected events to come.

To appreciate these events, we must put ourselves in the boots, waistcoats, and wigs of Beethoven's contemporary audience, hearing this symphony for the first time on December 22, 1808, in Vienna's Theater an der Wien.

"Crazy music. Don't really 'like' it, but, hey, we just heard theme one in the recapitulation, so the movement must almost be over. Now we expect the modulating bridge, theme two in the tonic key of C minor, cadence material in the tonic key of C minor, a brief coda, movement over, and none too soon!"

Beethoven completely dashes these expectations, because the dramatic context of the movement now demands that he go beyond the rituals and expectations of Classical era sonata form. Theme two and the ensuing cadence material are triumphantly stated not in C minor but in C major, a key entirely new to the movement!

"Sweet mother of marmalade! That's *not* how it's done! What does this *mean*?"

Beethoven's audience would have been completely flummoxed. What does C major have to do with *anything*? The answer to that question will be learned only in time.

Coda

The coda is no mere closer but, in reality, a second development section. During the coda, the process of disintegration that occurred in the development section is thrown into reverse, as all sorts of new melodic growth is generated from the fragments of the horn call motive.

As it turns out, the key of C major plays a decisive role in the dramatic narrative of the symphony. It is the key of hope, the key of life, and its unexpected appearance in the recapitulation brings hope, life, and new motivic growth back to the shattered landscape of the first movement.

The Big "Story Line"

It is the struggle between C minor and C major, between despair and hope, between death and life, that is the large-scale dramatic narrative in Beethoven's Fifth Symphony. It is a struggle that is won by C major during the third movement, a victory that is celebrated in the blaring and giddy fourth movement.

Beethoven's Symphony no. 5 begins darkly in C minor and ends triumphantly in C major. The catharsis it describes, of victory through struggle, is a mirror of both Beethoven's external environment and his post-reinvention heroic emotional landscape. It is a work in which the conventions of classicism are rendered secondary to Beethoven's dual artistic tenets of originality and profound self-expression above all else.

Beethoven's music was rooted in the forms and genres of classicism. But the overpowering, sometimes even demonic, entirely personalized expressive content of his music set it far apart from the Classical ideal. This is what Beethoven's contemporary Ernst Theodor Wilhelm (E.T.A.) Hoffman was getting at when he wrote that:

> Beethoven's music sets in motion the lever of fear, of awe, of horror, of suffering, and awakens just that infinite longing which is the essence of romanticism. He is, accordingly, a completely Romantic composer. (Grout, Palisca, 4th ed., 653)

When it comes to Beethoven, labels such as classicist and romantic are best avoided. His music was sui generis. He was a revolutionary man living at a revolutionary time, and in terms of his impact on the next generations of composers, he was, without a doubt, the single most disruptive and influential composer in the history of Western music.

CHAPTER 22

Isn't It Romantic?

The Music of the Nineteenth Century

The Romantic era is understood as running from the death of Beethoven in 1827 until 1900. Were we compelled to do so, we could come up with better dates. It is a compulsion we will, for now, ignore.

The adjective *romantic* comes from the noun *romance*. A romance was a story or a poem that dealt with legendary people and/or events written in one of the romance languages, that is, one of the languages descended from Roman (Latin). For example, the medieval poems about King Arthur were called Arthurian romances. As a result, when the adjective *romantic* was first used during the seventeenth century, it referred to something remote, legendary, fantastic, and marvelous, beyond the everyday world of real life.

When applied to the art and literature of the nineteenth century, then, the word *romantic* refers not to physical love or affection but rather to something that is beyond the everyday. Where a twenty-first-century individual, when met with something incredible, might say, "Far out, man," her nineteenth-century counterpart would have said, "Most romantic, dude."

The big difference between the music of the Classical era and that of the Romantic era has to do with expanded expressive content and the incremental changes to the musical language that were made in order to describe that expanded expressive content.

We must be wary of the word *inevitable*. In truth, few things are inevitable: death, perhaps (but certainly not taxes, not if you've got your money in a numbered account in the Cayman Islands). Nevertheless, given the social evolution that marked the European world from the seventeenth to the nineteenth century, there does appear to be a certain inevitability to the development of Romantic art.

The music of the Baroque era in general, and opera in particular, acknowledged and celebrated the individual human voice to a degree entirely new in the post-ancient world. During the Enlightenment, the dramatic and homophonic elements of Baroque opera were institutionalized in the instrumental genres and musical forms of classicism. Beethoven, having come to the conclusion that music was above all a self-expressive art, adhered to Classical era rituals only to the degree that they served his expressive needs.

In his lifetime, Beethoven was regarded by many as an eccentric modernist whose late music, in particular, could be written off as the product of a slightly crazy, hearing-impaired composer. However, it didn't take long for the generation of composers who came into

Liszt at the Piano, *by Josef Danhauser (1840)* The Teaching Company Collection

their prime immediately after Beethoven's death to embrace him as the Moses of new music, one that would lead them to an expressive promised land relevant to the changing social and economic realities of the 1830s and '40s.

Danhauser's painting *Liszt at the Piano* (1840) illustrates perfectly the Romantic era infatuation with the Beethovenian "ideal." Pictured is a Parisian salon filled with some of the greatest artists of the day. For his inspiration, Liszt is looking at a monumental marble bust of Beethoven perched on the piano. The bust is seen against a window, which frames a roiling and turbulent sky, as if to say that Beethoven is one with the gods, that he cannot be contained in a mere room. Typical of Beethoven's postmortem deification, the bust looks more like Tyrone Power than the short, ugly, smallpox-scarred Ludwig van Beethoven. For the great majority of composers and listeners of the mid- and late-nineteenth century, Beethoven was viewed as a spiritual guide, as a hero, as a deity, as a catalyst for the expressive evolution that we now call romanticism.

For the audiences of the Romantic era, music became the ultimate art form. The remote, boundless, ephemeral, nontactile nature of music, particularly instrumental music, made it the ideal art for the nineteenth century. Its detachment from the world, its mystery, and its incomparable power of suggestion—which works on the mind directly without the mediation of words—made it the dominant art, the one most representative among all the arts of the nineteenth century. According to the nineteenth-century English essayist Walter Pater, "All art aspires to the condition of music."

Ludwig van Beethoven (1770 1827) Library of Congress, Prints and Photographs Division, LC-USZ62-29499

Romantic Era Trends

There are four main Romantic era expressive trends. They are the fascination with extreme emotional states; musical nationalism; a glorification of nature, particularly the *wilder* aspects of nature; and a fascination with the macabre, the gothic, and the supernatural.

Let's compare three thematic melodies and ask what they are each "about," beginning with the first theme of the first movement of Haydn's Symphony no. 88 of 1787:

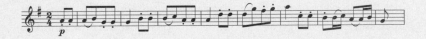

Back in chapter 20, we said that this Classical era theme was about "nice." Let us expand on that a bit. It is "about" an upbeat, motivic melody with balanced phrases set in the key of G major, a melody most easily discussed in purely musical terms as a piece of "absolute music."

We return to the opening of the first theme of the first movement of Beethoven's Symphony no. 5 of 1808:

Back in chapter 20, we observed that this turbulent, jagged, highly motivic theme set in C minor seems to represent some dark and dramatic experience or emotion. The exact nature of that experience or emotion is up to the individual listener. Expressively, the theme is best discussed as a metaphor.

Finally, we consider the second theme from Peter Tchaikovsky's Fantasy Overture to *Romeo and Juliet* of 1869:

There should be a parental warning label on that long, sprawling theme! The theme is known as "the love theme from Romeo and Juliet" because of what it *explicitly* describes: the love (and physical desire) between two starry-eyed and star-crossed teenagers. It's no accident that this theme has the expressive impact it does; Tchaikovsky, with great savvy and care, has built a lush theme filled with phrases that climb, climb, and climb some more, until it peaks with a frankly orgasmic climax

There is nothing abstract or metaphorical about the theme's meaning. It is *explicitly* about idealized love and almost unbearable physical yearning. This is the sort of extreme emotion *explicitly* portrayed that is typical of cutting-edge Romantic era music.

The second of the four major Romantic era musical trends is musical nationalism: the use of folk or folklike music in concert works. Such folkloric nationalism is a different thing from the language-based nationalism we observed in the Baroque era. The nineteenth century was an age of revolution and growing national pride and awareness, pride and awareness that manifested themselves in artistic nationalism: the celebration of ethnic and national character in the arts.

Folkloric musical nationalism became an important mode of self-expression and political expression for many nineteenth-century composers. It was a sort of expression that would have been unthinkable during the more cosmopolitan Classical era.

The third of the four major Romantic era trends was a fascination on the part of nineteenth-century artists and audiences with nature, particularly the wilder aspects of nature. It was a fascination that mirrored societal reality.

For many reasons, the industrial revolution among them, the population of Europe exploded during the nineteenth century. The population of England alone grew from ten million in 1800 to twenty-one million by 1850. Most of this population growth was in the cities; London and Paris both quadrupled in population between 1800 and 1880. As the powers of the provincial courts dwindled, most composers and musicians were drawn to major cities. The urbanization of the artistic community had a tremendous impact on the nature of the art this community produced.

During the nineteenth century, nature came to be worshipped and celebrated by artists as an ideal of purity. For these artists, nature inspired an awe that counterbalanced the artificiality of the city and of human society. Different works depict nature in different ways, from the bright and brilliant sunshine of Italy (in the first movement of Felix Mendelssohn's Symphony no. 4 of 1833), to the craggy mountain ridges of the Austrian Alps (the first movement of Gustav Mahler's Symphony no. 3 of 1896), to a summer evening's storm as a metaphor for the great flood (the fourth movement of Beethoven's Symphony no. 6 of 1808; see the following Music Box).

Beethoven, Symphony No. 6 in F Major, Op. 68 (1808)

Beethoven's Sixth Symphony, which is nicknamed the *Pastoral*, remains one of the great "back-to-nature" works of the nineteenth century. Over the course of its five movements, Beethoven describes a day in the country. The climax of the symphony is the fourth movement, which Beethoven entitles Sturm ("Storm"). What begins as a summer night's thunderstorm becomes a cataclysm, nature at its wildest and most uncontrolled, and a metaphor for humankind's powerlessness over its own fate.

- While listening to this movement, be aware that its theme is neither a melody, a harmony, nor a rhythm, but rather, the concept of the *storm*. The music is entirely programmatic in that it seeks to describe a visual/literary program using purely musical means. Program music is instrumental music that seeks to paint pictures and/or tell a literary story in strictly instrumental terms.
- Form in this movement is determined entirely by the programmatic story being told, from the distant thunderous rumbles and "pitter-pats" of drizzle that begin the movement; through its vicious, dissonant, lightning-slashed climax; to the arching string line and rising flute solo that depict, respectively, an early morning rainbow and the rising sun at the conclusion of the movement.

As the natural world and its mysteries were increasingly explained by science, and as the middle and upper classes were no longer awed by religious dogma, so audiences sought ever greater titillation through their entertainment.

This should sound very familiar. Modern audiences crave the same sort of incredible, imagination-stretching entertainment, featuring anything from giant reptiles to space aliens, nasty orcs to skeletal pirates, evil galactic emperors to chainsaw-wielding madmen.

The nineteenth century had gothic novels and poets and writers such as Edgar Allan Poe and Mary Shelley. It had music compositions such as Hector Berlioz's "Dream of a Witches' Sabbath," the fifth movement of his *Symphonie Fantastique*, and Franz Liszt's *Totentanz*, a piece of music based on the Black Death of the fourteenth century: art that titillates, terrifies, and amuses all at the same time.

All the Romantic era trends we've just observed were informed by a single overriding desire on the part of composers: to be personally expressive by creating a personal compositional sound. At the heart of the Romantic ideal lay this search for personal self-expression.

The music of the Renaissance, Baroque, and Classical eras is characterized by what is called period style, a relatively uniform approach to the musical language in terms of form and aesthetics. Yes, both Johann Sebastian Bach's and Wolfgang Mozart's music stands out from that of their contemporaries, but that's not because they made a purposeful effort to cultivate their own "sound"; they were just phenomenally great geniuses/artists.

However, starting with Beethoven, we are witness to a shift from period style to individual styles. Part of the cult of individual feeling that characterized romanticism made itself evident in a desire on the part of composers to find their own compositional voice, their own "sound." This is yet another aspect of romanticism that remained common currency through the twentieth century and up to today, as composers continue to cultivate a compositional voice of their own.

We can blame it on the Enlightenment. The Enlightenment's emphasis on the individual reveling in his individuality found full flower in the art of the nineteenth century, during which artists no longer conceived of themselves as servants to their patrons and audiences but, rather, as *artistes*, who had to follow their own muse.

CHAPTER 23

Structural Problems

Formal Challenges in Early Romantic Music

For cutting-edge Romantic era composers, the issue of musical form was a challenge. The spontaneity, individuality, and creative freedom treasured by so many nineteenth-century composers were at odds with the notion of conforming to a preordained musical form. Many early Romantic composers altered the traditional Classical era forms almost beyond recognition, while others abandoned them altogether. Thus the challenge: to find alternative formal structures that allowed composers the spontaneity and freedom of expression they craved yet still provided a measure of compositional coherence.

For some composers, Beethoven showed the way: using the Classical era forms contextually, according to expressive need.

For those composers who chose not to use the Classical era forms, the challenges were daunting. One need only remember that composers such as Haydn and Mozart, and yes, even Beethoven, employed these forms because they were a societal given, a common structural ground between themselves and their audiences. The artistic risk is clear: if a composer abandoned the forms, he abandoned that common ground.

Ah, the creative mind! Challenges were meant to be overcome, and with varying degrees of success, the 1820s and '30s saw a number of solutions to the formal challenges of the time.

Some composers chose to write "miniature compositions," and

thus dealt with the challenge of large-scale musical form by simply not dealing with it at all. Such composers created collections of very short pieces we now call miniatures, pieces that rarely run more than a few minutes in length. Miniatures are mostly songs and piano pieces, and they were constructed in such a way as to project a single mood or emotion to the listener. They also avoid entirely the issues of large-scale departure, development, and return.

At the other end of the musical spectrum are works that are now referred to as grandiose compositions. These are compositions that used orchestras, solo singers, choruses, and even narrators to create long, multimedia stage events in which the overall form was determined by the text. These were Romantic era oratorios, modeled in equal parts on the oratorios of Handel and on Beethoven's Symphony no. 9, and they included such works as Berlioz's *Romeo and Juliet* of 1839 and *The Damnation of Faust* of 1845, and Mendelssohn's *Elijah* of 1846. Such works were costly to produce, and they were undone by the overwhelming popularity of opera.

Which brings us to program music. Like the fourth movement "Storm" of Beethoven's Symphony no. 6, program music is instrumental music based on a poem, story, or some other literary source, composed in such a way as to project the action of the story. The musical form of such a piece is determined by the story being told. Unlike "grandiose compositions," which represented an evolutionary dead end, program music flourished in the nineteenth century. Indeed, it became the most important solution to the challenge of how to create a large-scale musical structure without having to fall back on the Classical era forms, since form was a function of the story being told.

For example, Richard Strauss's *Don Quixote* of 1897 is an orchestral composition that tells the story of Don Quixote in a series of ten episodes. A cello portrays the Don; other instruments portray other characters. Provided we know what parts of the story Strauss's episodes represent, we can follow along.

That's a mighty big proviso.

Clearly, there's a potential problem here. If we don't have a written program in front of us that describes the action as it unfolds in the music, we might easily become lost absent an abstract musical structure that makes sense unto itself.

Composers of program music were well aware of the perceptual problems inherent in program music, and so they developed the concept of thematic unity. Romantic era composers sought to create long-range structural unity by using certain themes cyclically. By returning to these themes throughout the multiple movements of a composition, they could create thematic continuity and coherence.

There were three basic genres of nineteenth-century orchestral program music: the program symphony; the concert, or symphonic overture; and the symphonic or tone poem.

A program symphony is a multi-movement work for orchestra that tells a single story. Beethoven's Symphony no. 6 and Hector Berlioz's *Symphonie Fantastique* (which we will examine in chapter 24) are two such works.

A concert or symphonic overture (the terms are synonymous) is a one-movement program composition for orchestra written in sonata form or some very close approximation of sonata form. We will meet and greet a concert overture in chapter 29, when we examine Nikolai Rimsky-Korsakov's *Russian Easter Overture* of 1888.

A symphonic or tone poem (again, the terms are synonymous) is a one-movement program work for orchestra in which the form is determined entirely by the story being told. The previously mentioned *Don Quixote* of 1897 by Richard Strauss is just such a tone poem.

The creation of program music as a solution to the formal challenges of romanticism should not make us think that the Classical era forms were discarded like some moth-eaten powdered wig as the nineteenth century progressed. In truth, the vast majority of nineteenth-century composers continued to use the Classical era forms in one way or another whenever it suited them.

Robert Schumann, Felix Mendelssohn, Peter Tchaikovsky, Antonin Dvořák, and Gustav Mahler composed both program works and more traditional works such as symphonies and concertos that employed, to some degree or another, the Classical era forms. And in writing program symphonies and/or concert overtures, these composers—and the vast majority of their colleagues—composed program music that, nevertheless, continued to follow the outlines of Classical era formal procedures.

Peter Tchaikovsky (1840–1893) The Teaching Company Collection

Johannes Brahms

The only major nineteenth-century composer who wrote no program music whatsoever was the Hamburg-born Johannes Brahms (1833–1897). This fact has prompted generations of writers on music to call Brahms a classicist, implying that he was composing faux-Haydnesque, ersatz Mozartean music.

Wrong.

Brahms's music did indeed adhere to genres and formal structures invented during the Classical era (and the Baroque era, too). But he used those forms in a thoroughly modern

Johannes Brahms (1833–1897) Library of Congress, Music Division

way, with a Beethoven-like flexibility and a most modern approach to melody, harmony, and expressive content. He was a nineteenth-century Romantic era composer who just happened to believe in the enduring quality and discipline of the Classical era forms and genres. But this doesn't make him a "classicist" any more than a modern painter who uses oils on canvas is a "Renaissance-ist."

The German Lied and the Instrumental Miniature

As we've observed, a miniature composition is a brief, self-standing work that evokes a single emotion, a single mood, a single state of mind. To give an example of such, we turn first to Franz Schubert and the lied ballad. A lied is a German song, for which *lieder* is the plural. A ballad is a long, story-like poem, a genre that became increasingly popular in England and Germany during the eighteenth century. These poems alternated narrative and dialogue in stories filled with romantic adventure and supernatural incidents, and were embraced by late eighteenth- and nineteenth-century German composers as vehicles for their increasingly personal, increasingly self-expressive music.

The masters of German language lieder reads like a Who's Who of great nineteenth-century Austrian and German composers. Franz Schubert (1797–1828), Robert Schumann (1810–1856), Johannes Brahms (1833–1897), Hugo Wolf (1860–1903), Gustav Mahler (1860–1911), and Richard Strauss (1864–1949) were all masters of the German lied. As an example

Franz Schubert (1797–1828) Library of Congress, Prints and Photographs Division, LC-USZ62-43355

Richard Strauss (1864–1949) Library of Congress, Prints and Photographs Division, LC-USZ62-110616

of the Romantic German lied, we turn to a lied by the *great one*, the incomparable Franz Schubert.

Lied Ballad *Erlkönig* (The Elf King) for Baritone and Piano

Franz Schubert (1797–1828)
Despite his terribly foreshortened life, Schubert was *incredibly* prolific. In his thirty-one years he composed at least thirteen operas and singspiels. He wrote hundreds of sacred and choral works, nine numbered symphonies (eight, in reality, but who's counting?), hundreds of chamber and piano works, and well over six hundred songs. The man was a machine, the Energizer bunny of composers, a compulsive creator.

Schubert composed *Erlkönig* in 1815, at the age of eighteen. It sets a ballad written by the German poet and polymath Johann Wolfgang von Goethe, who lived from 1749 to 1832. It is a poem of haunting and, finally, terrifying supernatural content. While riding through a dark forest at night, a father attempts, vainly, to save his young son from the clutches of the "Elf King."

Typical of German lieder, the piano is no mere accompaniment here, but rather a full musical partner to the voice. The hoofbeats of the father's horse, projected in the piano part, become the connective musical tissue that holds *Erlkönig* together. Once those hoofbeats start at the very beginning of the song, they do not flag until the father arrives home at the very end of the song, with the body of his dead son in his arms.

Erlkönig is a veritable one-person mini-opera, as the singer must project four distinct characters: the father, his son, the Elf King, and a narrator. The voice of the father is gruff and lies low in the baritone's range. The voice of the boy is set high; the voice of the narrator is set medium low; and the voice of the Elf King, unctuous and smooth, lies medium-high in the baritone's range.

Modest though the performing forces are and brief though the song may be, *Erlkönig* has an expressive punch equal to anything

we'll hear on the opera stage. If your eyes remain dry at the conclusion of this piece, you have no heart, none whatsoever. This is the
compact, expressive power of the German lied at its amazing best.

Typical of his remarkable compositional speed, the eighteen-year-
old Schubert tossed off *Erlkönig* in just a few hours. Schubert was one
thing and one thing only: an obsessive composer who went directly
from one piece to the next. He was small, round, shy, severely near-
sighted, unassuming, and lacked entirely the self-promotion gene.
He was surrounded by a circle of friends who treasured him and
his music, and if it hadn't been for these friends, much of his music
would likely have been lost. As it was, many of his greatest works—
including, for example, his incredible Symphony no. 9 in C Major,
"The Great"—were not discovered or performed until long after his
death.

From the lied, a miniature composition for voice and piano, we
move now to early Romantic instrumental miniatures for piano
alone.

Crazy 88s: The Piano Grows Up

A few words about a very special instrument: the nineteenth-century
piano.

By the 1830s and early 1840s, the Paris-based piano builders
Sébastien Erard and Ignaz Pleyel were turning out what we might
think of as proto-modern pianos: iron-harped, steel-stringed grands
using a mechanism very nearly the same as the one used today. These
French instruments were bigger, more sonorous, more responsive,
and more durable than the wooden harped pianos of just a generation before. They represented, truly, a brand-new instrument. As
with any new instrumental technology, someone was required to
test this new piano, to establish its limits, and to create a body of
work that would become the groundline standard on which others
could build.

The composer-pianists who defined the new piano were the Polish-born Frédéric Chopin (1810–1849) and the Hungarian-born Franz Liszt (1811–1886). To a remarkable degree, the piano music composed by Chopin and Liszt in the 1830s and '40s continues to define the piano and its limits to the present day.

Frédéric Chopin: Up Close and Personal

Chopin was born in Warsaw in 1810 to a French father and a Polish mother. His genius made itself apparent very early, and by the age of eight he'd published his first music. He moved to Paris in 1831, to seek his fame and fortune. He achieved both. He died in Paris in October of 1849.

Chopin was, first and last, a composer for piano, a composer whose maturity corresponded exactly with the development of the proto-modern piano.

His piano works together constitute an encyclopedia of modern pianism, and are a pillar of the modern piano repertoire. They include sixteen polonaises, four impromptus, twenty-one nocturnes, twenty waltzes, four scherzos, fifty-eight mazurkas, twenty-seven etudes, and twenty-eight preludes. (By definition, a prelude is something that precedes something else. Chopin's "preludes," however, precede nothing except the ether, the bleak empty canvas of time that mocks the futile strivings of humankind, the . . . whoa! I got a little wrapped up in a Romantic era thing. Sorry.)

Even the most cursory glance at his compositional output reveals Chopin's unwavering commitment to solo piano music. Except for his two early piano concertos, a small number of works for piano and orchestra, and a late sonata for cello and piano (the last of Chopin's works to be published in his lifetime), most of his music was for solo piano, primarily sets of miniature compositions. Brief and compact though Chopin's miniatures may be, let us not fall into the trap of thinking that they are somehow lesser works than, say, a symphony or a concerto. Frankly, Chopin could accomplish more in terms of compositional interest and expressive nuance in three minutes than many composers could in thirty.

Frédéric Chopin, Mazurka in A Minor, Op. 17, No. 4 (1833)

A mazurka is a three-step dance of Polish origin. Chopin composed fifty-eight mazurkas for the piano. Like Classical era minuet and trio form movements and Chopin's own polonaises and waltzes, Chopin's mazurkas are stylized dances, works meant to be listened to and not danced to.

Please note the following:

- In his Mazurka in A Minor, op. 17, no. 4, Chopin turns the right hand of the pianist into a world-weary chanteuse, as a supple, fluid melody line in the right hand is supported by quiet, throbbing harmonies in the left.

- Chopin's trademark use of rubato—stretching out one beat while shortening the next—gives this music the flexibility and nuance of song.

continued on next page

- The emotion projected by this miniature is one of exquisite, autumnal melancholy. There's a personal sound to the melodic writing, a complexity and idiosyncratic approach to harmony, and a sort of pianism that marks this music as Chopin's own. No one else could have written it.

CHAPTER 24

Going Beyond Beethoven

Hector Berlioz's *Symphony Fantastique* and the Program Symphony

T he rise of the middle-class individual that characterized the Enlightenment saw its denouement in the Romantic era cult of individual expression. Whereas the Classical era artist saw himself as a servant to his audience and patrons, the Romantic era *artiste* saw himself as a creative figure beholden to nobody but himself. When Franz Liszt said, "My talent ennobles me," he spoke for an entire generation of post-Beethoven composers who believed that God and nature had endowed them with a gift and a vision that had to be nurtured at any cost. The Romantic generation believed entirely in the meritocracy. It bears repeating: the notion of a fixed set of preexisting musical forms was at odds with the Romantic vision of the artist as a creative world unto himself. Thus, it fell to the generation of composers who followed Beethoven to reinterpret musical form in such a way as to allow themselves the expressive freedom their imaginations demanded while still creating coherent musical structures that an audience could follow.

Some composers, such as Chopin, turned primarily to composing sets of miniature compositions that avoided almost entirely the issues of large-scale, long-range structural departure and return. Many composers continued to use the Classical era forms, but with a freedom and flexibility that show the influence of Beethoven and his "contextual" approach to musical form.

Many composers turned to writing program music, in which the literary story being told determined the structure of the piece.

As often as not, these techniques were mixed and matched depending upon the expressive whim of the composer. For example, early in his career, Robert Schumann composed a series of wonderful piano works—*Papillons, Carnaval,* and *Kreisleriana*—that consist of a series of miniatures that collectively tell a programmatic story. Some composers wrote movements of program music that were nevertheless structured along the lines of sonata form: Felix Mendelssohn's *Overture to a Midsummer Night's Dream* and Peter Tchaikovsky's *Fantasy-Overture to Romeo and Juliet,* for example. Still other composers sought to build on the legacy of Beethoven by composing program symphonies—multi-movement orchestral compositions that, like Beethoven's Symphony no. 6, tell a literary story. Such a work is Hector Berlioz's five-movement *Symphonie Fantastique* of 1830.

Louis-Hector Berlioz

Hector Berlioz (1803–1869) was an early Romantic composer on a mission. He believed with the fervor of a biblical prophet that the future of music was tied to making it a composite art form, a marriage of literature and music with the whole a thousand times greater than its parts. Monsieur Berlioz was a fascinating character, the archetypal Romantic *artiste* and, as such, a prototypical man of his time.

Louis-Hector Berlioz (1803– 1869) Library of Congress, Music Division

Berlioz grew up in post-Revolutionary France. He was twenty-four years old when Ludwig van Beethoven died, and was thus a card-carrying member of that first generation of composers whose inheritance included Beethoven's legacy of self-expression and originality.

As a child, Berlioz displayed only limited musical gifts. He taught himself to play the flute and guitar, but had only the spottiest music education, if we can dignify it by calling it an education at all.

For the late-blooming Berlioz, ignorance was bliss. His approach to form, orchestration, harmony, and counterpoint were all self-evolved. Having never learned to do things the "right" way, he was able to make conceptual leaps and was willing to take creative risks that a proper music education would surely have inhibited him from doing.

Despite his passion for music, his parents sent him to medical school in Paris, which he hated from day one. He dropped out and, eventually, at the age of twenty-three, entered the Paris Conservatory. A full five years older than most of the other incoming students, Berlioz covered his insecurity with an overly aggressive posture and constant opinionating. At the opera, surrounded by fellow students, Berlioz held court as a kind of self-appointed critic, judge, and jury. The dramatist Ernest Legouve was at a performance of *Der Freischütz* by Carl Maria von Weber when he, Legouvé, was witness to a "disturbance" in the balcony.

> One of my neighbors rises from his seat and bending toward the orchestra, shouts in a voice of thunder: "You don't want two flutes there, you brutes! You want two piccolos! Two piccolos, do you hear? Oh, the brutes!" Having said this, he simply sits down again, scowling indignantly. Amidst the general tumult produced by this outburst, I turn around and I see a young man trembling with passion, his hands clenched, his eyes flashing, and a head of hair—such a head of hair! It looked like an enormous umbrella of hair projecting like an awning over the beak of a bird of prey. (Schonberg, 1997)

Hector Berlioz was a hypersensitive, self-indulgent, over-opinionated crazy living in an era that celebrated hypersensitive, self-indulgent, over-opinionated crazies. He fit perfectly the stereotype of the Romantic artist, the "Byronesque" hero, and he played it to the hilt. Of course, we can't help but wonder if it was all a put-on, a cover for Berlioz's insecurity over his lack of a proper musical education.

The *Symphonie Fantastique*

Berlioz began writing the *Symphonie Fantastique* in 1829 and completed it in 1830, the year he graduated from the conservatory at the age of twenty-seven. For the late-starting Berlioz, it is a youthful piece, and technically not his best work. But because of its sheer artistic boldness and imagination, it is his most popular and influential work, a testament to the fearlessness of youth! Put simply, the *Symphonie Fantastique* is a cutting-edge, experimental artwork in which Berlioz attempted to unite what were the four great loves of his life at the time: Shakespeare's plays and Shakespeare's dramatic sensibility, Beethoven's symphonies, the storytelling of opera, and his greatest love, himself. The *Symphonie Fantastique* is a symphonic autobiography.

Along with Beethoven's Third (1804), Fifth (1808), and Ninth (1824) symphonies and Richard Wagner's music drama *Tristan and Isolde* (1859), Berlioz's *Symphonie Fantastique* must be considered among the most groundbreaking and influential works composed in the nineteenth century. Thus this book has dedicated a commensurately big chunk of space to its examination.

The gestation of the *Symphonie Fantastique* starts with Shakespeare. A Shakespeare revival swept across Europe during the early nineteenth century. The composers of the time were particularly enthralled with expressive power and loose form of Shakespeare's plays, which resonated entirely with the post-Beethoven conviction that form should follow expressive content.

On September 11, 1827, Berlioz attended a Parisian performance of Shakespeare's *Hamlet*. The play was performed in English, a language Berlioz did not speak at the time. He followed the action from a crude translation. Nevertheless, he was bowled over, and not just by the play, but by a certain actress in the cast.

Her real name was Harriet Smithson (1800–1854), despite the fact that Berlioz insisted on calling her Henriette. Smithson was an Anglo-Irish actress who'd made her fame on the continent, where her Irish accent was less of an issue than in England.

Thus smitten, Hector Berlioz, stage door Johnny par excellence, spent the next few months trying to bring himself to Smithson's attention. Accurately speaking, he became a Harriet Smithson fanatic, a stalker, infatuated to the point of psychosis. On February 6, 1830 (a full two and a half years after first seeing Smithson), Berlioz wrote his friend Humbert Ferrand:

> After a period of calm, I have just been plunged again into the tortures of an endless and unquenchable passion, without cause, without purpose. She is still in London and yet I seem to feel her all around me. I hear my heart pounding and its beats set me going like the piston strokes of a steam engine. Each muscle of my body trembles with pain— useless, frightening, unhappy woman. If she could—for one moment—conceive all the poetry, all the infinity of such a love, she would fly to my arms, even if she must die from my embrace. (Cone, 7)

Reading this, we begin to suspect that Berlioz actually enjoyed his suffering. Clearly it inspired him, because the great fruit of all this suffering was the *Symphonie Fantastique*, the symphonic story of an artist in love.

Harriet and Hector

In 1832, two years after having written the desperate, previously quoted letter, Harriet Smithson and Hector Berlioz were married. He insisted on calling her Henriette, which drove her crazy. Within a few years, she'd aged past the ingenue roles on which she had built her career, and the roles disappeared. She turned to the bottle, becoming angry and shrewish to the point that the small and slight Berlioz was physically afraid of her. All in all, theirs was something less than a storybook ending.

The *Symphonie Fantastique* was composed at a time when Berlioz's unquenchable passion for Harriet Smithson was the central emotional issue of his life. Of all the elements and influences present in the *Symphonie Fantastique*—Shakespeare, opera, and Beethoven—it is the autobiographical information that is the generative expressive element of the piece.

The *Symphonie Fantastique* placed Berlioz at the forefront of the post-Beethoven avant-garde who believed the music of the future was a composite art form, a combination of music and literature.

The *Symphonie Fantastique* received its premiere on December 5, 1830. As the audience filed in, they were surprised—even shocked—to receive a printed program that described what each of the symphony's five movements was "about." This just wasn't done in 1830 in Paris, where a symphony was still considered an abstract art form. That program will provide us with our starting point.

The goals of this examination of this seminal work are three in number. First, we want to observe the degree to which Berlioz—and, by extension, the cutting-edge composers of the nineteenth century—managed to depict literary and autobiographical information in purely instrumental music. Second, we will observe how Berlioz manages to create thematic unity across the huge, five-movement span of the symphony. Third, we will observe how all of this is done within the framework of a multi-movement symphony.

Movement One: Berlioz's Program and the Idée Fixe
Berlioz's program for the first movement reads as follows:

> Reveries—Passions: The author imagines that a young musician afflicted with that moral disease that a well-known writer calls the *vague des passions* ["wave of passions"] sees for the first time a woman who embodies all the charms of the ideal being he has imagined in his dreams, and he falls desperately in love with her.

Translation: I, Hector Berlioz, saw "Henriette" Smithson. She is the ideal being I have imagined in my dreams and I have fallen desperately in love with her.

Berlioz's program continues:

> Through an odd whim, whenever the beloved image appears before the mind's eye of the artist, it is linked with a musical idea whose character, passionate but at the same time noble and shy, he finds similar to his beloved. This melodic image and the model it reflects pursue him incessantly like a double *idée fixe* [that is, a fixed idea].

Translation: There's a theme that represents *her*, the beloved image, Harriet, "Henriette," whomever. It is a theme that will appear in every one of the five movements of the *Symphonie Fantastique*, providing thematic unity and becoming the dramatic thread that holds together this sprawling and wholly original symphony.

The long, sighing, drooping, palpitating idée fixe first appears after a doleful introduction:

This melodic image and the [woman] it reflects pursue him incessantly. The passage from this state of melancholy reverie, interrupted by a few fits of groundless joy to one of frenzied passion, with its movements of fury, of jealousy, its return to tenderness, its tears, its religious consolations, this is the subject of the first movement. (Cone)

The first movement, presumably a sonata form, with the idée fixe as theme one, is in reality a stream-of-consciousness expressive roller-coaster with only passing resemblance to the structures and discipline of sonata form. Berlioz completes his description of the movement:

Movement Two: "A Ball"
Berlioz's description:

> The artist finds himself in the most varied situations. In the midst of the tumult of a party, in the peaceful contemplation of the beauties of nature, but everywhere in town, in the country, the beloved image appears before him and disturbs his peace of mind.

Translation: The "artist" goes to a dance party. Try as he might, though, he cannot stop thinking about "her."

The manner in which Berlioz projects this is brilliant. The movement is built around a dazzling waltz that represents "the party." However, every time the artist thinks of "her," the waltz music quiets and the idée fixe appears in nonimitative polyphony with the waltz music:

By setting the idée fixe against the waltz, Berlioz projects two different levels of experience *simultaneously*: the waltz represents the exterior environment while the idée fixe represents the artist's interior emotional landscape.

Movement Three: "Scene in the Country"
This central movement marks the point where the story line of the *Symphonie Fantastique* turns from hope to despair, from light to dark.
Berlioz's program:

> Scene in the Country. Finding himself one evening in the country, he hears in the distance two shepherds piping a [shepherd's song] in dialogue.
>
> He reflects upon his isolation; he hopes that his loneliness will soon be over. But what if she were deceiving him? This mingling of hope and fear, these ideas of happiness disturbed by black presentiments, form the subject of the [movement].

In this movement, Berlioz uses Nature as a metaphor for the soul of the artist, and a storm becomes a metaphor for the rising "storm of doubt" in the heart of the artist.
Berlioz depicts this "storm of doubt" by alternating increasingly

anxious phrases of the idée fixe—"she loves me" (see below)—with increasingly violent dissonances—"she loves me not!"

The storm of doubt reaches a climax on an explosive dissonance, followed by a dismal, weeping descent. In his program notes, Berlioz writes that as the movement concludes:

> [O]ne of the shepherds [as portrayed by the English horn] takes up again the [song]; the other [the shepherdess, as portrayed by the oboe] no longer replies. Distant sounds of thunder—loneliness—silence.

Bummer.

Movement Four: "March to the Scaffold"
Berlioz writes:

> Convinced that his love is unappreciated, the artist poisons himself with opium. The dose plunges him into a sleep accompanied by the most horrible visions. He dreams that he has killed his beloved and he is condemned and led to the scaffold and that he is witnessing his own execution. The procession moves forward to the sounds of a march, in which the muffled noise of heavy steps gives way, without transition, to the noisiest clamor. At the end of the march, the first four measures of the *idée fixe* appear like a last thought of love, interrupted by the fatal blow.

The "March to the Scaffold" is the most famous of all the movements of the *Symphonie Fantastique*. It's likely that Berlioz lifted a big chunk of it from an earlier work, but who cares? It works perfectly right here.

Structurally, the movement is a rather hackneyed sonata form: for Berlioz's critics, it is a perfect example of his inability to do things "correctly." To his fans, it's an example of his unwillingness to adhere to any compositional imperative other than good storytelling. Whatever. Berlioz creates here a glorious and compelling movement, one that could have only been diminished had he been concerned with being technically "correct."

The scene comes right out of the French Revolution, and the march that accompanies the condemned artist's cart ride through the streets of Paris remains the most famous tune Berlioz ever composed. As the movement approaches its conclusion, the artist "mounts" the scaffold. The artist is surrounded by a jeering mob (portrayed by the thunderous sound of massed brass), and descending string scales depict his neck being placed across the guillotine's block.

Suddenly, a hush falls and a solo clarinet begins to play the idée fixe. We are "hearing" the artist's last thought, and his last thought is of his beloved. Abruptly the idée fixe is brutally "cut short" by a fortissimo explosion in the full orchestra (the falling guillotine blade), followed by three descending plucked notes in the strings (the head of the artist falling into the waiting basket).

The movement ends with ferocious fanfare, and we can easily imagine the severed head of the artist being displayed to the howling mob.

Movement Five: "Dream of a Witches' Sabbath"

In this fifth movement, the artist's hallucination becomes even more bizarre.

> Dream of a Witches' Sabbath: He sees himself at the Sabbath in the midst of a frightful troop of ghosts, sorcerers, monsters of every kind, come together for his funeral. The beloved melody appears again, but it has lost its character of nobility and shyness; it is no more than a dance tune, mean, trivial, and grotesque; it is she, coming to join the Sabbath. A roar of joy at her arrival. She takes part in the devilish orgy. Funeral knell, burlesque parody of the *Dies irae*, Sabbath Round Dance.

In this fifth movement, Berlioz abandons any pretense to preexisting musical form. Instead, the movement is cast in three large "scenes." In scene 1, Berlioz depicts a dark, shattered graveyard and the ghoulish gathering come together for the artist's funeral. In scene 2, he parodies the Catholic plainchant *Dies irae* ("The Day of Wrath") from the Requiem Mass as the assembled nasties conduct the artist's funeral. In scene 3, entitled "Sabbath Round," the ghouls *party hearty*.

We turn our attention to "scene 1," during which the idée fixe appears. The beloved image, portrayed by a shrill E-flat soprano clarinet, approaches from the distance. Once "noble and shy," the idée fixe has been converted into an obscene little jig:

Despite the misgivings inspired by the "program," the grumblings from those members of the audience who believed pictorial (meaning program) music to be of low artistic merit, and the blasphemous (and sensational!) use of the *Dies irae* in the fifth movement "Witches' Sabbath," the premiere went brilliantly. Two days after the concert, Berlioz wrote his friend Humbert Ferrand.

> I had a furious success! The *Symphonie Fantastique* was welcomed with shouting and stamping; they demanded a repetition of the [fourth movement] "March to the Scaffold"; and the [fifth movement Witches'] Sabbath destroyed everything with Satanic effect! (Kelly, 223)

The *Symphonie Fantastique* is music of stunning originality and modernity. Thank goodness Berlioz never learned to do things the "right way": his vision of music as a composite of literature and music was incredibly influential, and the *Symphonie Fantastique* became a vanguard work for the Romantic era.

CHAPTER 25

Nineteenth-Century Italian Opera

Rossini and Bel Canto

We return to opera for the next two chapters. We will focus our attention on Italian and German opera (as opposed to French and Russian opera) for two reasons: because they are the most influential of the nineteenth-century operatic traditions, and because nineteenth-century Italian and German opera make a marvelous contrast. The former was grounded in tradition and commercialism, and the latter in Romantic expression and experimentation.

By the early nineteenth century, opera in Italy had become a de facto universally popular art. In addition to large cities such as Naples, Rome, Florence, Milan, and Venice, there were operatic performances in almost every Italian town of moderate size. Much of this popularity was attributable to the rise of opera buffa, opera that pretty much anyone could enjoy. Italian opera buffa made few intellectual demands on its audience, and it was perfectly suited to the Italian taste for wit, fast-paced dialogue, attractive tunes, and comic situations.

Opera seria continued to be cultivated mainly in the larger Italian cities, primarily under aristocratic patronage.

By the early nineteenth century, then, Italian opera was a high-profit media industry. The popular and therefore commercial nature of Italian opera had its good side and its bad side. Listeners and critics who like (who *love*) these operas will tell us that their popularity grounded them "in the life of the nation," and that since opera was far and away the preeminent musical media in nineteenth-century Italy, the creative genius of the nation was focused almost entirely on this one genre. However, the artistically conservative nature of early nineteenth-century Italian opera had its critics as well, among them Hector Berlioz, who spoke for many when he wrote that:

> Opera for the Italians is a sensual pleasure and nothing more. For this noble expression of the mind they have hardly more respect than for cooking! They want a score that, like a plate of macaroni, can be [digested] immediately without their having to think about it or even pay attention to it!

Berlioz objected to the lack of artistic risk and the overwhelming importance of the pleasure principle in early nineteenth-century Italian opera. For him, contemporary Italian opera was "opera lite": those very things that made it popular made it, for him, artistically unfulfilling.

The actual musical style of early nineteenth-century Italian opera emerged by 1810 and characterized both Italian opera buffa and opera seria. It was a style based on the deep-rooted Italian convictions that opera is the highest manifestation of the art of song and that its primary purpose is to delight and move the hearer with music that is tuneful, unsentimental, spontaneous, and in every sense of the word, popular. This operatic style is called bel canto opera, *bel canto* meaning "beautiful song" and, by extension, "beautiful voice."

The three principal composers of bel canto opera are Gaetano Donizetti (1797–1848), Vincenzo Bellini (1801–1835), and Gioacchino Rossini (1792–1868). Donizetti composed an astonishing seventy operas, more than one hundred songs, several symphonies, and various oratorios, cantatas, and chamber work. The guy must have had the most overworked espresso machine in all of Italy. By comparison, Bellini's output was downright spare, consisting of ten opera serie. Rossini composed thirty-five operas between 1810—when he was but a lad of eighteen—and 1829, when he completed his final opera, *William Tell*, at the age of thirty-seven. Rich and successful, the thirty-seven-year-old Rossini retired to Paris where he lived until his death, thirty-nine years later.

Gioacchino Rossini (1792–1868)
The Teaching Company Collection

Rossini Rocks!

Gioacchino Rossini is among the most quotable composers of all time. Of the hundreds of Rossini's anecdotes that have been recorded, I offer this one, told by Lillie de Hegermann-Lindencrone in her book, *The Courts of Memory*:

Baron James Rothschild sent Rossini some splendid grapes from his hothouse. Rossini, in thanking him, wrote: "Wonderful though your grapes certainly are, I don't take my wine in pills." This Baron Rothschild read as an invitation to send [Rossini] some of his celebrated Chateau-Lafitte.

The Business of Bel Canto Opera

Like most consumer product industries, nineteenth-century Italian opera demanded quick manufacture and turnaround to be profitable. Here's how things worked. A composer would show up at an opera house, be handed a libretto, check into a local hotel or *pensione*, and have about three weeks to compose the opera. He was typically required to conduct the first three performances, at which point he'd pack his bags and move on to the next opera house. Only rarely were these operas published, so composers had few qualms about passing off old material as being newly composed, knowing that the folks in Lucca, for example, hadn't a clue as to what was performed in Parma the previous month. Rossini was a master of such "selective reuse." For example, his *Barber of Seville* of 1816, which was composed for the Teatro Argentina in Rome, employs entire arias and ensembles originally written for an opera entitled *La Cambiale di Matrimonio* of 1810, and material from four other operas of his composition, including *The Barber of Seville*'s now-famous overture.

Not wanting to waste a good thing, Rossini then went on to use the *Barber of Seville* overture for his operas *Aureliano* and *L'Equivoco stravagante*. Talk about getting good mileage: Rossini thus used the same overture in four different operas! All in all, it took him just thirteen days to complete *The Barber of Seville*, which prompted his fellow composer Gaetano Donizetti to joke, "I always knew Rossini was a lazy man."

In 1900, the eighty-seven-year-old Giuseppe Verdi wrote his friend Camille Ballaigue:

> You may say things about Rossini and they may be true regarding the borrowings and the simplicity of the harmonies, the speed of composition and so forth, but I confess that I cannot help believing *The Barber of Seville* for abundance of ideas, for verve, [and] for truth of declamation the most beautiful opera buffa in existence.

Posterity agrees with Verdi. Along with Mozart's *Marriage of Figaro, Don Giovanni*, and *Così Fan Tutte*, and Verdi's own *Falstaff*, Rossini's *The Barber of Seville* is universally acknowledged as one of the greatest *opere buffe* ever composed.

Rossini was just twenty-four years old when he composed *The Barber of Seville*. The contract he signed with the Teatro Argentina in Rome to compose the opera was typical of its time. He had to accept whatever libretto was chosen by the local impresario, meaning that he had no choice or input in the words he was to set. He had to agree to any and all modifications requested by the singers. He had to lodge with the baritones so that the impresario could keep an eye on him. He had to be present for the rehearsals and the first three performances. Dates were specified for the completion of the first act and the opening night, and compensation was set at the equivalent of about two hundred dollars plus a coat with gold buttons.

The libretto given to Rossini was *The Barber of Seville*; it was prepared by Cesare Sterbini and based on the play by Beaumarchais. *The Barber of Seville* was the first of a trilogy of plays by Pierre Beaumarchais, written and originally produced in Paris between 1772 and 1792. The second play of the trilogy is *The Marriage of Figaro*, and the third is entitled *The Guilty Mother*.

Rossini and Sterbini were not the first operatic team to set *The Barber of Seville* to music. It had first been turned into an opera in 1782, thirty-four years before, by the composer Giovanni Paisiello and librettist Giuseppe Petrosellini. Paisiello's 1782 version of *The Barber of Seville* had been an audience favorite for many years, and Rossini tried to do the politic thing by writing the elderly Paisiello to assure him that he meant no disrespect by writing a similar opera.

Rossini's preemptive apology did *not* do the trick, and the first performance of his version of *The Barber of Seville*, on February 20, 1816, was a fiasco. As soon as the theater doors opened, a pro-Paisiello, anti-Rossini clique rushed the box office and filled the theater. By comparison, Rossini's clique was small and timid. The hissing and derisive whistling began the moment the curtain opened. Said one eyewitness, "All the whistlers in Italy seemed to have given themselves a rendezvous for this performance."

When the curtain fell on the first act, Rossini turned toward the audience, shrugged his shoulders slightly, and clapped his hands. The audience took this as a sign of contempt, with the result being that not a note of the second act that followed could be heard above the din. In the end, it was a case of much ado about *niente*. By the second performance, a couple of days later, the vast superiority of Rossini's *Barber* over Paisiello's was recognized, and Rossini's version has remained an audience favorite and a mainstay of the repertoire since that day.

MUSIC BOX

Rossini, *The Barber of Seville* (1816), "Una voce poco fa"

As an example of Rossini's *The Barber of Seville* and the bel canto style it represents, we turn to the cavatina, "Una voce poco fa," from act 1, scene 2.

A cavatina is a type of aria: one intended to show off a singer's ability to negotiate a long phrase with beauty of tone, nuance, and color. "Una voce poco fa" illustrates perfectly the beautiful melody, wit, and comic delineation that mark Rossini at his very best.

"Una voce poco fa," which means "a voice [I heard] a short while ago," is sung by a perky, adorable sixteen-year-old ingenue named Rosina. She is the ward of the evil Doctor Bartolo, who plans to marry her (yuck!) and steal her inheritance (hiss!). Rosina is in love with a handsome soldier (actually a nobleman in disguise), who has just serenaded her (his was "the voice [I heard] a short while ago").

This cavatina is Rosina's first number—her "entrance aria"—so it must tell us who she is, what she is, and what's going on in her head. Is she strong? Is she weak? Is she smart? Is she a ditz?

Rossini's setting of Rosina's cavatina is superb, and it immediately defines who and what Rosina is as a person and as a dramatic force. The cavatina alternates between firm, stentorian, almost militant rhythms (which depict Rosina's absolute conviction that she will have her way) and brilliant, virtuosic (or "coloratura") writing, which depicts Rosina as a joyful and quick-witted young lady. It is thanks to Rossini's music that we discover that while Rosina will play the role of an "innocent," underneath she's tough as tungsten and will become the driving force and most interesting character in the opera.

CHAPTER 26

Giuseppe Verdi

It's All About the *People*—Dramatic
Truth in Italian Opera

For all intents and purposes, the career of Giuseppe Verdi (1813–1901) is the history of Italian opera for the fifty years from 1850 to 1900.

Giuseppe Verdi. The name sounds so Italian, so European; to American ears, so formidable and elite. Signor Verdi was indeed a formidable man, but excepting his genius, he didn't have an elite bone in his body. Might I suggest that we think of him as Joe Green, the English equivalent of Giuseppe Verdi, as a man and composer completely lacking in pretense and artistic arrogance. He was direct, real, earthy, no-nonsense, and to the point. He composed twenty-six operas; the first, *Oberto*, premiered in 1839, when he was twenty-six years old, and his final opera, *Falstaff*, was completed in 1893, when he was eighty years old. All told, his was an incredible artistic lifetime.

Despite the fact that Verdi changed the nature of Italian opera, he was not a purposeful innovator or reformer. Rather, his evolution was toward inten- sification of dramatic line and literary truth. By the end of his career he had

GIUSEPPE VERDI oel 1898.

Giuseppe Verdi (1813–1901)
Library of Congress, Music Division

brought Italian opera to a level of dramatic and technical excellence never since surpassed.

Giuseppe Fortunino Francesco Verdi was born in October of 1813 in Le Roncole, a village in the Duchy of Parma. He had a middle-class upbringing, and his musical talent was diligently cultivated. He studied music with various local organists. When he was seventeen, the expenses of his music education were taken over by a wealthy local merchant and music lover by the name of Antonio Barezzi, who hailed from the nearby city of Busseto.

In 1831 Verdi traveled to Milan, to apply for entry to the conservatory of music. To his shock and eternal humiliation, he was not granted admission. According to the admissions committee, his keyboard skills were weak, his knowledge of music theory inadequate, and he was too old: at eighteen, he was already four years older than most of the incoming students. To his eternal credit, Barezzi insisted that Verdi remain in Milan and study privately at his expense. This Verdi did, and as part of his studies, he began work on an opera entitled *Oberto*. He returned to Busseto at the age of twenty, in 1833, and married Antonio Barezzi's daughter, Margherita. (We should all have a padrone like Barezzi. After having underwritten Verdi's musical education, he then gave Verdi his daughter as well!)

Oberto came to the attention of Bartolomeo Merelli, who was none other than the director of "the Theater of the Steps," Teatro alla Scala, in Milan. To *his* eternal credit, Merelli took a chance on an opera by a young and unknown composer. *Oberto* was well received, and Merelli offered Verdi a contract to compose three more operas at intervals of eight months. Verdi's second opera, the first of this La Scala commission, was an opera buffa entitled *Un Giorno di Regno* (*King for a Day*). (*Un Giorno di Regno* is one of only two *opere buffe* Verdi composed. The other was *Falstaff*, his final opera, completed some fifty years later.)

It was during this period of his life that a series of horrific tragedies struck Verdi and his family. In August of 1838, his sixteen-month-old daughter, Virginia, suddenly died. Fourteen months later, in October of 1839, his eighteen-month-old son, Icilio, died. Forty years later, in 1879, Verdi wrote, "The poor little boy, languishing, died in the arms of his utterly desolate mother."

Fate was not yet finished with the Verdi family. In June of 1840, just eight months after the death of Icilio, Verdi's wife, Margherita, died, stricken with encephalitis. In the span of twenty-two months, Verdi had lost his entire family.

The young composer was paralyzed with grief. He attempted to withdraw from the commission for *Un Giorno di Regno*, but once again Bartolomeo Merelli, the director of La Scala, did the right thing: he insisted that Verdi fulfill his commission. Incredibly, as if to prove to himself that he could, Verdi managed to finish the opera.

Un Giorno di Regno received its premiere on September 5, 1840, just three months after Margherita's death.

I wish I could tell you that *Un Giorno di Regno* was a triumph, but I cannot. It was a complete failure, and audience reaction to it colored Verdi's feelings about the public for the rest of his life. He wrote, "I accept their criticisms and jeers only on condition that I do not have to be grateful for their applause."

Verdi's third opera, *Nabucco* ("Nebuchadnezzar"), premiered in 1842. *Nabucco*, an opera seria, made a huge political statement. It's about the king of Babylon, Nebuchadnezzar, who, having defeated the nation of Israel, has taken into "Babylonian captivity" the surviving cream of the nation. At the time Verdi composed *Nabucco*, a growing and increasingly powerful Italian nationalist movement was advocating revolution against the foreign overlords who controlled most of Italy. *Nabucco*, with its story about a great and ancient nation held prisoner by a foreign king, could not have been more politically timely or provocative. Intentionally or unintentionally, Verdi became a major player in the Italian nationalist movement. Eventually, even his name became a symbol for the movement. "Viva Verdi!" became a common graffito in Italy, an acronym for *Viva Vittorio Emmanuele, Re d'Italia*, "Long live Victor Emmanuel, King of Italy."

Nabucco made Verdi famous.

From the start, what distinguished Verdi from his bel canto colleagues was his preoccupation with dramatic truth and momentum. By the time he composed *Macbeth* in 1847, just five years after *Nabucco*, dramatic issues had completely replaced the niceties of the bel canto style in Verdi's operas.

When *Macbeth* went into rehearsals in Paris, Verdi wrote a long letter to the director. It's a revealing document that illustrates well his priorities regarding dramatic veracity versus the bel canto style. He wrote:

> They gave the role of Lady Macbeth to Eugenia Tadolini and I'm very surprised that she consented to do the part. You know how much I admire Tadolini and she knows it herself, but in our common interest we should stop and consider: Tadolini's qualities are too great for this role. . . . Tadolini's appearance is good and beautiful, and I would like Lady Macbeth to be twisted and ugly. . . . Tadolini has a marvelous, brilliant, clear, powerful voice, and for Lady Macbeth I should like a raw, choked, hollow voice. Tadolini's voice has something angelic. Lady Macbeth's voice should have something devilish. (Schonberg, *Lives*, 2nd ed.)

While this makes sense to us, it's not the kind of thing we would expect to hear from a composer involved in the bel canto Italian operatic industry.

Just as Mozart left the operatic pack far behind him in 1781 with the composition of *Idomeneo*, so Verdi left his bel canto contemporaries behind in the years between 1851 and 1853, with the composition of *Rigoletto* in 1851 and *Il Trovatore* and *La Traviata* in 1853.

Bel canto opera—both opera buffa and opera seria—was characterized by the traditional divisions of aria, recitative, and ensemble, divisions that had existed in some form or another since the mid-seventeenth century.

Incrementally, Verdi broke away from these traditional operatic divisions. In the operas of 1851 to 1853, the divisions between aria, recitative, and ensemble are almost completely indistinguishable, subsumed in the name of ever greater dramatic thrust and continuity.

Verdi's mature operas were often harshly criticized, though he could not have cared less. Certainly part of his attitude toward the public and the critics was forged by the *Un Giorno di Regno* fiasco. But much of it was due to his own personality. He was a man who kept his own counsel and refused to be bullied by anyone.

Verdi seems genuinely not to have cared what the critics said, positive or negative. His single most famous letter echoes exactly these sentiments:

March 7, 1853

Dear Emmanuele Muzio:
    La Traviata *last night, a fiasco. Was it my fault or the singers? Time will decide.*
                                    Always yours, G. Verdi. (Verdi)

Verdi's mature operas share several characteristics. Human emotions and relationships lie at the heart of his mature operas. These mature operas deemphasized almost entirely the old divisions of aria, recitative, and ensemble in favor of continuous dramatic line. In them, the orchestra, as an entity, plays a much more important role than in bel canto opera, in which the orchestra is essentially an accompaniment to the voices. Finally, Verdi insisted on setting good libretti, libretti often based on standout literature by such authors as Friedrich Schiller, Victor Hugo, Alexander Dumas, Lord Byron, and Shakespeare.

As an example of Giuseppe Verdi at the very top of his game, we turn to what is arguably his most famous opera, *Aida,* of 1871. Its libretto was written by Antonio Ghislanzoni and is based on a scenario written by the French Egyptologist Auguste Mariette.

Aida (1871)

Aida unites the heroic quality of grand opera with the sound dramatic structure, vivid character delineation, pathos, and melodic, harmonic, and orchestral color that show us Giuseppe Verdi at his best.

On the surface, *Aida* is a magnificent, cast-of-thousands opera seria. It was written to celebrate the opening of the Suez Canal, and thus its ancient Egyptian locale. However, for all its magnificence, *Aida* is about three flesh-and-blood people whose feelings and actions come to life through Verdi's music.

The plot revolves around a love triangle. At the top of the triangle is the heroic Egyptian general Radames. He and Aida, an Ethiopian princess turned slave, are secretly in love. Unfortunately for them, Amneris, a jealous Egyptian princess with serious anger management issues, also loves Radames. Radames is tricked into revealing a battle plan to Aida. Amneris eavesdrops on their conversation and reports Radames's indiscretion. Accused of treason, Radames is tried, convicted, and sentenced to die via suffocation by the all-powerful priesthood of Ptah.

MUSIC BOX

Giuseppe Verdi, *Aida* (1871), Act 4, Scene 2 ("Tomb Scene")

The final scene of *Aida* offers in microcosm the visual magnificence and the emotional intimacy that lie at the heart of *Aida*. The lower half of the stage bears the tomb in which Radames has just been sealed. Above him is the interior of the Temple of Ptah. The chanting of its priests becomes part of the background fabric of the scene.

Radames discovers Aida, who has hidden in the tomb; they will die together. They sing of their love; their music ranges from the

continued on next page

mournful to the ecstatic, as they anticipate life together at a higher metaphysical plane.

Note that the differences between recitative, aria, and duet are completely obscured, as pretty much everything they sing has the melodic richness of aria and is accompanied by the orchestra.

Above them, in the temple, a grief-struck Amneris sits huddled on the floor, begging the gods for peace. Eventually, Radames and Aida stop singing; they are unconscious. Amneris moans with grief. The priests chant. The opera ends with the violins quietly playing the heavenly melody sung moments ago by the doomed lovers, telling us that Aida and Radames have passed and "transcended" to a higher place.

For all of *Aida*'s spectacle, this final scene is neither grandiose, heroic, nor even tragic. Rather, it is intensely quiet. For all the magnificence of the set, our attention is riveted on the emotions and actions of three characters with whom we identify deeply.

Verdi was a dramatist of the greatest genius. His characters resonate with us as few operatic characters do, and no matter how steamy the melodrama—and Verdi wrote some real potboilers—his characters and their emotions always strike us as real. In all of his mature operas, from *Nabucco* to *Falstaff*, we are witness to a refinement of compositional detail and an elemental emotional force delivered with a fundamental simplicity of utterance. For Verdi, it's all about the humanity of his characters and the thrust of the drama.

CHAPTER 27

Nineteenth-Century German Opera

Von Weber and Wagner, Nationalism and Experimentation

t is a *fact*: for all the hundreds (thousands?) of German-language operas written in the seventeenth and eighteenth century, for all the popularity of Mozart's wonderful *The Magic Flute* (of 1791) inside and outside of Germany/Austria, for all of this, a truly German-language national opera tradition did not come into existence until 1821, with the premiere of Carl Maria von Weber's *Der Freischütz* in Berlin.

Some might question this "fact." So, let's take a moment and trace a brief history of German-language opera. In doing so, we'll create a few distinctions that will allow us to contextualize and accept my statement for the uncontestable fact that it is!

The first German-language opera was Heinrich Schütz's *Dafne*, an opera based on the Orpheus legend, which was first performed in 1627. While we can start the history of German-language opera in 1627 with Schütz's *Dafne*, we cannot claim that it initiated a tradition of German-language opera. It was strictly an imitation of Italian models, something that was true of most of German-language opera composed during the seventeenth century.

Italian opera seria dominated German and Austrian opera stages for the first half of the eighteenth century. The exception was the Hamburg Opera, Germany's most important civic stage, where a long list of German composers tried their hands at composing German-language opera. In the end, the German-language operas produced in Hamburg could not compete with Italian-language opera, and the house closed in 1738.

The watershed event that created the first real stirrings of pan-German political nationalism—which in turn led to the cultivation of an authentically German form of opera—was the Seven Years' War (known in America as the French and Indian War). The war, which took place between 1756 and 1763, involved all the major powers of Europe and was the first war in history to be fought across the globe.

The big winners were Great Britain and Prussia. The Treaty of Paris that concluded the war saw Prussia gain a degree of influence and prestige in Europe that, in hindsight, can be seen as the beginning of the modern German state.

One of the many upshots of this new, pan-German nationalism was the cultivation of a German-language musical theater genre called the singspiel.

Singspiel means, literally, "a spoken play with singing," and that's precisely what a singspiel is: a partly sung, partly spoken German theatrical genre that has its roots in popular culture. In England, such a work is called a ballad opera or an operetta. In the United States, it's called a musical. There is no equivalent in Italian musical theater, because all such Italian works—light or heavy, serious or comic—are sung in their entirety.

The singspiel became increasingly popular as a public entertainment in German-speaking lands, even as Italian opera seria continued to be cultivated by the German aristocracy. Mozart's *The Abduction from the Harem* of 1782 and *The Magic Flute* of 1791—both of which use spoken dialogue in place of recitative—elevated the genre of singspiel to the level of high art.

However, these two Mozart operas spawned neither a school nor imitators. It wasn't until the uniquely German aspects of the singspiel were combined with the mystical, Gothic, and supernatural elements of romanticism that a truly German national opera came into being. This event occurred in 1821, with the production of

Carl Maria von Weber's opera *Der Freischütz* ("The Freeshooter") in Berlin.

Weber's *Der Freischütz* was the breakaway piece: that German-language opera that recognized and celebrated the idiosyncrasies of the German language and employed plot elements and character types identifiable as being uniquely German. It was a fabulously popular opera from the moment of its premiere, and it spawned an entire German-language Romantic opera school, capped forty years later by the "music dramas" of Richard Wagner.

German Romanticism

German romanticism in general and German Romantic opera in particular grew out of a late eighteenth-century German literary movement known as *Sturm und Drang*, or "storm and stress." Sturm und Drang, which flourished in the 1770s and the early 1780s, arose as a revolt against Classical restraint. The movement drew its inspiration from Jean Jacques Rousseau's belief that feelings serve us more reliably than reason. Sturm und Drang authors advocated free expression in language, dress, behavior, and love. Pre-Romantic German hippies.

The movement's outstanding writer was Johann Wolfgang von Goethe, who lived from 1749 to 1832. Goethe was a dramatist and poet of tremendous influence who proved the German language capable of the highest level of literary beauty and expression. He became an advocate for German-language literature and German-language vocal music by creating a body of German-language poetry that would be set to music by the next four generations of composers.

Sturm und Drang's emphasis on feeling—the volatile emotional life of the individual—and the supernatural powerfully influenced a number of young, early nineteenth-century German composers. From the standpoint of opera, the most important of these was Carl Maria von Weber. Generally speaking, music that reflected the spirit of Sturm und Drang—such as the "Storm" movement of Beethoven's Sixth Symphony—put expressive extremes ahead of the rituals, expressive niceties, and melodic fluency of classicism. Sturm und Drang music tends to be dominated by minor (meaning darker) keys areas, melodic fragmentation, and a powerfully dissonant harmonic palette. Listen to a good horror movie soundtrack and you'll hear the sorts of devices employed in Sturm und Drang, which influenced works by such composers as Carl Maria von Weber during the early nineteenth century.

Weber's *Der Freischütz*

Der Freischütz was the definitive work that established German romantic opera. In discussing the characteristics of German Romantic opera as exemplified by *Der Freischütz*, let us be aware of how very different they are from Italian bel canto opera and the operas of Verdi.

- German Romantic opera plots are drawn from medieval history, legend, or fairy tale, and generally take place in some sort of mythical time of the past.
- The stories of German Romantic opera typically involve supernatural beings and happenings.
- German Romantic opera typically features a background of nature—wild, mysterious, and uncontrolled.
- German Romantic opera employs supernatural events not as incidental elements but as essential plot elements intertwined with the fate of human characters.
- The human characters in German Romantic operas often become agents for supernatural forces, and their conflict represents nothing less than the conflict of good versus evil. Thus, the triumph of good over evil is often interpreted in terms of salvation or redemption, which creates in these operas vaguely religious overtones.

Carl Maria von Weber

After Beethoven, Carl Maria von Weber (1786–1826) was the composer most idolized by the early Romantics. He was a bundle of talent: a virtuoso pianist; a composer of what was considered music advanced for its day; a writer of sharp and pitiless criticism; and an outstanding conductor. Sadly, he also suffered from tuberculosis and died at the age of thirty-nine. It is no small irony that this first of the great "post-Beethoven" German Romantic composers actually predeceased Beethoven by nine months.

Carl Maria von Weber (1786–1826) The Teaching Company Collection

In 1817—a full forty years before Richard Wagner pronounced his idea of the *Gesamtkunstwerk* (the "all-inclusive artwork"), Weber had expounded upon his Germanic operatic ideal, in which he sought to create:

> . . . a fully rounded and self-contained work of art in which all the ingredients furnished by the contributing arts disappear in the process of fusion, and in thus perishing help to form an entirely new universe. (Schonberg, *Lives*, 3rd ed.)

Der Freischütz Story Line

Der Freischütz exemplifies the trends and content of pre-Wagner German Romantic opera.

The story features four main characters: Samiel, Max, Agathe, and Caspar. Samiel is a wild huntsman who is the devil in disguise. Max is a young huntsman in love with Agathe, the daughter of the hereditary forester. Caspar is Max's "friend" who, unbeknownst to all, has sold his soul to Samiel.

In order to marry Agathe, Max has to win a shooting contest. Inexplicably, he has found himself incapable of hitting the broad side of a barn, and in desperation he turns to his friend Caspar. Caspar promises to make magic bullets that never miss their target, provided that Max comes to the haunted Wolf's Glen in order to forge them. It is during the course of the famous "Wolf's Glen Scene" that Caspar casts the bullets under the most terrifying circumstances. According to his dastardly plan, the first six bullets will hit their intended targets, but the seventh bullet will strike Agathe. As it turns out, Samiel has his own plan, and the seventh bullet takes out Casper, who dies cursing and screaming. Max owns up to what he has done and is pardoned. In the end, *Der Freischütz* is about mercy, redemption, and, most important, the triumph of good over evil.

MUSIC BOX

Der Freischütz, Act 2 Finale, the "Wolf's Glen Scene"

The impact this scene had on contemporary audiences was incredible. Men hid their eyes; women fainted. Based on the instant popularity of the opera, we must assume they loved every minute of it.

Please note the following while listening and reading the libretto:

- The free mix of spoken dialogue and singing over the course of the scene. Samiel, the devil, only speaks, and never sings.
- Much of Caspar's dialogue is accompanied by the orchestra, creating something called a "melodrama."
- Harmonic dissonances rarely resolve during the course of the scene, creating a sense of pervasive tension.

Nineteenth-century Italian versus German Opera

The business and expressive/dramatic content of nineteenth-century Italian and German opera is a study in contrast.

Nineteenth-century Italian opera was a highly profitable popular entertainment rooted in tradition, a fact that encouraged conservatism and discouraged experimentation. Nineteenth-century Italian opera was about people: their emotions and their relationships.

German Romantic opera was an experimental Romantic art form. Unlike Italian opera, it was not limited by tradition or an industry intent on maintaining its profit margin. Free from the anchor of tradition, nineteenth-century German-language opera was free to develop as a cutting-edge Romantic era art form. It was with the operas and music dramas of Richard Wagner that German opera, German musical nationalism, and German romanticism reached their thunderous, gut-wrenching climax.

Richard Wagner (1813–1883)

What Beethoven was to the first half of the nineteenth century, so Richard Wagner was to the second half: the single most influential, revolutionary, controversial, and talked-about composer of his time. Wagner was the darling of the Romantic avant-garde, a prophet, an idealist, and a genuine musical revolutionary. His music redefined what was considered expressively possible in the opera house and, by extension, the symphony hall.

Richard Wagner (1813–1883) The Teaching Company Collection

Wilhelm Richard Wagner was born in Leipzig on May 22, 1813. Richard's legal father was Karl Friedrich Wagner, though it is almost certain that his biological father was an actor and painter named Ludwig Geyer, with whom his mother was having an affair. Wagner's paternity was something he obsessed over his entire life.

At the age of fifteen Wagner decided to become a composer, despite the fact that he could hardly play any musical instrument and knew next to nothing about the mechanics of music. He turned out to be the most amazing adolescent prodigy in the history of Western music. Within five years, by the age of twenty, he had composed his first complete opera, an entirely credible work entitled *The Fairies*.

Wagner later claimed that his two greatest musical influences were Beethoven's Symphony no. 9 and Carl Maria von Weber's opera *Der Freischütz*. Because Wagner considered Beethoven's Ninth to be the essential antecedent of his own dramatically charged music, he claimed to be the only legitimate musical offspring of Beethoven. (It was a typically "Wagnerian" statement of paternity: "If I can't be sure who my father is, he'll be whoever I want him to be!")

From the beginning Wagner wanted to write operas, and from the beginning of his operatic career he was his own librettist, and thus controlled virtually every aspect of his works. In total, he created thirteen complete musical-dramatic productions. The first, *The Fairies*, was completed in 1833. The last, *Parsifal*, was completed in 1882.

Wagner's career was an object lesson in perseverance. After an extremely rocky start, he landed a plum job in 1842, at the age of twenty-nine: as assistant director of the Dresden Court Opera. Unfortunately, he was never one to keep his enthusiasms to himself or his mouth shut, and his outspoken political activism during the failed Dresden uprising of May 1849 got him into very hot water with the authorities, who issued a warrant for his arrest. With the help of his future father-in-law, Franz Liszt, he escaped Dresden and hightailed it to Switzerland, where he remained in exile for twelve years. It was while in Switzerland that Wagner took a five-year hiatus from composing, during which he reevaluated his career and the nature of the music he wanted to write.

Wagner came to the conclusion that French and Italian opera were degenerate art forms, fossils from the past and not harbingers of the future. What was required, he asserted, was a musical-dramatic revolution that would create a comprehensive art form "in which all the resources of drama, poetry, instrumental music, song, acting, gesture, costumes, and scenery would combine in the presentation and celebration of myth." Far from being mere entertainment, such productions would have the power and impact of religious celebrations.

According to Wagner, the artist of the future (and we don't have to guess who the artist of the future was in Wagner's mind) would combine the achievements of ancient Greek drama, myth, Shakespeare, and Beethoven into a single art form: something that, drawing an analogy with poetic drama, Wagner called music drama.

The term Wagner coined for such an artwork was *Gesamtkunstwerk*, the all-inclusive artwork: *Gesamt*, "all-inclusive"; *kunst*, "art"; *werk*, "work."

Tristan und Isolde (1859)

As an example of Wagner's ideas-in-action, we turn to *Tristan und Isolde* of 1859. With Beethoven's Ninth Symphony, it was the most influential musical work of the nineteenth century.

The major characters: Isolde is an Irish princess. Tristan is a knight and a nephew of King Mark of Cornwall, in southern England. Brangäne is Isolde's maid.

Deep background: While campaigning in Ireland, an army led by Tristan devastates Isolde's homeland. Tristan personally kills Isolde's fiancé, a gent called Morold, while he himself is grievously injured in the process. Isolde, who hails from a long line of Celtic healers and pharmacists, nurses Tristan back to health. Tristan tells her that his name is Tantris, which are the syllables of "Tristan" inverted. Isolde is nobody's fool, and she figures out pretty quickly who this Tantris actually is. Try as she might, however, she cannot kill him, for they have fallen in love.

Healed, Tristan leaves, and demonstrates his gratitude to Isolde by returning some years later in order to carry her off to Cornwall, there to marry his uncle, old King Mark.

The opera begins on board Tristan's ship as it approaches

Cornwall. Isolde is in her stateroom, livid with rage. She's determined to kill Tristan and then commit suicide. She orders her maid,
Brangäne, to mix a death potion. Brangäne, not wanting to join the
ranks of the unemployed, mixes a love potion instead.

Isolde sends word to Tristan that he should come to her stateroom
for a quaff. Tristan is conflicted: he understands what Isolde is up to,
but his shame demands that he comply. So they drink to each other,
each expecting to be dead within seconds. But of course, they don't
die. Instead, after a bit of convulsing and gyrating, they find themselves joined at the pelvis, hopelessly in love with each other. It is a
love, a passion, that remains unconsummated over the remainder
of the opera. In the end, Isolde expires in an orgasmic haze over the
recently deceased Tristan, and they are joined at a higher metaphysical plane, having transcended corporeal reality.

Wagner's music-dramas exhibit three major innovations that are
all in evidence in *Tristan und Isolde*:

- Music in the service of drama: Wagner's music-dramas are about
  continuous, nonstop music in the service of continuous, nonstop
  drama. Consequently, in his music-dramas, there is no distinction
  between aria and recitative, and only on the rarest of occasions
  does more than one singer sing at the same time.
- The orchestra as a "character": The orchestra becomes an actual
  character in a Wagner music-drama, playing a role analogous to that
  of the chorus in a Greek drama. In a Wagner music-drama, the music
  played by the orchestra is, more often than not, different from and of
  equal dramatic import as that being sung onstage. Sometimes what
  the orchestra plays even contradicts what is being sung, and reveals
  emotions that the character may not consciously acknowledge or
  understand. Thus, the instrumental music played by the orchestra
  becomes the alter ego of the drama unfolding onstage. In order to
  achieve this, Wagner de facto invented the concept of leitmotif.
- Leitmotif: A leitmotif is some sort of musical idea—a motive, a thematic melody, a particular harmony, or a harmonic progression—that

represents a person, a thing, or even an idea. The meaning of a particular leitmotif is established with the leitmotif being sounded, typically in the orchestra, when the person, thing, or idea it represents first appears (or is mentioned), and then repeated at each subsequent appearance (or mention).

The key leitmotif in *Tristan and Isolde* is the so-called drink-death leitmotif: it's that musical idea that represents the drink that Tristan and Isolde think is poison but is actually a love potion that, once consumed, will lead to their deaths anyway, thus signifying "death through love" *and* "love through death": a convention/theme particularly popular with composers of the Romantic era. (Got that?) Other dramatic ramifications of the drink are projected by this leitmotif, including endless longing, death, and corporeal negation.

When it is first sung, the leitmotif is heard in association with the words "I drink to you!"

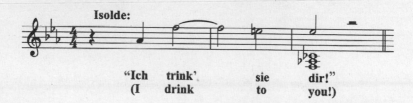

However, long before the leitmotif is sung, it appears in this form at the very beginning of the overture:

This version of the leitmotif describes three distinct dramatic elements. The first element is the rising minor sixth that describes the physical act of lifting the cup:

The second element is the downward chromatic line that describes the flow of liquid:

The third element is the downward chromatic descent to a harmonic dissonance:

Since the Renaissance, a descending chromatic line has been emblematic of death. The descending chromatic ending on a dissonance (the example just given) indicates that the erstwhile "love potion" will, in the end, be as deadly as poison. As such, love and death are here made equivalent, representing in this music-drama two sides of the same dramatic coin.

But wait! There's more! From the very beginning of the overture, the drink-death leitmotif is linked with a chromatically rising motive, a second leitmotif, one that represents mutual longing:

The linkage of the falling drink-death motive followed by the rising mutual longing motive creates three additional meanings: one, that the drink itself will be the cause of that longing; two, that death (the falling chromatic line) and desire (the rising chromatic line) are mirror images of each other; and three, that only through death can transcendent love be realized.

These leitmotifs and many others we have not discussed will be repeated, varied, fragmented, and developed, often in the voice, but most often in the orchestra, with each permutation offering up some new and subtle twist of meaning. Often they will be linked together to create, like those long composite German words, entirely new meanings.

Even the most prepared listener cannot possibly decode all of the leitmotifs as they fly by, and Wagner does not expect us to. What he wants is for us to react, consciously and unconsciously, to the dramatic truth the orchestral leitmotifs provide in tandem with the singers. Thus, the orchestra becomes the unconscious truth behind the words of the characters on stage.

Arthur Schopenhauer

*T*ristan and Isolde was singularly influenced by the nineteenth-century German philosopher Arthur Schopenhauer, who lived from 1788 to 1860. Schopenhauer asserted that only instrumental music could express both the full range of human emotions and impressions and the greater truths that lie behind the façade of everyday life:

> Instrumental music is entirely independent of the phenomenal, that is, the conscious, everyday world. It ignores it altogether. It is a copy of the will, the great inner truth itself. . . . Thus, the creator of [instrumental] music reveals the inner truth of the world.

Did this ever ring Wagner's chimes! Schopenhauer's belief that only instrumental music was capable of telling the great and hidden truths helped Wagner shape his concepts of the leitmotif and the orchestra.

For Wagner, the orchestra becomes the voice of inner truth. As a result, a Wagner music-drama unfolds at two very different levels. The singers onstage present the "phenomenal" world of the everyday, replete with the half-truths and the delusions that characterize our conscious interaction. The orchestra, by employing leitmotifs and speaking without the intervention of words, tells the truth.

That Wagner was an often hateful human being whose nationalistic, often jingoistic, and sometimes genuinely depraved work was hijacked by Hitler and the Nazis must be acknowledged. But none of this changes the fact that Wagner created entirely new worlds of experience and meaning in his music-dramas, which remain the most extreme examples of the Romantic doctrine of expressive inclusivity. Even more than that, by dint of his mythical settings, his highfalutin' use of language, and his overwhelmingly powerful music, Wagner created an alternative reality, one that arouses in us the mystical and sensuous ecstasy that is the essence of romanticism.

CHAPTER 28

Of Thee I Sing

Musical Nationalism in the Nineteenth Century

I n 1848, the European world was turned upside down as revolutions and nationalist movements broke out across Western and Central Europe. By the summer of 1849, the revolutions had, one by one faltered and then failed.

Why?

First, the old governments were stunned but not broken. Second, the revolutionaries themselves tended to be writers, professors, and students: people with ideas but lacking almost entirely practical political experience and economic clout. Finally, the armies—with their officer corps drawn from the old aristocracies—remained loyal to the old governments.

In the wave of repression that followed, overt political nationalism was outlawed. Among the results was that the nationalist aspirations unleashed by the failed revolutions of 1848–1849 found expression instead in the arts: in literature, in visual art, and in music.

The year of failed revolutions gave impetus to a musical movement called nationalism, which saw the incorporation of folk music or folklike music into concert works, songs, and operas. Program compositions and operas were based on stories drawn from national traditions, and very often these stories were reinforced by the inclusion of actual folk melodies in the works themselves. The result was music and opera that stirred powerful nationalistic feelings at home and made a strong ethnic impression abroad.

How was this different from the language-based musical national-ism of the Baroque era and nineteenth-century musical nationalism? In chapter 7, you'll recall we discussed the development of a German musical style during the sixteenth and seventeenth centuries based on the nature and idiosyncrasies of the German language. Nineteenth-century musical nationalism is different, as its basis is folk music rather than the idiosyncratic nature of a language. We refer to nineteenth-century musical nationalism as folkloric nationalism, which was, at least initially, as much a political movement as an artistic one.

This chapter and the next will examine nineteenth-century musical nationalism (and exoticism) through musical examples provided by Frédéric Chopin, Franz Liszt, Johannes Brahms, and the group of composers known as the Russian Five.

Frédéric Chopin (1810–1849)

Frédéric Chopin was born in 1810. His own nationalist impulse predates 1848 but was itself a patriotic tribute to his Polish home-land, a country partitioned and occupied in Chopin's time by Russia. The distinctly Pol-ish aspects of Chopin's music include not only the sound and Polish-language-derived rhythmic character of its melodies but even the compositional genres with which he worked. For example, Chopin's polonaises and mazurkas are stylized Polish dances, works that display the expressive spirit and rhythmic character of Polish national dance music.

Frédéric Chopin (1810–1849) Library of Congress, Prints and Photographs Division, LC-USZ62-103898

Frédéric Chopin, Polonaise for Piano in A Major, Op, 40, No. 1 (1838)

A polonaise is a stately Polish processional dance set in triple meter; that is, it is a three-step, like a waltz. By definition, a polonaise will be characterized by the following rhythm:

Chopin's sixteen polonaises, composed across the span of his all-too-brief career (he died at the age of thirty-nine) constitute the jewel in his nationalistic musical crown, and they run the expressive gamut from the tragic to the heroic. The Polonaise in A Major, op. 40, no. 1 is the most heroic of them all: proud, explosive, and gloriously lyric.

Note the following:

- The expressive spirit is unrelentingly magnificent, a worthy demonstration of Chopin's pride in his Polish heritage.
- Typical of the great bulk of Chopin's solo piano music, the polonaise can be considered an instrumental miniature, with a straightforward internal musical form of A-B-A.
- Chopin uses the entire keyboard of the piano, and milks every last bit of resonance out of the instrument. This is piano music that could not have been conceived before the invention of the metal harped piano.

Chopin's final illness was indirectly brought about as a result of the revolutions of 1848. He made his living giving piano lessons to the rich daughters of Parisian high society. In the spring of 1848, in response to political upheavals in Paris, that aristocratic class vamoosed; no reason to tempt fate by hanging around Paris during yet another revolution, right? Chopin, who lived high, saw his income dry up overnight. He was forced (or so he felt) to take up an invitation to concertize in England and Scotland in order to get by. Concertize he did, though he hated every minute of it. He was frail and consumptive to start with, and the concert tour finished him off. When he returned to Paris in 1849, he was so weakened that he died soon after of advanced pulmonary tuberculosis and possible tubercular enteritis.

Frédéric Chopin, small, slim, and sickly, played the piano with exquisite gentleness; we read that the volume of his playing rarely rose above piano, meaning "quiet." His friend Franz Liszt *thundered* on the piano, and while some auditors (usually envious ones) bemoaned Liszt's "tastelessness," Chopin openly envied him, famously saying in a letter that "Liszt is playing my etudes and putting honest thoughts out of my head. I should like to rob him of the way he plays my [music]!" (Walker, *Liszt*, vol. 1, 184)

Ferenç Liszt (1811–1886)

Ferenç, or Franz, Liszt was born in Hungary 1811 in and died in Bayreuth, Germany, in 1886 while attending an opera festival staged by his son-in-law, Richard Wagner.

Liszt was an extraordinary piano prodigy and began touring professionally at the age of eleven. By the age of sixteen he had burned out. He settled in Paris, where he studied composition, taught piano, concertized privately in salons, and generally kicked

Franz Liszt (1811–1886) Library of Congress, Music Division

around like the semi-slacker he was, unsure of where his life was headed.

This all changed in April of 1832, when Liszt heard the violinist Niccolò Paganini play a concert at the Paris Opera House. Liszt was floored by the sheer, awe-inspiring, head-shaking virtuosity of Paganini's violin playing. Talk about hair-raising: thanks to Paganini, Liszt had what the fight promoter Don King would call an "epiphanous realization of magnanimous importitude." Liszt realized that the "Paganini of the piano" had yet to appear, and he vowed to become that person: a virtuosic hero in whom man and instrument would be united as one!

His underachiever days over, Liszt later claimed to have spent the next five years practicing the piano ten to twelve hours each day, mastering every conceivable technical challenge and, at the same time, building up what became his legendary endurance. He also began to compose works for piano that took advantage of his developing technique, works of often intractable difficulty.

In 1838, Liszt began to tour again and became a legend. He was the greatest showman of his age, a one-man circus: Elvis, Sinatra, P. T. Barnum, Liberace, and KISS all rolled into one. He virtually invented the "solo piano recital," refusing, as he did, to share the stage with anyone (to which we ask, Who, in their right mind, would want to have to share the stage with Franz Liszt?). His recitals created riots (see below). The poet Heinrich Heine coined a term for it all, calling it Lisztomania.

There would seem to be a direct correlation between the ongoing diminution of religious institutions and the aristocracy and the concurrent rise of secular heroes after 1800. It was in this atmosphere that Franz Liszt came to define the instrumental virtuoso as a hero, even as a god.

Liszt's concerts were orgies. Women would scream and faint and throw precious tokens of their esteem onto the stage. Liszt would casually flick his cigar butts into the audience, and women would tear each other to shreds to get a hold of such a treasure.

Other such trophies included Liszt's gloves, which he would casually toss into the audience, and even the broken piano strings that had not been equal to Liszt's playing. Sometimes Liszt would himself stage a faint at the conclusion of a recital, just to freak out the audience.

Meanwhile, we can well imagine Liszt, sitting in his dressing room a minute or two later, with a cigar and brandy, counting that night's receipts. Because of such antics, many of his more serious contemporaries believed him to be a charlatan and a con man. That he was. But he was also one of the greatest pianists who ever lived, and a composer capable of first-rate work when he put his mind to it.

In 1848 Liszt stopped touring, as European travel was too dangerous during that revolutionary year. Instead, he took the city of Weimar up on a standing job offer and moved there in 1849, to live and work for the next ten years as Weimar's composer-in-residence. It was during his time in Weimar that Liszt began to compose orchestral music as well as piano music. Among the works published while he lived in Weimar was his Hungarian Rhapsody No. 2, one of nineteen he composed between 1846 and 1885.

Liszt's Hungarian Rhapsodies were his attempt to elevate what he believed to be Hungarian folk music. In reality, they are settings of gypsy (Romani) melodies, a far cry from genuine Magyar (Hungarian folk) music. If Liszt's ethnomusicological knowledge left something to be desired, his heart was in the right nationalist place.

There's no great pretense to high musical art in Liszt's Hungarian Rhapsodies. They are essentially medleys of gypsy tunes structured along the lines of a Hungarian dance called a *verbunkos*. But what wonderful tunes they are, and how wonderfully arranged for the piano! If this music is the train wreck that so many academes claim it to be, then I would suggest there's much to be salvaged from the wreck. Mostly, the Rhapsodies are fun: filled with engaging melodies, ethnic color, rhythmic energy, and extraordinary pianism. They are also a wonderful example of nineteenth-century folkloric nationalism: concert works that feature folk or folklike music. For the Hungarian-born Liszt, this presumably Hungarian music also made a powerful personal and political statement: "This is who I am, and this is a culture of which I am proud!"

Liszt, Hungarian Rhapsody No. 2 in C-sharp Minor

The most famous of Liszt's nineteen Hungarian Rhapsodies is the second, which was ingrained forever on the public's consciousness in 1946, when it was simultaneously used in a Warner Bros./*Bugs Bunny* cartoon called "Rhapsody Rabbit," and a MGM/*Tom and Jerry* cartoon called "The Cat Concerto." Warner and MGM were each convinced that they had been plagiarized by the other.

Note the following two points:

- The *Rhapsody* is dance music that evokes a physical response.
- The constant shifts between major and minor, and the manner in which short, punchy motivic ideas and phrases are repeated, help to imbue this music with an "accent," a sense of locale that is neither Italian, Austrian, nor German, but rather, stereotypically central European.

Exoticism

By the 1860s or so, the language of concert music had been profoundly enriched by folkloric nationalism. Polish, Bohemian, Hungarian, Russian, Moravian, Spanish, and other nationalist composers brought all sorts of new melodic and rhythmic resources to the compositional table, and it didn't take long for their musical "ethnicisms" to became part of the common musical language, a composer's country of origin notwithstanding.

We see the beginnings of what we might rightly call musical globalism in the 1860s and '70s as composers, entranced by the ethnic sounds of other nations, began incorporating such ethnicisms in their own music.

For example, Johannes Brahms was born in 1833 in Hamburg, a city of upright, conservative, and solid Lutheran stock. Brahms was a young musician of extraordinary promise who, as an adolescent, found his home town and its good people a bit stiff, a bit unyielding, and *boring*. Well, not after 1848 he didn't, when thousands of Hungarian refugees fleeing their failed revolution arrived in Hamburg, either to stay or sail off through the seaport. Suddenly, at the most impressionable age of fifteen, Brahms was surrounded by all of these exotic and wonderful people who wore their emotions and their cultures on their sleeves. Brahms fell in love with their passion, their emotionalism, and, especially, their music.

The Hamburg-born Johannes Brahms became a Hungarophile. His mature compositions are filled with Hungarian gypsy-like music. Brahms's Hungarian Dance No. 5 (see the next Music Box) is but the most famous of his Hungarian works. Other examples include the fourth movement of his Piano Quartet in G Minor of 1861; the third movement of his magnificent Violin Concerto in D Major of 1878; and the second movement of his Clarinet Quintet in B Minor of 1891, one of my personal desert island pieces. We could go on, but there's no need to; with all due respect to Franz Liszt, perhaps the greatest nineteenth-century composer of Hungarian gypsy-inspired music is the German Johannes Brahms!

MUSIC BOX

Brahms, Hungarian Dance No. 5 (1869)

With apologies to Franz Liszt, no nineteenth-century composer wrote better Romani-flavored music than Johannes Brahms. Note the following:

- This Hungarian "dance" is precisely what it purports to be: dance music that evokes a physical response.
- Of Brahms's composed twenty-one Hungarian dances, only three are entirely original compositions: nos. 11, 14, and 16.
- Brahms's ethnomusicological research skills were no better than Liszt's. Brahms thought that the melody he set as dance no. 5 was a traditional folk song, when in truth it is a Hungarian dance known as the Csárdás by a composer named Kéler Béla entitled "Bártfai emlék." (Walker, *Liszt* vol. 1, p. 341)

Exoticism, then, is the use by a composer of one nationality of the ethnic musical elements of another nationality. Other examples of exoticism include the Russian composer Nikolai Rimsky-Korsakov's Arabian-flavored *Scheherazade*; the Russian composer Peter Tchaikovsky's *Capriccio Italian*; and the French composer Maurice Ravel's Spanish-flavored *Bolero*. For many Romantic and early twentieth-century composers, folkloric nationalism and exoticism became modes of heightened self-expression in an era that valued self-expression above all other things.

CHAPTER 29

Romantic Nationalism, Russian Style

Nineteenth-century Russian musical nationalism was also an artistic response to political events: Russia's entry into the larger European community and the subsequent desire on the part of Russian musicians to ensure the preservation of their unique musical heritage in the face of what they considered Italian and German musical dominance.

Czar Peter I (the "Great") lived from 1672 to 1725. In his effort to move his country out of its Middle Ages to join the family of European nations, Peter transformed Muscovite Russia into a major European power.

To this end, he founded (in 1703) and built a spanking new capital city. Named for his patron saint, Saint Peter the Apostle, St. Petersburg was inspired by Venice and Amsterdam and is itself a city of canals. But even more than just a new capital city (which it remained until the capital was returned to Moscow after the Revolution in 1917), St. Petersburg was to be Russia's so-called Window to the West. To achieve this, Peter stocked it with the best foreign artists, musicians, and teachers his rubles could buy. St. Petersburg became, and remains, the most Westernized city in all of Russia.

From the city's beginning, the cultural life of St. Petersburg was controlled by the Russian aristocracy and not the Russian Orthodox Church. Through the beginning of the nineteenth century, the cultured music one would have heard in St. Petersburg consisted of the same Italian opera that was popular with aristocratic classes across Europe, light Viennese and Italian instrumental music, and aristocratic amateur concerts.

This began to change as a result of two galvanizing events, events that thrust Russia into the forefront of the European community. The first was the defeat of Napoleon in 1812 and the second was the Decembrist Revolution of 1825 The defeat of Napoleon in 1812 raised Russian national pride and prestige through the roof. Perceived as the saviors of Europe, Russian politics and culture became even more enmeshed with those of Western Europe.

The Decembrist Revolution was a failed attempt to create a constitutional monarchy based on the ideals of the French Revolution. While the revolution might have failed politically, the spirit of individual freedom and nationalism it engendered electrified the intellectual and artistic classes of Russia. After 1825, many Russian writers, poets, and musicians made a conscious effort to cultivate a uniquely Russian artistic tradition.

Preeminent among these new Russian nationalists was the poet and author Alexander Sergeyevich Pushkin (1799–1837). Through the model of his own work, Pushkin did for the Russian language what Goethe did for the German language: he gave an artistic legitimacy to a language that had, up to his time, not been considered fit for fine literary expression. Pushkin's influence was not limited to the world of letters; many of his literary works were turned into operas, including *Eugene Onegin* and the *Queen of Spades* by Tchaikovsky; *Boris Godunov* by Mussorgsky; and *Ruslan and Lyudmila* by Mikhail Glinka.

Mikhail Ivanovich Glinka (1804–1857)

The history of a truly Russian concert music begins with Glinka. He was born into a wealthy, landowning family, and his early musical education consisted of the piano and violin lessons typical for a young man of his class.

In 1824, at the age of twenty, Glinka became a civil servant, taking a job in the Ministry of Ways and Communications in St. Petersburg. He continued to dabble in music until 1834, when, inspired by the nationalist literature of Pushkin and Nikolai Gogol, he got it into his head to compose an opera on a Russian subject and in the Russian language.

As we have observed, nothing is more basic to a nation's culture than its native language, and nothing will shape the sound of a particular nation's music more than musical structures based on the idiosyncrasies of that native language.

Glinka's opera, entitled *A Life for the Tsar*, received its premiere on December 9, 1836, and it was a gigantic success. Yes, the opera owes much to Italy, and it employs the large choruses and dance segments characteristic of French opera. But in composing it, Glinka devised a very flexible and highly idiosyncratic style of recitative that grew out of both the rhythms and inflections of the Russian language and filled it with tunes that have the rhythmic oomph and melodic character of Russian folk music. It is not an overstatement to say that Russian national concert music began with Mikhail Glinka's *A Life for the Tsar* in 1836.

Glinka's music provided a model for a Russian national music that would inspire the next generation of Russian composers. When he died in February of 1857 he was canonized, even deified. Among those who believed most fervently in Glinka's musical godhead was a twenty-year-old pianist and composer living in St. Petersburg by the name of Mily Alexeyevich Balakirev (1837–1910).

The Mighty Handful: The Russian Five

Despite his minimal musical training, Balakirev set himself up as a music teacher and managed to become the successor of Glinka: the Tsar of Russian Music. During the 1860s, Balakirev gathered around himself a group of young musical hobbyists whose day gigs had nothing to do with music. They were César Cui (1835–1918), a career army officer; Modest Mussorgsky (1839–1881), an army ensign who resigned from the army and took a job at the post office; Nikolai Rimsky-Korsakov (1844–1908), a naval officer; and Alexander Borodin (1833–1887), a doctor and chemist.

This group of composers came to be known as The Mighty Handful, or simply, The Five. Not since the Florentine Camerata had a group of dilettantes so profoundly affected the history of Western music. In his memoirs, César Cui described what they did:

> We formed a close-knit circle of young composers and, since there was nowhere to study—for us the conservatory did not exist—our self-education began. It consisted of playing through [on the piano] everything that had been written by all the greatest composers, and all works were subjected to criticism and analysis in all their technical and creative aspects. We were young and our judgments were harsh. We were very disrespectful in our attitude toward Mozart and Mendelssohn. [No surprise there; The Five had a really bad attitude toward Austrian and German composers.] We were very enthusiastic about Liszt and Berlioz. [No surprise there either; The Five adored the Romantics.] [And] we worshipped Chopin and Glinka. We carried on heated debates; we discussed musical form, program music, vocal music, and especially opera. (Grout, Palisca, 4th ed.)

Self-taught and proud of it, The Five considered their technical ignorance an asset and raised the flag of their dogmatic nationalism at every opportunity. To them, the great enemies of Russian music were the Rubinstein brothers, Anton and Nikolai. Anton Rubinstein, a pianist and composer, founded the St. Petersburg Conservatory in 1862. His brother Nikolai, a pianist and conductor, founded the Moscow Conservatory in 1866. As far as the members of The Five were concerned, the Rubinsteins, who represented the Western European academic tradition, were an ongoing threat to Russian music. Mily

Balakirev considered the St. Petersburg Conservatory "A plot to bring all Russian music under the yoke of the German generals!"

Thanks to The Five, the ancient and enduring tradition of Russian xenophobia was applied to nineteenth-century concert music as well! A characteristically Russian music emerged from The Five based on the model of Glinka. It was music that, one, employed Russian folk melodies or melodies built to sound like folk melodies; two, was overwhelmingly expository (meaning thematic) in nature and featured little or no development in the German sense; and three, was rhythmically powerful and sharply accented, based on the rhythmic character of the Russian language itself.

Nikolai Andreyevich Rimsky-Korsakov (1844–1908)

By the 1880s, the once-amateurish Rimsky-Korsakov had become the most technically polished composer of The Five. This was due, in no small part, to a job he took in 1871, one that irked some of his colleagues in The Five to no end: he accepted a position teaching orchestration and composition at Anton Rubinstein's St. Petersburg Conservatory. For all the rancor this caused, Rimsky-Korsakov's new day job was a giant step forward for Russian music. In order to stay ahead of his students, Rimsky-Korsakov finally had to learn proper compositional technique, for which, as it turns out, he had a genius. As a teacher, Rimsky-Korsakov managed to bridge the gap between The Five and their nationalist agenda with the traditional European musical establishment. His professorship

Nikolai Andreyevich Rimsky-Korsakov (1844–1908) Library of Congress, Prints and Photographs Division, LC-USZ61-560

enabled him to become an influential teacher, taking the message of
The Five to the next generation of Russian composers, a generation
properly grounded in technique. Among Rimsky-Korsakov's great
students were Igor Stravinsky, Sergei Prokofiev, and Alexander Glazunov; and Glazunov's greatest student was Dmitri Shostakovich.

Today, we in the West know Rimsky-Korsakov as the composer of
a number of incredibly popular orchestral works: The *Capriccio Espa-
ñol*, *The Russian Easter Overture*, and *Scheherazade*. However, in his
lifetime and in Russia today, Rimsky-Korsakov is known primarily
as a composer of operas, thirteen in all, the same number as Richard
Wagner and two more than Vincenzo Bellini.

MUSIC BOX

Nicolai Rimsky-Korsakov,
Russian Easter Overture (1888)

Rimsky-Korsakov's *Russian Easter Overture* is an example of late
nineteenth-century Russian nationalism and Rimsky-Korsakov
at their best.

The *Russian Easter Overture* is a concert overture, a one-movement program work cast in sonata form and intended as a curtain
raiser for an orchestral concert.

It is nationalistic in two distinct ways. The first is programmatic:
the overture tells the story of a Russian Easter Day from dawn to
dusk. The second way it is nationalistic is through the musical means
with which Rimsky-Korsakov tells the story: the four main themes
of the piece are all Orthodox chants drawn from a collection of
melodies published in 1772 called the *Obichod*, the first music actually printed in Russia.

Note the following:

- The preexisting chants on which Rimsky-Korsakov bases the
  overture are motivically related to each other, which creates an

continued on next page

extraordinary degree of thematic unity across the span of the overture. By fragmenting and developing motives drawn from these chants, it becomes virtually impossible to tell where the preexisting materials leave off and where Rimsky-Korsakov's new material begins.

- Like Hector Berlioz before him, Rimsky-Korsakov played the orchestra the way another musician might play the piano or the flute. He had an extraordinary ear for instrumental combinations and "color," and like Berlioz he even wrote an important and influential book on orchestration. In the Russia of Rimsky-Korsakov's time, Easter was celebrated at around the same time as the beginning of spring. Thus, the rebirth intrinsic to spring becomes, by extension, a metaphor for Christ's resurrection, which lies at the heart of the Easter celebration.

In many ways, the spirit of romanticism—of supra-self-expression, heightened emotional states, and self-identification through nationalist (or exotic) musical content continued through 1939, and ended only with the advent of World War II. However, the musical language with which Western composers expressed themselves underwent a sea change in the first years of the twentieth century, as the very syntax of music became contextual and subject to the expressive vision and requirements of the composer. Our next chapter will explore some of the cultural, technological, intellectual, and philosophical currents that contributed to this reevaluation of the musical syntax around the turn of the twentieth century.

CHAPTER 30

A Modern Music for a
Modern World

The twentieth century was a time of terrific (and often terrifying) change. If music is indeed a mirror, we would expect musical style to have gone through a period of accelerated change
during the twentieth century. And that it did.

We will ease our way into the twentieth century, as the average
listener has a problem with most twentieth-century concert music,
and most twentieth-century concert music has a problem with the
average listener. The aim of this chapter is to create a context for the
stunning musical innovations that occurred during the first years of
the twentieth century.

For those who turn to concert music as a refuge from the complexities of modern life, much of the music of the twentieth century
might appear to be painfully dissonant and even incomprehensible.
To these good folks, I would suggest that many of the best things in
life—including the music of the twentieth century—are acquired
tastes. If this were not true, then every ten-year-old would be as
sophisticated as every fifty-year-old, something I personally would
find intolerable. The kids have their hair, their teeth, their eyesight,
and their knees, but we grown-ups know the difference between
taupe and *tan* and between Southern Comfort and a smoky Islay
single malt. Life experience is everything, and real wisdom comes
only with time and experience.

We often forget that the music we turn to as a refuge was, at the time it was created, considered by many to be painfully dissonant and/or incomprehensible new music. In their own lifetimes, Johann Sebastian Bach's music was criticized for being impenetrably complex; Haydn's for being too facile; Mozart's for being overly long and complicated; Beethoven's for being virtually unfathomable and without melody; and hey, Johannes Brahms was called a "giftless bastard," by the composer Peter Tchaikovsky no less! The point: the same things that make a piece of contemporary music new and exciting also make it different, and lacking a context to understand its differences, an audience will often dismiss such a work. Lacking historical perspective, a contemporary audience is in no position to tell what music will stand the test of time and what music will not.

However painfully dissonant and incomprehensible the music of the twentieth century might sound to some listeners, we here in the twenty-first century have all the historical context we require to understand the expressive impetus behind and the meaning of the music of the twentieth century in general, and of the first decades of the twentieth century in particular. In order to contextualize the vast changes in Western concert music that took place during the first two decades of the twentieth century, let us first take a few baby steps backward.

Across the span of this book, we've examined music that served the spirit and the Church, both Catholic and Protestant. We've examined music that, at different times and places, served the word, the stage, the aristocracy, and the middle class.

Not until the early nineteenth century do we encounter music in which the principal expressive aim was to serve the particular emotional needs of the composer himself. The glorification of the individual that marked the Enlightenment, the growing social and economic power of the middle class, the almost inconceivable societal disruptions caused by the French Revolution and the subsequent Napoleonic age; these and various other circumstances combined to create the conditions for an expressive musical revolution, one that would see a composer assert that musical expression must serve the individual composer himself.

That composer was Ludwig van Beethoven, an unhappy man of genius whose investment in the status quo—in the Classical style— was minimal at best. Beethoven's volcanic personal issues required an outlet, and that outlet was his music.

Revolutionary as his music appears, Beethoven was, like his contemporary Napoleon, a quintessential man of his time: a middle-class man who attained the rank of a creative hero thanks to his own industry and genius, an example of the post-Enlightenment meritocracy in action.

The same societal conditions that allowed Beethoven to frame his seemingly revolutionary attitude toward musical expression led to that expression-at-all-costs movement known as "romanticism." With Beethoven as their poster child, cutting-edge Romantics valued extreme, supra-personalized expressive content above all things.

The increasingly extreme range of Romantic expression required increasingly extreme musical means to depict that expression. To make their new and original expressive points, Romantic composers had to go ever further beyond the bounds of the traditional musical language to achieve their expressive ends, something called the "abortive gesture": that is, doing the "wrong" thing for the "right" expressive reason.

For example, take the first movement of Gustav Mahler's Symphony no. 9 of 1908. Despite the fact that the symphony dates from the early twentieth century, it is, in terms of its musical language, a Romantic era composition. Once again, temporal reality intrudes on the chronological convenience of period dates. Mahler was born in 1860; his musical inheritance was that of Beethoven, Berlioz, Weber, and Wagner; his expressive impulse was formed by nineteenth-century German Romanticism. So despite the fact that he completed his Ninth Symphony in 1908, it is a work that must be observed through the lens of romanticism.

Gustav Mahler and the Abortive Gesture

Gustav Mahler (1860–1911) was a complex and difficult man. Born to Jewish parents in Bohemia in 1860, he was a prototypical alienated individual. His famous rather self-pitying statement says it all: "I am thrice homeless: as a Bohemian in Austria, as an Austrian among Germans, as a Jew throughout the world, everywhere an intruder, never welcomed."

Gustav Mahler (1860–1911)
Library of Congress, Music Division

Though a composer of genius, Mahler was "forced," as he would tell it, to conduct for a living. He was almost as good a conductor as he was a composer, and in 1897 he accepted the job of a lifetime: principal conductor and, within a short period of time, music director of the Vienna State Opera. Five years later, in 1902, he impregnated and married (in that order) a woman nineteen years his junior. Alma Schindler—who would eventually number among her surnames Mahler, Gropius (as in the architect Walter), and Werfel (as in the poet Franz)—was one of the most desirable, talented, and intelligent women in all of Vienna. She gave Mahler two daughters: Marie in 1902, and Anna in 1904.

Mahler's world fell apart in 1907. In the spring of that year, he was forced to resign his position at the Vienna State Opera; the endless battering he received at the hands of the anti-Semitic Viennese press had simply become too much for him to bear. Then, during the summer, his daughter Marie, just five years old, died of either scarlet fever or diphtheria; and two weeks after that, he was diagnosed as having a serious heart condition.

Distraught, grieving, and filled with premonitions of his own death, Mahler composed his Ninth Symphony, completing the score in 1908.

The introduction that begins the first movement is pregnant with meaning. It begins with a low repeated note in the cellos that is "echoed" by a horn:

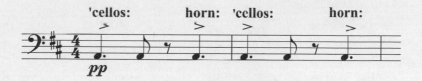

The repeated notes in the cellos are meant to depict Mahler's own heartbeat. The echo in the horn depicts the echo in Mahler's heartbeat, the result of the valvular defect diagnosed in the summer of 1907. The heartbeat and echo music is followed by a series of quivering viola tremolos, which depict ventricular fibrillations attributable to his heart disease:

Finally, theme one begins: a sighing, resigned melody characterized by a "hanging dissonance" that never resolves. The melancholy tension of this theme is a direct response to the heart disease–related introduction that precedes it.

Two thirds of the way through the movement, the music slips and spirals downward into the abyss, and at the bottom of that abyss appears a terrible and shocking dissonance heard between sustained horns and trombones in the heartbeat rhythm:

This dissonance is something called a tritone, and it never resolves. It is simply used as a sonic *object* to describe something ugly and terrifying: a fatal heart attack. In this case, we know it's a fatal heart attack because Mahler indicates that the passage of music that follows be performed *Wie ein schwerer Kondukt*, "Like a heavy, ponderous funeral cortege." Mahler has composed his own death, and to make it as shocking and as gritty as possible, he has used an abortive gesture—an unresolved tritone.

Romantic hyperexpressivity required increasingly extreme musical means to make increasingly extreme expressive statements. Given the Romantic emphasis on self-expression and originality, sooner or later the expressive desires of composers were going to outstrip the ability of the traditional tonal language to describe them. This expressive Rubicon—the abandonment by some composers of the traditional tonal language—was crossed during the first ten years of the twentieth century.

The late nineteenth and early twentieth century was a period of incredible intellectual, scientific, and technological change. Even a short list of the technical and scientific discoveries, innovations, and changes of the period should make us shake our heads with wonder.

1892: The first automatic telephone switchboards go into
action.

1894: Louis Lumière invents the cinematograph.

1895: Guglielmo Marconi invents radio telegraphy.

1895: Wilhelm Roentgen discovers X rays.

1896: Henry Ford builds his first car.

1897: J. J. Thomas discovers the electron.

1898: Pierre and Marie Curie discover radium and polo-
nium.

1899: The first magnetic recordings of sound.

1902: The first Classical 78 rpm records—of Enrico Caruso
singing Italian opera arias—are made by the Emil Ber-
liner Gramophone Company.

Hello, Mass Media! Hello, Couch!

We contemplate the invention of commercially recorded music.
On the one hand, it is a wonderful thing. Commercial record-
ing made it possible for anyone to hear anything, anywhere. But,
unfortunately, the record industry also created the passive listener:
the couch potato. With the availability of commercial recordings, it
was no longer necessary to attend a concert or learn how to play an
instrument yourself if you wanted to hear music. You didn't even
have to pump the pedals of a player piano. All you had to do was toss
a few cents on the counter, take a record home, wind up the gramophone, and veg out while the machine did all the work. I love my
hi-fi, but recorded music has been a mixed blessing for our culture,
our world, and for music itself.

Recordings, telephones, airplanes, cars, electric power, motion
pictures, motorcycles: these are not just technologies; they are

creations that affect the very way we as a species perceive time, space, and distance. I would suggest that our perceptions of time and distance were conditioned by the speed at which we could travel and communicate. Two hundred years ago, people thought nothing of sitting in a carriage for 5 days to travel 250 miles; of taking 30 days to cross the Atlantic; of writing a letter and having it answered months later; of reading 2,000-page novels.

I can climb into a jumbo jet in Paris and be home in the San Francisco Bay Area, with the time change, two hours later. The speed with which we move today, the rapidity with which we communicate, the tempo of our lives, and what we expect from our lives have changed so dramatically that if we brought someone forward from two hundred years ago she'd probably OD from overstimulation within hours.

One of the victims of the speed of twentieth- and twenty-first century life is large-scale musical repetition. In a world where every second counts, where time is money, where information turnover is often more important than information content, we cannot, for better or for worse, expect the *same* sort of phrase repetition, structural repetition, and leisurely musical development in twentieth- and twenty-first century art music that we were witness to in the seventeenth, eighteenth, and nineteenth centuries.

The accelerated rate of change that kicked in around the turn of the twentieth century has affected everything: our way of thinking, our sensory perceptions, our ability to process information, our art, and our music.

In 1900, Sigmund Freud published his *Interpretation of Dreams* and Max Planck presented his quantum theory. In 1905, Albert Einstein had his *annus mirabilis*, his "miraculous year": he formulated the special theory of relativity, established the law of mass energy equivalents, expounded on the Brownian theory of motion, and formulated the photon theory of light. Whoa.

Freud, Planck, Einstein: these men penned esoteric treatises that weren't filed and forgotten but forced us to reconsider the way we perceived the workings of our minds, and the nature of time, matter, and the universe.

By 1905, with expressive content and the "abortive gesture" pushing the traditional tonal language to the brink, with a new century and an increasingly new scientific, technological, and intellectual reality around them, many young composers were simply unwilling to continue writing music the likes of which they believed had "already been written."

The French modernist composer Claude Debussy wrote, "I want my music to be as relevant to the twentieth century as the aeroplane." In a new century dominated by a heady sense of change, the desire to be relevant was overwhelming. The time was ripe for a new set of approaches to melody, harmony, and rhythm.

CHAPTER 31

Revolutions, Evolutions, and "-isms" Galore

The Making of a New Music in the Early Twentieth Century

The French Musical Revolution

The challenge of replacing the principles and structures of the common practice with new approaches to melody, harmony, and rhythm occupied many of the best musical minds in the years around 1900. The first big break with the common practice occurred in France.

Speaking generally but not inaccurately, French music is a relatively insular and self-evolved tradition. Some have gone so far as to label France the musical marsupial of Europe, a comparison that might seem unkind until we contemplate just how special marsupials can be.

(On these lines, some observers have mistakenly compared this Gallic insularity with Russian artistic xenophobia. This is not correct. Such Russian nationalists as The Five rejected Western musical models out of fear of Western artistic domination, whereas French composers—Hector Berlioz being an exception—generally rejected non-French musical models out of simple disdain for anything not French.)

However, nineteenth-century French and Russian music are very much alike in their shared emphasis on thematic material and their relative lack of emphasis on development. Nineteenth-century French music generally displays a slower harmonic turnover than

German music. Finally, French music has historically celebrated timbral nuance—the color of musical sound itself—to a degree far greater than Germanic or Italian music.

The gulf between German music and French music—indeed, between those things French and those things German—was widened exponentially by the humiliating French defeat at the hands of Prussia during the Franco-Prussian War of 1870 and '71. French culture turned more inward than ever, and the nationalist cultivation of things French, already evident for hundreds of years, took on a new intensity. The inspiration at the core of this cultivation of things French was the French language itself.

The French sensitivity toward musical timbre is a direct outgrowth of the French language. The French language is itself about nuance: about color, vowel, and diphthong. It's a language characterized by extraordinary rhythmic flexibility; a language almost entirely free of sharp accents and harsh consonants. The unique sound and beauty of the French language—limpid, elegant, finely shaded, and slightly blurred—is a source of singular pride to the French nation. For the French, how you say something is as important as what you say: style (timbre) is as important as substance (pitch and rhythm). By the late nineteenth century, the time was ripe for French music to capture what French visual art (impressionism) and literature (symbolist poetry) had captured already: the essence of the French language itself.

Achille-Claude Debussy (1862–1918) Library of Congress, Prints and Photographs Division, LC-USZ62-44510

The French composer whose music marked the definitive break with the common practice, with both traditional tonality and Austrian-German compositional models, was Claude Debussy.

Debussy's music—characterized to its core by finesse and nuance (*finesse* and *nuance*: two French words, we would note)—is the French language in musical action.

Achille-Claude Debussy (1862–1918)

Debussy was Paris born, bred, and dead. As a true Parisian of the "Belle Epoque," he could not tolerate being anywhere else. As a true Frenchman of the post–Franco-Prussian War era, he professed to hate almost everything German, Johann Sebastian Bach being the exception.

Debussy's French-language-inspired love of color and nuance developed at a very young age. A great anecdote, told by Alma Mahler in her biography of her husband, Gustav: the Mahlers were in Paris in April of 1910 for a performance of Mahler's Symphony No. 2:

> While the rehearsals were on, Pierné gave a party in Mahler's honor and invited Debussy, Dukas, Gabriel Fauré, Bruneau, and the Clemenceaus. Debussy's strong personality and the beauty of his head were very impressive. [Alma is referring to Debussy's double forehead.]
>
> Debussy brought his second wife, who was said to be very wealthy. He sat next to me at dinner and I noticed that he took only the minutest helping of any dish. When Madame Pierné tried pressing him, his face took on a look of pain. Dukas [Paul Dukas, the composer of *The Sorcerer's Apprentice*] told me in an undertone that when they were schoolboys together and provided by their mothers with money to buy their mid-morning lunches, they all selected the largest confections, except Debussy. He always chose the smallest and most expensive, for even as a child he was nauseated by bulk. That evening, too, we were told of Debussy's ill treatment that had almost been the death of his first wife. It was a youthful marriage and they were very poor. She couldn't endure her life with him or life

without him, so she took poison. Debussy found her apparently unconscious on the floor. He went up to her very calmly and took what money she had on her before sending for a doctor. She heard and saw all of it, for she was not unconscious but simply temporarily paralyzed. She recovered from the poison and was cured, too, of her love of Debussy, from whom she was divorced. (Mahler)

Debussy might have been a selfish, ironic, unpleasant man with the morals of a tomcat, but he had the compositional imagination of an angel.

His major compositional influences were:

- The French language, with its blurred edges and infinity of nuance;
- Romantic expression: Debussy grew up during the nineteenth century, and the overwhelming bulk of his music is programmatic;
- Romantic literature extolling expression and descriptive images, in particular, the symbolist poets Mallarmé, Verlaine, and Rimbaud; and
- French impressionist painting: "Impressionism" is a visual manifestation of the French language, an art movement that celebrates light, blended and nuanced color, blurred edges, and objects in flux, art in which the perception of an image is more important than the substance of image itself.

The term *impressionism* was originally applied as a critical pejorative to Monet's painting *Impression: Sunrise* of 1874, but the word stuck. Debussy claimed to hate the word *impressionism* and didn't want to be associated with the movement. Whether he liked the term or not, his music evokes the same water-dominated, brilliantly colored, subtly shaded, blurred-edge imagery as does impressionist art.

Debussy's incredibly original approach to timbre, rhythm, melody, harmony, and musical form created a music the likes of which no one had ever heard before. In this, he is one of the great originals in the history of Western music and, along with Igor Stravinsky and Arnold Schoenberg, one of the most influential composers of the twentieth century.

"Nuages," from Three Nocturnes for Orchestra (1899)

A nocturne is a piece of "night music," and *nuages* means "clouds."

Night clouds. It's hard to imagine a more impressionistic image than moonlit clouds scudding across the night sky. That's what this movement is about, and it is stunning in its beauty and originality.

The piece is cast in seven parts. Parts one through four consist of a thematic statement (part one) and then a series of elongations and intensifications of that theme. Part five introduces a contrasting theme. Part six sees a return to the first theme; and seven, the quiet conclusion of the piece. We will focus our attention on the nature of the themes themselves.

"Nuages" begins with an ostinato, a repeated melodic pattern in the winds:

An English horn cuts in with a nondescript melodic idea using an eight-pitch collection called an octatonic scale.

Finally, high, sustained violins accompanied by a quiet roll in the timpani bring this opening part to its conclusion.

The sixty-four-dollar question is: What constitutes "theme" in this music? It's not a tune, or a key area, or even a harmonic progression. What constitutes "theme" is the actual sounds of the music materials just heard: the gently undulating wind ostinato; the piercing, nasal sound of the English horn; and the icy sound of the high strings. Timbre has here been elevated to a point equal to pitch, rhythm, and harmony. This is quintessentially *French music*, and typical of Debussy.

Part five offers a contrasting theme, played by a single flute and the harp, that uses a five-pitch collection called a pentatonic scale.

Neither of Debussy's themes is set in "major" or "minor," the basic, seven-pitch collections that served the common practice for hundreds of years. Instead, he creates contrast by basing his first theme on an eight-pitch (octatonic) collection and the second theme on a five-pitch (pentatonic) collection. This is stunningly original music, and the result is stunningly exotic: music that simply doesn't "sound" like anything else.

Debussy's approach to the orchestra is as delicate and nuanced as his thematic ideas. He uses it as if it were a huge chamber group consisting of eighty-five individual instruments that can be used singly or grouped in any way he pleases. His innovative approach to the orchestra offered him a virtual infinity of possible instrumental combinations and colors and has made him the single most influential and imitated orchestrator in the last one hundred years.

We have observed only what Debussy is doing "up top" in "Nuages," with his themes. However, his harmonic usage and mode of accompaniment are just as innovative and influential as his approach to theme and instrumental timbre. In place of traditional "chord progressions," he employs long, sustained harmonies called pedals, or repeated melodic patterns called ostinatos. These pedals and ostinatos give his music a static quality, a sense of musical time that is not so much "narrative"—as in progressing from point A to point B—as experiential, in that we as listeners are content to sit quietly and revel in the timbral beauties around us.

Finally, Debussy employs traditional-sounding harmonies, but he does not "deploy" them in traditional ways. For example, about two thirds of the way through "Nuages," the following series of chords moves in lockstep downward in the strings:

Each of these chords is a dissonance—a dominant ninth chord—a chord that in traditional tonal harmony is supposed to *resolve*. But these dissonant harmonies do not resolve; they simply move from one to the next. Debussy isn't using them as dissonances; he's using them because *he likes the way they sound*, and by putting a string of them together, he gets a wonderful "smear" of harmonic color. For Debussy, these harmonies are objects that can exist by and of themselves. It's a perfect example of how Debussy uses a traditional construct—for example, a dominant ninth chord—in a completely untraditional way.

Claude Debussy is among the most original composers in the history of Western music. It almost goes without saying, then, that the critics savaged his music. Of the legion of nasty, smart-alecky reviews he received, we'll read just one, written in response to Debussy's opera *Pelléas et Mélisande,* by Arthur Pougin, published on May 4, 1902, in the Parisian journal *Le Menestral:*

> Rhythm, melody, tonality: These are three things unknown to Monsieur Debussy and deliberately distained by him. His music is vague, floating, without color and without shape, without movement and without life. What a pretty series of false relations. What adorable progressions in parallel motion. What a collection of dissonances. No, decidedly, I will never agree with these anarchists of music. (Slonimsky)

As is so often the case, it was the youngsters—the kids born in the 1880s like Béla Bartók and Igor Stravinsky—who worshipped Debussy's music. They heard in it the same sense of novelty, truth, and relevance the young 'uns had heard in Beethoven's music exactly a century before. The next generation of composers saw Debussy as a compositional Messiah who could lead them from the bondage of traditional tonality to a promised land of new music, music relevant to the new truths and realities of the new twentieth century.

CHAPTER 32

From Russia with Rhythm

Igor Stravinsky

S travinsky tells us this story about his teacher Nikolai Rimsky-Korsakov:

> The following is illustrative of the attitude of the old master toward Debussy. [In 1907], at a concert where one of the latter's work was on the program, I asked Rimsky-Korsakov what he thought of it. He answered in these very words, "Better not listen to him; one runs the risk of getting accustomed to him and might even end up liking him." (Stravinsky, 18)

Born on June 17, 1882, in the resort town of Oranienbaum, about thirty-five miles west of St. Petersburg, Stravinsky grew up in St. Petersburg; he sat out World War I in Switzerland; moved to France and became a French citizen after the Russian Revolution; moved to the United States and became an American citizen after the Nazi invasion of France; spent the bulk of his American years living in Beverly Hills; and died in New York City in 1971.

Stravinsky's long life was complemented by an equally long creative career, one marked by the creation of one masterwork after another, from *The Firebird* of 1910 to the *Requiem Canticles* of 1966.

Stravinsky came from a musical background: his mother was a pianist and his father a bass baritone in the St. Petersburg Opera. Stravinsky was a small, sickly child; intelligent but certainly not a prodigy or an academic overachiever. He was a decent pianist who nursed a powerful desire to be a composer. Not a chance, said his father, Fyodor, who did not believe his son's talent was equal to his ambition. Stravinsky was sent to St. Petersburg University to study law.

It was while at the university that Stravinsky met one of the sons of Nikolai Rimsky-Korsakov. Stravinsky desperately wanted to meet the grand old man himself and managed to do so in 1902. The twenty-year-old Stravinsky played some of his early compositions for Rimsky-Korsakov, who, to Stravinsky's dismay, told him that he needed to thoroughly study harmony and counterpoint. Rimsky-Korsakov offered to recommend a teacher if Stravinsky wanted to take some lessons.

In the time-honored tradition of old pros dealing with young wannabes, Rimsky-Korsakov blew Stravinsky off: "Don't go away mad, kid; just go away." But Stravinsky refused to be either blown off or discouraged. Even as he continued to attend law school, he pursued the lessons Rimsky-Korsakov recommended, and he turned out to be a late bloomer of genius. When he returned to Rimsky-Korsakov three years later, in 1905, RK was stunned by Stravinsky's progress. He immediately accepted Stravinsky as a student (thus ending Stravinsky's legal career), and they worked together until Rimsky-Korsakov's death three years later, in 1908.

In 1909, Stravinsky came to the attention of Serge Diaghilev, one of the great movers and shakers of the twentieth century. Diaghilev was a lapsed musician who had an almost unparalleled ability to spot talent, bring it together, get funding, and put on productions that were the marvel his time. He commuted between Paris and St. Petersburg, banking off decadent, bourgeois Paris's hunger for Russian art. In 1906, he founded the *Russian Art Journal,* and in 1908 the Russian Ballet; in French, the Ballets Russes.

The avowed mission of the Ballets Russes was to bring Russian dancers to Paris between May and July to perform cutting-edge productions that, when possible, would be choreographed, designed, and composed by Russian artists.

In 1909, the young, tiny, and theretofore untested Igor Stravinsky came to Diaghilev's attention. Based on two brief orchestral works called *Fireworks* and *Scherzo* and a couple of orchestration exercises, Diaghilev hired this nobody to compose the music for the "big" production of the 1910 Ballets Russes season: a ballet called *The Firebird*.

We can almost hear Diaghilev's financiers screeching "Igor *who?*" But Diaghilev had the eye, that sixth sense that separates a mere producer from an impresario. He insisted on going with the kid, and the result was Stravinsky's first major commission and his first masterwork.

At the time he composed *The Firebird*, Stravinsky's compositional toolbox contained orchestration skills gleaned from his studies with Rimsky-Korsakov: a harmonic language based largely on the music of Richard Wagner, a Debussy-inspired attitude toward the thematic possibilities of pure timbre, and his Russian roots and the rhythmic asymmetry of Russian-language folk music.

The Firebird

The Firebird is based on a Russian folk tale. An evil ogre holds thirteen pretty princesses captive. Good Prince Ivan captures the mythical Firebird. The Firebird offers to help the Prince free the princesses in exchange for her own freedom; deal. Ogre dies, Firebird flies, Prince picks a chick, happy ending's the trick.

Diaghilev put together his usual all-star cast for the production: Michel Fokine wrote the scenario and did the choreography. Leon Bakst designed the costumes, and Alexander Golovine designed the production. Tamara Karsavina danced the lead as the Firebird.

Just before the premiere, Diaghilev was giving an interview to a number of journalists when he pointed to Stravinsky on the stage and told them, "That is Stravinsky. Mark him well. He is a man at the eve of great celebrity." As usual, Diaghilev was right.

Stravinsky's score for *The Firebird* both draws on tradition and displays moments of innovation. Like so much nineteenth-century Russian nationalist music, Stravinsky employs preexisting traditional Russian folk music in *The Firebird*. However, *The Firebird* also features moments that are pure twentieth-century modernism, moments of innovation that indicate, with twenty-twenty hindsight, Stravinsky's artistic trajectory. Such a passage is the "Infernal Dance," during which the monsters that guard the Ogre's castle dance until they drop, exhausted.

MUSIC BOX

Igor Stravinsky, *The Firebird*, "Infernal Dance"

The opening section of the "Infernal Dance" offers a brilliant example of the sort of Russian-language-inspired rhythmic asymmetry that will become the trademark element of Stravinsky's music.

Note the following:

- The dance is indeed infernal, characterized by a throbbing, nonstop beat.
- Certain beats are irregularly, asymmetrically accented.
- The asymmetrical accents fall faster and faster, squeezing the music like a tube of toothpaste into a climax of purely rhythmic manufacture. These inward telescoping accents create an irregular rhythmic strata of their own, layered atop the steady beats of the dance.

The Rite of Spring (1912)

Stravinsky's early experiments with rhythmic asymmetry reach a peak in *The Rite of Spring* of 1912. (The hoity-toity call the piece by its French name, *Le Sacre du printemps*, though the hoityest of the toity simply call it *Sacre*.)

The Rite of Spring is probably the single most influential musical composition of the twentieth century.

The "rites" invoked by the title are various rituals that presumably accompanied the advent of spring in Bronze Age Russia. The first half of the ballet consists of a series of scenes that describe a variety of different "rites," from mating rituals to sun worship. The second half is about human sacrifice, during which the chosen virgin dances herself to death. In the words of one observer, it's all dubious anthropology but very good theater.

Stravinsky's job was to compose music that somehow evoked the spirit of tribal, Bronze Age Russia. Given the unfortunate dearth of either recorded or notated music from that era, Stravinsky was pretty much on his own in trying to create modern music played by a modern orchestra that could evoke Bronze Age Russia. If he was to create a musical environment the likes of which no one had ever heard before, he was going to have to create a musical vocabulary the likes of which no one had ever used before. That challenge fired his imagination in a way that nothing else might have. In *The Rite of Spring*, Stravinsky created a work that—for all of its debt to Debussy and Russian nationalism—sounded utterly new.

Et tu, Brute?

*T*he Rite was also powerfully influenced by an art movement called primitivism. Primitivism had been inspired by the West African tribal art that took the Parisian art community by storm in the early years of the twentieth century. The Parisians perceived in this African art ritual power and human sexuality reduced to its basic components, presented in highly stylized, sometimes almost abstract forms. (In reality, there is nothing primitive about this remarkable art, but that's a discussion to be had at another time.) This African art powerfully influenced many artists at the turn of the twentieth century. There was even a group of artists who called themselves Les Fauves, that is, "The Brutes," whose

African-inspired aesthetic sought to create art that would obliterate the trappings of Victorian repression still evident in early twentieth-century European culture. *The Rite of Spring* is a product of the primitive, *Fauvist* spirit of the day.

It Don't Mean a Thing If It Ain't Got That Swing!

More than anything else, *The Rite of Spring* is about asymmetrical rhythm elevated to the point of dramatic narrative.

For example, the episode called the "Dance of the Adolescents" is characterized by a single bitonal harmony that is literally *drummed* into our heads. The harmony (or better, the "sonority") consists of an E-flat dominant seventh chord heard over an E major triad; a sonority that projects no familiar tonal reference whatsoever:

This sonority is employed as neither a consonance nor a dissonance. Rather, it simply "exists" as it is pounded out with nonstop metronomic regularity 180 times over the first half of the "Dance of the Adolescents."

What renders the repetitions of the bitonal sonority interesting is their asymmetrical accentuation, a series of irregular (and thus unexpected) accents that cannot be anticipated. As a result, we sit riveted to our seats, not knowing when the next rhythmic bomb will drop.

In traditional tonal music, dramatic narrative is a product of thematic variation, contrast, or development; of modulation and contrasting key areas, and so forth. In the "Dance of the Adolescents," dramatic narrative is created almost solely by rhythmic asymmetry. This is Russki rock 'n' roll, and in 1912 it was sensationally original. What Debussy did for timbre—elevating it to a level equal to rhythm, pitch, and harmony—so Stravinsky did for rhythm, by demonstrating how rhythm *alone* could be used as a thematic, dramatic, narrative, and developmental musical element.

With the premiere of *The Rite*, Igor Stravinsky replaced Claude Debussy as the enfant terrible of Parisian music. *The Rite of Spring* triggered an opening night riot on May 29, 1913. A large proportion of the opening night audience at Paris's Théâtre des Champs-Élysées, convinced that it was a purposeful insult to dance and music as they understood them, made their displeasure loudly known, their whistles, boos, and hisses often drowning out the orchestra. And despite the fact that Stravinsky honored Debussy by giving him the pencil score of *The Rite*, Debussy was not at all happy about Stravinsky's newfound notoriety.

To which we all say to Monsieur Debussy, *tant pis, mec* (too bad, dude).

CHAPTER 33

No Waltz in the Park

Arnold Schoenberg's Vienna and Expressionism

A t the turn of the twentieth century, Vienna was Paris's only musical rival, the heart of the great Austrian-German musical tradition.

The advent of Viennese musical modernism represents a very different sort of musical revolution than that in Paris. While Debussy and Stravinsky both grew out of Romanticism, their musical debts to the past were ultimately less important than their innovations. This is not so with the music of Arnold Schoenberg, whose music is a clear and purposeful continuation of the great tradition of German music we've discussed since chapter 7.

Two Peoples *Connected* by a Common Language

Let's address this now, so that we needn't keep saying "*Austrian-German* music." The word *Austria* is an Anglicization of the German word *Österreich*, which means "eastern realm" or "eastern empire." The name refers to the eastern realm of the Holy Roman Empire, the pan-German empire that was ruled—excepting one brief interlude—by the Habsburg family from 1438 to 1806. While Germany and Austria are today separate national entities, for hundreds of years they were not. And whatever their real or perceived differences, Germany and Austria speak the same language and thus share a common cultural heritage. For our purposes, Austrian music is German music and vice versa.

Arnold Schoenberg's music is a purposeful continuation of the tradition of German music. Among the basic elements of the "greater German" compositional tradition are the role of music in the Lutheran Church, the Classical era instrumental musical forms, musical unity through motivic development, and a Romantic expressive urge to plumb the deepest levels of the human psyche. Let's examine these elements one at a time.

The Lutheran Church emphasized the use of vernacular language and did not discourage—as did the Catholic Church—the use of polyphony and musical instruments in its liturgical music. As a result, complex polyphony and instrumental music were cultivated to a much greater degree in central and northern Germany than in the south. The Lutheran Church's emphasis on vernacular worship and congregational singing also helped to foster a characteristically German-language style of melody on the part of certain German composers, a style of melody characterized by syllabic text settings, clarity, punch, and concision.

The Classical era instrumental forms evolved in and around Vienna in the 1740s, '50s, and '60s, forms that synthesized Germanic compositional rigor with Italian melodic fluency.

Beethoven's tenets of musical unity through motivic development, music composition as self-expression, and originality as an artistic goal became the underpinning of German music through the nineteenth and early twentieth century.

Last, there is the expressive nature of late nineteenth-century German Romantic art, with its tendency to turn inward to the recesses (the often dark recesses) of the human psyche for inspiration. The artistic movement associated with this "inward psychological investigation" is called expressionism.

Expressionism may be understood as the German answer to French impressionism. Where French impressionism celebrated light, movement, and an expressive substance divined from the outside world, German expressionism drew its expressive substance from the deepest reaches of the soul. In the same Vienna that saw Sigmund Freud attempt to understand, clinically, the shadowy terrain of the unconscious, so Expressionist artists attempted to capture it in their art.

Arnold Schoenberg and his students Alban Berg and Anton Webern are often referred to as the second Viennese school (the "first" consisting of Haydn, Mozart, and Beethoven). Collectively, the music of Schoenberg, Berg, and Webern constitutes the core repertoire of German expressionist music. What Monet, Cezanne, and Manet were to Debussy, so Kandinsky, Kokoschka, Kirchner, Nolde, Munch, and Schiele were to Schoenberg: post-Romantic artists dealing, in some way, with the innermost regions of the human psyche.

Arnold Schoenberg

Arnold Schoenberg was born in 1874 in Vienna and died 1951 in Los Angeles. For all the misconceptions and miscomprehensions about Schoenberg and his music, he was, expressively, a pure Romantic. He wrote, "There is only one greatest goal toward which the artist strives: to express himself."

Schoenberg came from a poor Orthodox Jewish family and grew up in the Leopoldstadt in Vienna: the old Jewish ghetto. He took up the violin at the age of eight, and began composing soon after. As a composer, he was almost entirely self-taught. His only lessons consisted of two years of counterpoint with the composer Alexander Zemlinsky. After those two years, Schoenberg's amazing talent mandated a reversal of roles, and Zemlinsky became the student and Schoenberg the teacher!

Schoenberg's real musical classroom was the city of Vienna and its amazing musical environment. Schoenberg's Vienna was the city of Brahms, Mahler, Bruckner, Wolf; for Schoenberg it was like living in a chocolate factory where an endless supply of free samples was available 24/7.

Financial necessities forced Schoenberg to take a variety of jobs, including bank clerk, an orchestrator of operettas, and a composer of cabaret songs (the latter of which powerfully influenced his *Pierrot Lunaire*, which we will discuss here).

Schoenberg's earliest works, like *Transfigured Night* and his String Quartet no. 1, were composed within the late nineteenth-century Romantic tonal tradition. However, in 1900, several of Schoenberg's songs provoked a scene at a Viennese concert and, to quote Schoenberg, "since that day, the scandal has never ceased."

For Schoenberg, the years between 1908 and 1913 were about what he called "the emancipation of dissonance." He was increasingly convinced that the future of German music lay in preserving its craft, its polyphony, its motivic development, its spirituality and expressive content, but not the dense harmonic underbrush that, according to him, constrained genuine melodic development. In 1908, Schoenberg decided that the solution was to *simplify*: to eliminate the difference between consonance and dissonance, which he had come to believe were arbitrary designations that only constrained melodic development.

Consequently, between 1908 and 1913, Schoenberg experimented with suspending the rules of traditional tonal harmony and composed music in which melody, polyphony, and motivic development and transformation were the be-alls and end-alls. Instead of calling these years "the emancipation of dissonance," Schoenberg might more accurately have called this period "the emancipation of melody."

Schoenberg created a type of music ruled not by the constructs of tonal harmony but by pure melodic development and transformation. He saw himself as a simplifier; someone who'd gone back to basics, back to the root source of all music: pure melody. The so-called freely atonal works he composed between 1908 and 1913 include the

Five Pieces for Orchestra, Erwartung, and *Pierrot Lunaire,* works that changed the course and history of Western music.

Pierrot Lunaire (1912)

Pierrot Lunaire is a set of twenty-one "songs" for female voice and chamber ensemble. It is the crowning achievement of Schoenberg's "emancipation of dissonance" period. In terms of its influence and importance to the music of the twentieth century, it is second only to Stravinsky's *The Rite of Spring.*

In 1959, Igor Stravinsky wrote:

> The great event in my life, then, in 1912, was the performance of *Pierrot Lunaire* that I heard in December of 1912 in Berlin. Ravel was quickly contaminated with my enthusiasm for *Pierrot,* too, whereas Debussy, when I told him about it, merely stared at me and said nothing. Is this why Debussy later wrote his friend Godet that Stravinsky is inclining dangerously toward the direction of Schoenberg? (Stravinsky/Craft, *Expositions,* 67)

Pierrot Lunaire was commissioned by an actress named Albertine Zehme. Madame Zehme, who was not a singer, requested a piece with a musical background against which she could recite or speak rather than sing. Schoenberg created a vocal part using a technique drawn directly from German cabaret music—something he called *Sprechstimme,* or "speech voice"—a recitative-like technique halfway between singing and speaking. The first key to understanding, appreciating, and even enjoying *Pierrot Lunaire* is to perceive it as a set of extremely sophisticated cabaret songs.

The poems themselves come from a collection entitled *Moonstruck Pierrot,* by Albert Giraud. Of the fifty original poems, Schoenberg set twenty-one of them. *Pierrot Lunaire* just happens to be his opus 21, and this is the sort of numbers game that composers generally find irresistible. Schoenberg groups the twenty-one poems into three sets of seven. The first set is expository in nature; the second set grim and exceedingly dark; and the third set expository once again. The second key to understanding, appreciating, and enjoying *Pierrot Lunaire*: from a literary point of view, the grouping of the poems outlines a large-scale A-B-A form. Each of the poems of *Pierrot Lunaire* is structured as a rondeau.

Each poem is thirteen lines long: lines one and two are repeated as lines seven and eight, and line one is repeated as line thirteen. Key number three to understanding, appreciating, and enjoying *Pierrot Lunaire*: there is a structural consistency between all the songs, and the three-part structure created by the repeated lines in each poem reflects, on the small scale, the large-scale, A-B-A structure of the piece.

The instrumental ensemble Schoenberg calls for in *Pierrot Lunaire* has become so standard today that its simply called a *Pierrot* ensemble: a total of five instrumentalists playing a piano; a flute doubling on piccolo; a clarinet doubling on bass clarinet; a violin doubling on viola; and a cello.

Pierrot Lunaire constitutes a virtual encyclopedia of Schoenberg's "emancipation of dissonance" compositional techniques. We'll hear a tremendous amount of word painting, and be witness to all sorts of polyphonic constructs, including canons and fugues.

Pierrot: Up Close and Personal

Pierrot is the white-faced clown that is a stock character in almost every Western culture. Sometimes a rascal, sometimes sad-faced, Pierrot is capable of extraordinary pathos and violence, an archetype of both the best and worst of who we are. There are all sorts of national variants: in Italy, he is known as Pulcinella, Pulcinello, or Pedrolino; in Russia as Petrushka; in England as Punch or Punchinello.

The title *Pierrot Lunaire* may be translated in a number of different ways: as either "moonstruck Pierrot," as in "Pierrot in love"; or "mooning Pierrot" (meaning "melancholy" or "moping Pierrot"); or, last, as "lunatic Pierrot." Each of these characterizations finds its way into Giraud's poems and Schoenberg's songs.

Pierrot Lunaire must be approached through its poetic texts. If we understand the poetry, we will understand why the music sounds the way it does. And that is key number four to understanding, appreciating, and enjoying *Pierrot Lunaire*: the songs sound the way they do *for expressive reasons.*

MUSIC BOX

Arnold Schoenberg, *Pierrot Lunaire*, No. 1, "Moondrunk" (1912)

The poem on which this first of the songs is based reads, in translation, as follows:

The wine that only eyes may drink
Pours from the moon in waves at nightfall,
And like a spring flood overwhelms
The still horizon rim.

Desires, shivering and sweet,
Are swimming without number through the flood waters!
The wine that only eyes may drink
Pours from the moon in waves at nightfall.

The poet, by his passion driven,
Grows drunken with the holy drink,
To heaven he rapturously lifts
His head and reeling sips and swallows
The wine that only eyes may drink.

Please note the following:
* The guiding poetic allusion here is liquid. That liquid—"the *wine* that only eyes may drink"—is moonlight. This liquid moonlight is portrayed throughout the song by a descending ostinato:

continued on next page

This is ethereal moonlight: ghostly, silvery, and liquid; the moonlight/wine on which the poet of line number nine grows drunk. (The seven-note motive that generates this ostinato has come to be called the "*Pierrot* motive," because it reappears, in some form or another, across the span of the entire piece, helping to tie the twenty-one songs together into a single *composition*.)

- There's lots of other word painting heard during the song: for example, when the singer sings, "Desires, shivering and sweet," a trilling flute will properly "paint" the word for "shivering": *schauerlich*.

- The poem reaches its climax in the third part. "The poet, by his passion driven, grows drunken with the holy drink." Who is that poet? While Albert Giraud, Pierrot, and Schoenberg all qualify, I opt for Schoenberg. By choosing to begin his song cycle with this particular poem, Schoenberg creates an introductory context for everything that follows: "I, the poet-slash-composer, grown drunken on the moonlight, will now wax uninhibited on Pierrot Lunaire!"

Relevance versus Coherence: The Dilemma of Modern Art

Lacking familiar harmonic landmarks and marked by almost constant melodic development, *Pierrot Lunaire* is an entirely self-referential work—it sounds only like itself. Repeat listening will never make this music sound conventional *because it will always sound only like itself*. So despite the fact that it was composed while William Howard Taft was president of the United States and a portrait of "Liberty" graced the obverse side of an American nickel, *Pierrot Lunaire* is the soul of modernity and will likely always sound that way.

Which forces us to ask the question: Have modernity and the endless search for novelty and self-expression destroyed the social compact between composers and their essential audiences?

I don't think so, but they have made the relationship between the composer and her audience more complex. When composers abandoned the traditional tonal system of the common practice in the early years of the twentieth century, they were casting off the musical language they had shared with their audiences for hundreds of years.

And yet that common syntactical ground that was traditional tonality had—like the horse and buggy, gas lamps, Soviet communism, dial-up modems, and, yes, disco—run its course. For many composers, it had simply become irrelevant.

Once, after a performance of Edvard Grieg's magisterial Piano Concerto of 1868, Schoenberg turned to his friend, the composer Roberto Gerhard, and said wistfully, "That is the kind of music I should really like to write."

So why didn't he?

Because it wasn't relevant: Grieg's tonal, nineteenth-century musical language simply wasn't relevant to Schoenberg's world as he perceived that world. More than fame and fortune and even popularity, what composers seek is relevance: relevance to their time, their place, and their expressive vision.

Blame it on the Enlightenment, with its emphasis on the individual reveling in her individuality. Blame it on Beethoven; with his self-expressive article of faith that expressive context must determine content, rather than the other way around. Blame it on Wagner and *Tristan und Isolde*, in which even tonality became contextual, to be used or temporarily abandoned depending upon the expressive needs of the moment. Blame it on Gustav Mahler and all the other late Romantics who came to depend on the abortive gesture in order to make their expressive points. Or blame it on a twentieth century in which the very language with which composers worked was contextual.

So, back to Arnold Schoenberg and *Pierrot Lunaire*. Tough music? Yes, no doubt. Exquisite music? Brilliant music? Epochal, earth-shaking, often drop-dead gorgeous and deeply moving, German expressionist music at its zenith? Absolutely. On that you have my word.

Postlude

H aving navigated the contents of this book, I trust the reader
will have come to accept (if not perhaps celebrate) its titular
conceit. A more accurate but ungainly to the point of tears
title would be *How to Listen to and Understand Some of the Great
Music of the Common Practice Period*. There's a title sure to scare off
almost any potential reader, but if it is truth in advertising we seek,
then it's the real deal.

This book is based on a simple but all-encompassing premise: that
music in the Western world has been a mirror of the social, cultural,
religious, political, and economic world around the composer since
the High Middle Ages, and that changes in musical style—that is, the
sound and expressive content of a given era's music—are a function
of the larger environment and a composer's response to that environment. That this is true can be confirmed with a simple hypothetical,
the likes of which we indulged earlier in this book but which bears
indulging once again: what if Wolfgang Mozart had been born not in
1756 but in 1874, and Arnold Schoenberg had been born not in 1874
but in 1756? Would they still have composed the music they did?
The answer, of course, is no, no, a thousand times *no*. Schoenberg
could not have conceived of *Pierrot Lunaire* in 1787 any more than
someone of that time could have conceived of laptop computers. Had
Mozart been born in 1874, with the combined legacies of Beethoven
and romanticism as part of his heritage, he could not have composed

Don Giovanni in 1912 any more than we would ride a horse and buggy across the George Washington Bridge. Musical style is indeed a mirror of its time, and thus, to understand a particular musical style we must first understand the cultural circumstances that gave root and branch to that style.

This book has focused primarily on the musical styles of the common practice, that system of harmony and melody generally referred to as the tonal system. The common practice is generally— *generally*—understood to have run from 1600 to 1900, three centuries that span the historical periods called the Baroque, Classical, and Romantic eras. The common practice saw the invention of those musical genres and institutions that continue to dominate the world of concert music to this day: the compositional genres of opera, symphony, and concerto; the instrumental genres of chamber and orchestral music; and such performance institutions as the opera house and the public concert hall.

Our current musical epoch began in roughly 1600, with the ancient Greek–inspired invention of opera and its recognition of the individual and individual emotions as being the primary expressive goal in music. What this means is that the music of the common practice is our immediate musical heritage, and should be perceived as such. This means that opera houses and concert halls are not musical museums where lumps of old, dated sound are framed and mounted and observed by the aurally curious. Rather, this magnificent musical tradition is quite contemporary: a living, breathing expression of *our time as well as of its own*. That's because great art is universal; it transcends its immediate time and place and is relevant and revelatory for all times and all places. In truth, opera houses and concert halls are not museums or, worse, mausoleums, but rather, reanimation facilities, where the spiritual essence of a composer and his or her time, distilled and refined into a piece of music, comes back to life in all its original intensity, expressivity, and glory.

This is a very good thing, because music—the most abstract of all of the arts—is capable of transmitting an unbelievable amount of expressive, historical, allegorical, metaphorical, metaphysical, and even philosophical information to us, provided that our antennae are up and pointed in the right direction. That is why we listen, constantly, to music. Yes, to be entertained and amused, but even more, to be thrilled: to be enlightened, edified, reminded of our humanity, and to experience that white hot jolt of wordless inner truth that is the special province of musical expression.

This book has sought to create a context for the thrill by providing knowledge and tools that will help us to hear certain representative works with the ears of their contemporary audiences. When we listen contextually, we hear, know, and feel what Bach's, Beethoven's, and Schoenberg's audiences heard and knew and felt. In the process, their worlds become our own, and we are richer for it. When we listen contextually—with the life and times of the composer in mind—we realize that no great piece of music is conventional. At the time of its creation, each such work was new music, and it mirrored its contemporary world in its own special way.

For thousands of years, cultures have celebrated themselves (and, in the case of disco, punished themselves) through their music. Let us always be willing to join that celebration by listening as carefully as we can to what, through music, we have to say to one another. Our lives will be more complete, more deeply lived, more profoundly felt for the effort of having listened well.

Music Selections

Johann Sebastian Bach
Brandenburg Concerto no. 2
Fugue in C Minor, *Well-Tempered Clavier*, Book One
Cantata no. 140, *Wachet auf* (Sleepers Awake)
Passacaglia in C Minor for Organ
The Brandenburg Concertos

Ludwig van Beethoven
Symphony no. 5 in C Minor, op. 67
String Quartet in E-flat Major, op. 74
Piano Sonata in G Major, op. 49, nos. 1 and 2
Symphony no. 5 in C Minor, op. 67
Symphony no. 1 in C Major, op. 21
Symphony no. 2 in D Major, op. 36
Symphony no. 3 in E-flat Major, op. 55 (*Eroica*)
Symphony no. 6 in F Major, op. 68 (*Pastoral*)
Symphony no. 9 in D Minor, op. 125 (*Choral*)
Concerto in D Major for Violin and Orchestra, op. 61
Fidelio
Missa Solemnis (Mass in D Major, op. 123)
Diabelli Variations for piano (33 Variations on a Waltz by
    Diabelli in C Major, op. 120)

Hector Berlioz
Romeo and Juliet
The Damnation of Faust
Symphonie Fantastique

Johannes Brahms
Hungarian Dance no. 5
Piano Quartet no. 1 in G Minor, op. 25; the fourth movement
Concerto in D Major for Violin and Orchestra, op. 77; the third movement
Clarinet Quintet in B Minor, op. 115; the second movement
Piano Quartet no. 1 in G Minor, op. 25; the fourth movement

Frédéric Chopin
Mazurka in A Minor, op. 17, no. 4
Polonaise in A Major, op. 40, no. 1 (*Military*)

Claude Debussy
Three Nocturnes for Orchestra, "Nuages"

Mikhail Glinka
A Life for the Tsar

George Frideric Handel
Messiah, Overture
Messiah, "Hallelujah Chorus"

Joseph Haydn
Symphony no. 92 in G Major, *Oxford* (London symphony)
Symphony no. 88 in G Major; the third movement

Léonin
Organum Duplum on "Alleluia Pascha nostrum" ("Hallelujah, Our Passover")

Franz Liszt
Totentanz
Hungarian Rhapsody no. 2 in C-sharp Minor

Guillaume de Machaut
"Quant en moy"

Gustav Mahler
Symphony no. 3 in D Minor
Symphony no. 9 in D Major

Felix Mendelssohn
Symphony no. 4 in A Major, op. 90 (Italian)
Elijah

Claudio Monteverdi
La favola d'Orfeo
The Coronation of Poppea

Wolfgang Mozart
Eine kleine Nachtmusik
Twelve Variations on *Ah vous dirai-je, Maman*, K. 265
Symphony no. 40 in G Minor, K. 550
Symphony no. 39 in E-flat Major, K. 543
Symphony no. 41 in C Major, the *Jupiter*
Piano Concerto no. 17 in G Major, K. 453
La clemenza di Tito, or The Mercy of Titus
Idomeneo

The Abduction from the Seraglio (Harem)
The Magic Flute
La finta semplice, "The Pretended Simpleton"
The Marriage of Figaro
Don Giovanni
Così fan tutte (roughly, "Thus All Women Do")

Giovanni Battista Pergolesi
La Serva Padrona (*The Maid Turned Mistress*), Recitative
    and Aria, "Son imbrogliato io gia"

Jacopo Peri
Euridice

Nikolai Rimsky-Korsakov
Russian Easter Overture

Gioachino Rossini
The Barber of Seville, "*Una voce poco fa*"

Arnold Schoenberg
Pierrot Lunaire, no. 1, Moondrunk

Franz Schubert
Erlkönig (The Elf King) for Baritone and Piano
Symphony no. 9 in C Major (*The Great*)

Richard Strauss
Don Quixote

Igor Stravinsky
The Firebird, "Infernal Dance"
Le Sacre du printemps (The Rite of Spring)

Peter Tchaikovsky
Romeo and Juliet, Fantasy Overture

Giuseppe Verdi
Aida, Act 4, Scene 2 (the "Tomb Scene")

Antonio Vivaldi
L'Olimpiade, "Siam navi all'onde algenti" ("We are ships on silver waves")
The Four Seasons
Concerto no. 1 in E Major: La Primavera ("Spring")

Richard Wagner
Tristan und Isolde
The Valkyrie, "Ride of the Valkyries"

Carl Maria von Weber
Der Freischütz (*The Freeshooter*), Act 2, Scene 4, Finale, "Wolf's Glen Scene"

Thomas Weelkes
"As Vesta Was from Latmos Hill Descending"

Glossary

Aria: Originally a song sung by a single voice with or without accompaniment. Now taken to mean a lyric operatic number for solo voice generally having two contrasting parts, ending with a literal or elaborated repeat of part one. The aria first developed into this form in the early operas; the arias found in an opera, cantata, or oratorio usually express intense emotion.

Bel canto: A style of singing that emphasizes the beauty of sound throughout the entire voice range. Specifically, an elegant Italian vocal style characterized by florid melodic lines delivered by voices of great agility, smoothness, and purity of tone.

Cadence: A harmonic or melodic formula that occurs at the end of a phrase, section, or composition that conveys a momentary or permanent conclusion; in other words, a musical punctuation mark.

Cantata: A poem set to music to be performed by voices and instruments; usually has several movements, airs, recitatives, and choruses.

Chord: The simultaneous sounding of three or more different pitches.

Closed cadence: Equivalent to a period or exclamation mark; such a cadence ends on the tonic and gives a sense of rest and resolution.

Coda: The closing few measures of a composition; usually not a part of the main thematic groups of the standard form of a composition but a finishing theme added to the end to give the composition closure.

Concert overture: Music preceding an opera or play, often performed as an independent concert piece.

Conjunct: Refers to a melodic contour that generally features steps between notes; such a melody will usually sound smooth and controlled.

Deceptive/false cadence: Equivalent to a colon or semicolon; such a cadence does bring resolution but not to the expected tonic harmony.

Disjunct: A melodic contour that generally features leaps between notes; such a melody will usually sound jagged and jumpy.

Dominant: The note and the chord five notes above a given tonic note/chord. The dominant harmony is the chord most closely related to the tonic chord in a given key; the dominant chord will almost always immediately precede an appearance of the tonic chord.

Duplum: In twelfth-century organum, the duplum was the part immediately above the tenor. If a third part was present, it was called the triplum. In the thirteenth century, the duplum came to be known as the motetus.

Frequency: The rate of vibration of a string, column of air, or other sound-producing body.

Fugue: Important Baroque musical procedure in which a theme (or subject) is developed by means of various contrapuntal techniques.

Functional harmony: Harmonic usage that was standardized and codified into a fully coherent system during the Baroque period. This method is still used by modern arrangers and orchestrators. The basic concept used in functional harmony is that all harmonic sounds used in music may be classified in three large groups. These groups derive their names from the three important roots of the traditional harmonic system: the tonic, dominant, and subdominant. In this way, they are comparable to the three primary colors used by the artist: red, yellow, and blue.

Fundamental frequency: The rate of vibration of the full length of a sound-producing body and the sound created by that full-length vibration.

Gesamtkunstwerke: Wagner's projected all-inclusive art form.

Hocket: A medieval practice of composition in which two voices would move in such a manner that one would be still while the other moved, and vice versa. Sometimes this was achieved by breaking a single melody into short one- or two-note phrases, then dividing the phrases between the two voices so that a quick back-and-forth movement of the melody would be heard.

Homophonic texture/monophony: Texture in which one melodic line predominates; all other melodic material is heard as being secondary or accompanimental.

Idée fixe: A recurring theme that appears in many movements of the same composition.

Intermezzi/Intermedi: (1) An instrumental interlude between the acts of a performance; (2) a comic play with music performed between acts, popular in the sixteenth and seventeenth centuries in France and Italy; (3) a short lyric composition, often for the piano; (4) in the old dance suite, two to four short dance movements between the sarabande and the gigue.

Isorhythm: A medieval principal of construction that was used most often in motets. This construction is based on a repeating rhythmic pattern in one or more of the voices.

Kanon: Strict counterpoint in which each voice exactly imitates the previous voice at a fixed distance. In English, *canon*.

Klangfarbenmelodie: A term coined by composer Arnold Schoenberg to describe a style of composition that employs several different kinds of tone colors to a single pitch or to multiple pitches. This is achieved by distributing the pitch or melody among several different instruments.

K. numbers: Köchel numbers, named after Ludwig von Köchel, who catalogued Mozart's works.

Leitmotif: A recurring motif in a composition (usually an opera) that represents a specific person, idea, or emotion. This term was first applied to the operas of Richard Wagner.

Madrigal: A vocal music form that flourished in the Renaissance, originating in Italy. The madrigal is generally written for four to six voices that may or may not be accompanied. (In modern performance, madrigals are usually presented a cappella.) Madrigals are usually set to short love poems, though the words are occasionally about death, war, or other topics; they were extremely popular in England and Italy and were also produced in France, Germany, and Spain. The madrigal is characterized by word painting and harmonic and rhythmic contrast. In the madrigal, each line has its own tune, rather than the entire composition having a single tune with harmonic accompaniment.

Melisma: A group of many notes (usually at least five or six) sung melodically to a single syllable. Melismas are found especially in liturgical chant.

Melody: Any succession of notes.

Minuet: A dance of the seventeenth and eighteenth centuries, graceful and dignified, in moderately slow, three-quarter time.

Monophonic texture/monophony: Texture consisting of only a single, unaccompanied melody line (Gregorian chant, for example).

Motet: A polyphonic vocal style of composition. The motet was popular in the Middle Ages, when it consisted of a tenor foundation on which other tunes were added. The texts of these voices could be sacred or secular, Latin or French, and usually had little to do with one another, with the result that the composition lacked unity and direction. During the fourteenth century, isorhythm and other rhythmic refinements came into use, somewhat unifying the sound and texture of the motet. By the Renaissance, the separate voices of the motet had adopted the same text (by this time, the texts were religious almost without exception) and each voice was considered a part of the whole rather than a whole in itself, thus finally giving the motet unity and grace.

Motive/motif: A brief succession of notes from which a melody grows through the processes of repetition, sequence, and transformation.

Musica reservata: "Serious music," emphasizing clearly articulated words to ensure that the expressive message of a piece of music is understood by the audience.

Note: A sound with three properties: a single, singable fundamental frequency; timbre; and duration.

Octatonic scale: A scale of eight pitches per octave arranged by alternating half steps and whole steps. There are only three different arrangements of this scale.

Open cadence: Equivalent to a comma; such a cadence pauses on the dominant harmony without resolving the tonic harmony, creating tension and the need to continue.

Oratorio: Large-scale dramatic composition originating in the seventeenth century with text usually based on religious subjects. Oratorios are performed by choruses and solo voices with an instrumental accompaniment and are similar to operas but without costumes, scenery, or action.

Organum: The earliest kind of polyphonic music. Organum developed from the practice of adding voices above a plainchant (cantus firmus); at first, these added voices ran parallel to the plainchant at an interval of a fourth or fifth. Later, they began to move about more freely. Organum was in use from the twelfth through the thirteenth century.

Pentatonic scale: A scale of five tones. It is used in African, Far Eastern, and Native American music. The pentatonic scale has been used in twentieth-century compositions as well.

Pitch: A sound with two properties: a single, singable fundamental frequency and timbre.

Plagal cadence: So-called amen cadence; when used, a plagal cadence will generally occur as a musical postscript following a closed cadence.

Plainchant: Also called the Gregorian or Old Roman chant, this is one of the earliest surviving styles of music in Western Europe, attributed to Pope Gregory I. In reality, Gregory probably had little to do with the chant we know today, because the chants that survive in manuscript form date from the eleventh to the thirteenth century, and Gregory died in the year 604. The surviving chants are modal, with monophonic melodies and freely flowing, unmeasured vocal lines. Most chants belong to the Mass or to the daily offices.

Polyphonic texture/polyphony (contrapuntal texture or counterpoint): Texture consisting of two or more simultaneous melody lines of equal importance.

Pythagorean comma: The discrepancy between the opening pitch and the last pitch in a circle of fifths, making the final pitch about an eighth of a tone sharp.

Schmerz: German; pain or sorrow, angst.

Singspiel: German-language musical comedy, usually romantic or farcical in nature, with spoken dialogue. Popular in the eighteenth century.

Sonata: A piece of music, typically in three or four movements, composed for a piano (piano sonata) or a piano plus one instrument (violin sonata, for instance).

Sprechstimme: A vocal style in which the melody is spoken at approximate pitches rather than sung on exact pitches. The Sprechstimme was developed by Arnold Schönberg.

Sturm und Drang ("Storm and Stress"): Pre-Romantic artistic movement bent on expressing great personal feelings and emotions.

Texture: The number of melodies present and the relationship between those melodies in a given segment of music; the three textures discussed in this book are monophony, polyphony (counterpoint), and homophony.

Theme: The primary musical subject matter in a given section of music.

Timbre: Tone color.

Tonal/Tonality: The sense that one pitch is central to a section of music, as opposed to atonal/atonality.

Tone poem: Also called a symphonic poem. A one-movement orchestral genre that develops a poetic idea, suggests a scene, or creates a mood. The tone poem is generally associated with the Romantic era.

Tonic: The home note and chord of a piece of tonal music. Think of the term as being derived from *tonal center (tonic)*. For example, if a movement is in C, the note C is the tonic note, and the harmony is built on C, the tonic chord.

Trio: (1) Ensemble of three instruments; (2) composition for three instruments; and (3) type of minuet, frequently rustic in nature and paired with a second minuet to form a movement in a Classical era symphony.

Triple meter: A metrical pattern having three beats to a measure.

Tune: A generally singable, memorable melody with a clear sense of beginning, middle, and end.

Bibliography

Books of General Interest

Grout, Donald, and Claude Palisca. *A History of Western Music*. New York: Norton, 2005. The standard college music history textbook, the Grout/Palisca is currently in its seventh edition and is accompanied by a CD set and an anthology (the Norton Anthology of Western Music, or NAWM) of all the works discussed in the text.

Kelly, Thomas. *First Nights—Five Musical Premieres*. New Haven: Yale University Press, 2000.

Kerman, Joseph. *Listen*, 3rd ed. New York: Worth, 1980. Perhaps the single most intelligent general music history ever written. Kerman is a genuine polymath, and he manages to contextualize the development of Western music into the greater scheme of Western culture and history.

Lang, Paul Henry. *Music in Western Civilization*. New York: Norton, 1997. A landmark achievement, the most complete, single-volume history of Western music available.

Schonberg, Harold. *The Lives of the Great Composers*. New York: Norton, 1997. A series of superb and incisive pocket biographies/portraits of the great composers from Monteverdi to the minimalists.

Weiss, Piero, and Richard Taruskin. *Music in the Western World*. New York: Schirmer, 1984. A fascinating history of Western music in original documents.

Books on Particular Historical Eras

Bukofzer, Manfred. *Music in the Baroque Era: From Monteverdi to Bach*. New York: Norton, 1947.

Downs, Philip. *Classical Music: The Era of Haydn, Mozart, and Beethoven*. New York: Norton, 1992.

Heartz, Daniel. *Haydn, Mozart, and the Viennese School: 1740–1780*. New York: Norton, 1995.

Plantinga, Leon. *Romantic Music: A History of Musical Style in Nineteenth-Century Europe*. New York: Norton, 1984.

Reese, Gustave. *Music in the Renaissance*. New York: Norton, 1959.

Salzman, Eric. *Twentieth-Century Music: An Introduction*. Englewood Cliffs, N.J.: Prentice Hall, 2001.

Books on Particular Composers

Cone, Edward. *Berlioz Fantastic Symphony*. New York: Norton, 1971.

Mahler, Alma. *Gustav Mahler: Memories and Letters*. University of Washington Press; 3rd Revised and enlarged edition, June 1968.

Robbins Landon, H. C. *Beethoven: His Life, Work and World*. London: Thames & Hudson, April 1993.

Slonimsky, Nicolas. *Lexicon of Musical Invective: Critical Assaults on Composers Since Beethoven's Time*. New York: Norton, 2000.

Solomon, Maynard. *Beethoven* (Revised edition). New York: Schirmer, 2001.

Stravinsky, Igor, and Robert Craft. *Expositions and Developments*. University of California Press, 1981.

Walker, Alan. *Franz Liszt, Volume 1: The Virtuoso Years, 1811–1847* (1988); *Franz Liszt, Volume 2: The Weimar Years, 1848–1861*(1993); and *Franz Liszt, Volume 3: The Final Years, 1861–1886* (1997). Ithaca, N.Y.: Cornell University Press.

Walsh, Stephen. *Stravinsky, Volume 1: A Creative Spring, 1882–1934* (2002) and *Stravinsky, Volume 2: The Second Exile, 1934–1971* (2006). New York: Knopf.

Index

Note: Page numbers in *italics* refer to illustrations. Page numbers followed by a *t* refer to text boxes.